WHAT THE DE

A CRITIQUE FROM

WILLIAM (LEZ) HENRY

PREFACE BY PAUL GILROY

Learning By Choice!

Nu-Beyond Ltd

First published 2006 by Nu-Beyond Ltd: Learning by Choice!
PO Box 39266, Blackheath, London SE3 8XQ, UK

ISBN 13 978-09554094-0-0
ISBN 10 0-9554094-0-3

A Cataloguing in Publication Data record for this book is
available from the British Library

www.nubeyond.com

Acknowledgements

Rasspeck to the Mother/Father/Male/Female Creation Principle that is responsible for all things in and at all times: Amen-Ra-Amen. One Iternal love to Miss Dotty (Earth Mother) and Sweet Sixteen (Earth Father) for bringing us forth through love for one another and to the Ancestors who saw fit to choose me as a vessel for our liberation in this dread time. To my siblings (with whom I learned to debate, argue, wrangle, haggle and fight for what you believe is just) and their families (name too nuff tuh mention di whole ah dem): Novelette, Joe, Barry, Georgie, Victor, Christine, Steve, Jasmine and June, I give thanx for our constant reasonings and the conscious vibes and inspiration that I know was crucial to my reaching this point. To my children, Damian, Leanne (my precious proof-reader extraordinaire), Dane, Courtney, Daron, Sabrina, Chiamah and Khafarae, for their intellect, wisdom and support, including tossing me a lifeline and keeping 'mad-dad' in check during those moments when I choose to swim in the pool of insanity. And to my blessed granddaughter, Araya, who begins the completion of my cycle in this place at this time!

To my family and friends, heartical bredrin and Sistrin, especially those inveterate Reggae fans and people who love the business, like myself, who have empowered me on this journey (anyweh them deh ah-Yard or ah-broad) I give thanx that I am blessed enough to know you, and want you to know that you are loved and appreciated. To all the Africentric ones out there remember I AM WE!!!

I also want to hail up Ras Cosmo (my first Afrikan teacher), Prof. Ekwe Ekwe (my mentor and the master teacher), Rey Bowen (Mr Kemit/Egypt) and of course to Jean Besson for introducing me to academic rigour. To my 'soul sisters': Stella, Dawn, Maureen, Gbemi, Omo, T Banton, Carole, Kentura, and Angela who reasoned with me when others would run. To my 'soul brothers': Derek, who loaned me 'one bag of cassettes', Terry, Johnny T, Mickey B, Maurice and Rupert whose reasonings strengthened my resolve. Dalewyn (me little breddah), Bill, Mad Mikey Simpson and Kimani Nehusi for being the kind of bredrin that can only be described as rock-solid and heartical, whose reasonings, comments and constructive critiques were a constant inspiration to me.

X amount ah shout to Prof. Smart (keep the faith), Prof. Cooper and all the U.W.I. Massive and the staff and students at Goldsmiths College, and other places who have assisted me on my Journey, especially Magna, Winston, Mwalimu Shujaa, Tina, Ove, Hazel, Rupert, Colin, Nici, Victoria, Brian Morris, Fran, Denise, Sireita, Martin, Paru, Tim, Yasmeen, Ada, Thomas, Karen, Doreen and Violet (who always makes me smile). Also to the Hung Kuen, Kung-Fu Club, London (who keep me fit and healthy).

Nuff Rasspeck to Paul Gilroy who opened up a world of literature to me and to Les Back who was clever and patient enough to make sense out of my PhD ramblings that form the basis of this work, although it must be noted that I am solely responsible for the argument that is contained herein (an mi nuh tek back nuh talk). Honour to the Nu-Beyond staff team, the R.D.C. young researchers and to the B.L.A.K. FRIDAY massive; forward ever. Thanks also to the ESRC who funded the research degree that formed the basis of this work.

Finally, this book is livicated to Deborah Glasgow, Trevor Natch, Johnny Ringo, Little Mr Palmer, and Mrs Irie, I had the pleasure of performing with you all and know that your light still shines bright on all who were touched by your wise words. Hotep!

Table of Contents

B~SIDE Drama Pon Plastic: Critique from the street

To **Marlene,** without whose love and inspiration I would have achieved none of this!

Preface

This is a unique and special book. It is by turns insightful and moving. It is also consistently acute in its rich and diverse observations about music, language and the wider historical and political predicament of black people in Britain during the second half of the twentieth century.

Dr. Lez Henry has succeeded by filling in a large part of the historical and analytical gap which surrounds the dynamic fact of an irremovable black presence in this country. That central concern is framed here by a host of wider arguments which are addressed to the recent cultural life of the African diaspora into the western hemisphere. In particular, Dr. Henry is interested in the place of Jamaican music and playful, poetic, black Atlantic freedom-language in the global circuitry through which they now flow. They offer not just a distinctive soundtrack but something like a universal, humanistic idiom that has become meaningful to sufferers everywhere. In drawing attention to this, Dr. Henry shows us some of the contemporary consequences of the old idea that slavery would yield a special consciousness of freedom which would resonate all over the planet. He suggests not only that this oppositional mentality has a philosophical depth, but also that it has become allied with a range of special cultural tactics which are strengthened rather than limited by their origins in the slave ships and plantations of the New World.

Adopting a vindicationist and resolutely Africentric approach, Henry considers the modes of resistance and transcendence with which black people in Britain have answered their long victimisation. He is, above all, a highly skilled historian and anthropologist of black vernacular culture, but this rare project is not just of historical importance. The analysis he provides, aims at more than merely enumerating the sequence of past conflicts. In other words, his wise reflections are oriented by the demands of a future which the victims of Britain's persistent racism and growing inequality find hard to imagine. That inability is a measure of their powerlessness but Henry suggests that glimpses of a distant alternative world - ruled more justly than this one and purged of white supremacy - can be glimpsed and felt where the emergent future is pre-figured in the cultural life of the communities that strive for it. The hidden social world of the sound systems provides him with the means to examine those dynamics.

Alongside a subtle and lively "ethnographic" exposition, Henry articulates a grounded interpretation of Britain's living black culture which is rescued from the hostility, condescension and ridicule it has suffered at the hands of its more orthodox sociological and anthropological interpreters. He challenges those orthodoxies and reveals the mechanisms which have made them complicit with racism over a long period of time. The racist assumptions that survive today are, in his view, still marked by the after-effects of slavery and imperial rule which turn out to be much closer to the present than many people like to imagine.

This insurgent, oppositional account has been carefully flavoured by the author's autobiographical reflections on his own life as a youth, a worker, a student, a toaster, a dancehall DJ and a critical practitioner/historian inside the sound system scene. Though the power of the sound systems seems to have grown in proportion to their makers' exile from the official world of work and wages, Henry finds that the systems become and create rewarding forms of cultural work. The struggle to bring dignity and value to this worthless world of word and sound and to invest deep community-building historicity in its seeming ephemera has been enriched by a playful blend of ethics and aesthetics. That signature combination helps him to define the alternative public sphere that the systems bring alive.

The darkened space of the dance is both sacred and profane. Protest is there braided with carnivalesque affirmation. Revolutionary hope is, in this dread soundscape, knotted together with resignation, consolation and bitter accommodation to transitory unfreedoms. This complexity is mirrored in the way that the book has been structured.

Henry adopts a double perspective that corresponds imaginatively to the two sides of an old vinyl record. Those paired recordings are similar but they are emphatically not the same. Together they comprise an open and unfinished musical event that differs from itself and, in doing so, offers us a valuable lesson about the limits and the mutability of identity. There is not just passing pleasure but a deep, abiding joy to be found in the interplay of difference and sameness. One rhythm can have an infinite number of versions. Each is specific, made from and oriented by particular historical circumstances. Thus Henry's embrace of dancehall doubling is more than just a neat way to manage the combined political and historical dimensions of the cultural scene that he's concerned with. That formal device folds celebration and interpretation into a single process which is always more than the sum of its parts. But those two unstable halves, like the different versions of a single tune, are also a profound sign that Henry has risen to the challenge which this restlessly creative culture extends when it demands to be interpreted but simultaneously forbids interpretation.

His grasp of its fundamental creativity gets conveyed in the way that his own methods have been adapted to match the shape-shifting character of the dancehall form. If it is not to be sold short, the creative character of this culture demands a parallel act of creativity on the part of its would-be advocates and interpreters. Henry pulls off that difficult trick. He manages to let the political dimensions of this exemplary story appear clearly while not allowing them to stifle or compromise his tale. This living art has political aspects and consequences, but is stubbornly committed to being more than politricks could ever be.

This is also a local narrative. The author has stayed faithful to a finely grained account of sound system competitions in south-east London. If that supplies the spatial core of his book, its temporal focus is equally specific. He is centrally concerned with the experience of a transitional generation. These pivotal people were not the post-1945 settlers and migrants but rather their children, either born in Britain or brought here while young. Their experiences can be distinguished by a feeling of entitlement and ambiguous belonging that is quite different from anything encountered either by their parents or later by their children for whom Ethiopianism was not usually an immediate concern and blackness is as likely to have sources in the US as in the Caribbean. Here then, is a detailed survey of the embattled space between migrancy and mainstreaming both of which are seen differently as a result of Henry's intervention.

The intermediate group came of age during the 1970s. They were engaged in a great and historic conflict with the institutions of the British state which were apparently intent on a process of mis-education and criminalisation. Henry escaped that fate himself and clearly wants his book to demonstrate how an unvalued and underestimated, but nonetheless potent, culture sustained and nurtured the oppositional consciousness of that generation. The original courage of the 1950s settlers and the Thatcherite wheeler-dealing of their grandchildren have squeezed out this story, with the result that the intermediate group has usually been written off. The official line about them still suggests that their lives were destroyed by being caught between a Victorian parental culture and its flimsy English successor. Many who should know better, have been content to accept the portrait of pathological family life, mugging and nihilism, which was served up during the 70s and 80s by academics, politicians and community leaders alike. It is not only that Henry sees the sound system as a place where the antisocial effects of poverty, hopelessness and joblessness might be offset. His argument is deeper than that. The alternative public world created around and through these encounters with music and language became a vital source of improvised solidarity, wisdom and critical hope.

This wonderful book is livicated to the task of transmitting that precious legacy to subsequent generations and translating it into fresh terms that even might win an appropriate measure of recognition for a history of conflict which changed Britain irrevocably. These tasks are very important now. Too many young people lack even the most basic historical and cultural resources with which to comprehend their own fate and reflect upon their experience. For them, the mainstreaming of black culture brings the exaltation of ignorance and violence, disenchantment and despair. That mix of responses proceeds easily, hand in hand with the mistaken belief that the US somehow represents Britain's racial future and the related error that sees American blackness as the special centre of diaspora sensibility worldwide. Henry's greatest achievement is to show that there are powerful local reasons to hope for other outcomes.

Step Forward

Burning an illusion for me was the recognition of self. Black people in this society have become almost emasculated from who they are. They have become separated and caught up in kind of thinking that in order for them to become; they had to become somebody else. They had to kind of put on a mask and that mask would become who they are. And what's happening in that process is that you then lose your self and then you also become disconnected from reality...whether it's a male or it's a female... in order to be true to who you are, in order to be realistic in terms of how you see your relationship with each other you have to first know yourself. You have to come to that point because without that everything else is an illusion. Menelik Shabazz

The above quote from Menelik Shabazz (2005), Director of Burning An Illusion (1981) and Blood Ah Goh Run (1982), is lifted from the 2005 DVD release of these films that represent a seminal moment in the black British social, cultural and political experience. These films perfectly capture what it was like to be considered an unwanted worthless nigger, other, in the land of your birth and how this reality impacted on wider community relations during that historical moment. That was/is the reality Shabazz speaks of when suggesting black people can only 'burn the illusion' when alternative knowledge of self is used as the fuel for the fire. This book is forged in the fire and spirit of his libratory perspective and will present notions of resistance and transcendence that are missing from many accounts that sought to explain OUR behaviour during the 'crisis' period of the early 1970s – mid 1980s. I will speak from the inside, to counter much that has been suggested from the outside, demonstrating that there are ways the downpressed can resist and transcend their social, cultural and racial predicament which are deliberately 'hidden' from the wider public gaze. I will do so by using the lyricism of the Reggae-dancehall Deejays who were, in many respects, the mouthpiece of the black community during this moment. Thereby presenting an argument that will reappraise 'black youth' identifications with particular types of Afrikan, rhythmic, cultural expression, especially Jamaican Reggae-dancehall Deejaying. The same Deejaying that is now, in much the same way as it was then, coming under so much fire from many of those the form was created to chant down in the first place. You see, let's be clear that Deejaying in all of its manifestations (call it toasting, MCing, rapping, freestylin, head-toppin, grime or whatever) was, and is, a medium for challenging the downpressor on the terrain of language; no matter what colour or race that downpressor happens to be. Moreover I will detail how Reggae Sound System culture and Deejaying gave all black youth, irrespective of where in the Afrikan Diaspora either they or their parents came from, a voice that spoke to their immediate concerns that was totally uncompromising.

In fact, because many black youth chose to rebel and use Patwa to voice their disapproval of an inherently racist society and system, our endeavours were regarded by many white and black colonial minded individuals, as ignorant 'jungle talk' that had no social, cultural or political value whatsoever. Consequently the aim of this work is to refute these gross misrepresentations by presenting an account of the 'conscious' thought and action of several Deejays as a means of illuminating a 'hidden', but ironically well-documented, history of the black British experience. An experience featured within the alternative public arenas that are the Reggae-dancehalls where we control the airwaves. I will therefore argue that there is within the Deejay performance, as act, a notion of 'conscious choice' which, once fully appreciated, demonstrates how black youth in Britain had a language and a vocabulary to chant down Babylon in all of its manifestations. For there are ongoing reasonings, across the 'black Atlantic' (Gilroy, 1993a), that link the disparate elements of our fragmented and fractured being, thus making us, as Afrikans, outernational and therefore whole.

Introduction: thinking about "thoughtists"

> Them (the police) throw me in ah van and tek me down ah station,
> them insult me intelligence when them question me, ah treat me like
> ah animal ah call me monkey, them want me sign statement which
> wasn't written by me, but me nuh rob people fi get my money, so hey
> officer address me properly, cau me nuh born big me nuh drop out
> ah tree, I am more intelligent than you'll ever be, cos ah street life
> educate me, ah hard life educate me. (Lezlee Lyrix, Put Back You
> Truncheon, 1985)

The above lyrical extract was taken from the B-side of a track that I
voiced for Greensleeves Records, 'UK Bubblers Label', during the mid
1980s, which, incidentally, was the high point of British Deejaying. This
was when, according to a good friend and an ex sparring partner who
has now joined the ancestors, Trevor Natch, 'everyone want tek up mic
and seh them can Deejay'. Trust me, Trevor's words were no
exaggeration because everywhere you went in urban Britain in the early
1970s, where black people dwelled, you would find a Sound System.
Even if it was a small Sound System with a handful of speaker boxes
and 'one and two tunes', as long as there was a roof and four walls so
they could string-up inside (you know the one about the weather in
Britain; well, add racist club owners and an ever hostile police presence
to this and the choice makes perfect sense), 'dance can run'. And dance
did run in houses, flats, basements, youth clubs, halls - especially
church halls - garages, warehouses; anywhere you could think of was
turned into a place to rave. In fact, a popular venue at the time was the
'Crypt' in Deptford, south-east London where the spirits of the dead
were regularly replaced by the spirits of the living-black, tomb-ravers.
The 'Crypt' really was an underground tomb that was no longer used to
house the dead and, if you know how black people are said to be fraid
ah duppy (ghosts), raving in the Crypt shows you how committed we
were to supporting and promoting Reggae music. As long as we could

3

hear Reggae music being played by our favourite Sound Systems we would turn-up and 'tune-in till ah morning', as Gregory Isaacs reminds us, to hear our music.

Yes I make no apologies for the fact that I consider Reggae to be 'our' music, black music, for despite its international appeal, well some of it anyway, it was born out of the Afrikan struggle in Jamaica for self-determination in a white supremacist world. What is even more remarkable is how a microdot of an island, Jamaica, has had such a prominent and shaping role in global black popular culture, which in my opinion is still not fully appreciated. That is why I have written this book and began this Reggaematical journey with a lyric I used to chat in places like the Crypt, because the language I used is fundamentally Jamaican, Patwa. The language that I learned from my parents and older siblings that many use in Britain, in some way shape or form, regardless of where we or even our parents hail from. Of even more significance: it was the language that made me feel like I belonged to a community that could think and feel in ways that the white world did not appreciate and could never, in my opinion, truly overstand.

This said, the lyric was based on an incident that happened to me as a sixteen-year-old 'black youth' in the 1970s whilst on my way home from a youth club with my twin brother. We had just left the 'Moonshot' youth club in Deptford, south-east London and were on a bus making our way home on a winter's evening with a group of friends of similar age. Obviously, we were excited—something to do with Jah Shaka Sound System's latest earth-shaking session—and were involved in the usual loud, and possibly rowdy, behaviour one would expect from adolescent youths sitting upstairs at the back of the bus. Anyway the bus conductress, a black woman who I actually met at a party a few years later (and informed her of the outcome of this little saga) decided I was messing her around when I pointed to my brother and said "he's paying." The next thing I knew, she scolded me with her beautiful Grenadian accent (I recognised it as my then girlfriend's parents were from Grenada) and called the police on me. Some of the other youths who were on the bus got off and started 'trodding it' home, but I said "I aint going nowhere cos I haven't done anything", so my brother, our friends and myself stayed put. When the two 'bull' as we called them then arrived, they came upstairs, beckoned for me to follow them downstairs to answer a few questions and planted me with weed. The way they did it was so stupid that I was actually laughing at first until I realised they were serious, because one of them pretended to put his hand in my pocket, presented his palm which had a draw of weed in it and said "wot 'ave we 'ere then, sunshine?"

My saving grace, and the reason why I know I did not end up in some type of penal institution, was that at the time of my arrest I was employed as a solicitor's clerk and my boss refused to accept that I was stupid enough to walk the streets of London with 'weed' in an outside coat pocket. Furthermore, he was aware of the unjust treatment I received from the police as I, like many other black boys during this time and including my older brother had to have a letter from him stating my business in the West End of London. Think about it for a moment: as we are not talking about apart-hate South Africa in the early 1970s, we are talking about a young black boy 'suited and booted', carrying a brown leather briefcase in the streets of central London. Yet the reality is that the 'dutty Babylon' harassed me so often that I made this request to my boss as it was/is embarrassing to be treated in this fashion just for being born in what, for them, was obviously the 'wrong' colour skin.

These incidents demonstrate the reality of what it was, and still is, to be regarded as a 'social problem', rendered 'voiceless' and therefore at the mercy of those who are in a position to do something about this perceived 'problem'. For not only did the two officers plant me with 'weed', arrest me and take me to Forest Hill Police Station, south-east London, they also tried to make me confess, 'them want me sign statement which wasn't written by me', to robbing a local florist by constantly stating, 'will he own up'? 'Course he will.' The officers believed they could force me to 'speak' with their 'voice', which is why I informed them that 'I am more intelligent than you'll ever be, ah street life educate me' and I therefore have my own reasoned opinions.

Ironically, their unjust and decidedly criminal behaviour (I went to court and won that case) actually worked in my favour as it opened up my father's eyes to the extent of police corruption, as he was used to being stopped by them when driving, but thought that was it. In fact they stopped my father so many times, in the early 1960s, that he bought himself a PINK VAUXHALL CRESTA (his version of the much sought after Pink Cadillac) so they would know that he was legit and therefore would let him be. Nonetheless he would more often than not believe their accounts of what happened if any of his children had a run-in with them: 'yuh mussi do supn fi mek them trouble yuh'. That was until the day they planted me with weed and I still remember sitting in a cell and being reassured when hearing his booming voice (my father had a huge and intimidating physical presence with a voice to match) echoing around the police station proclaiming my innocence:

> Me want back me son! Oonuh can tell me anything bout me pickney them, but nuh tell me seh them ah fool, cau only ah fool ah goh stan-up and know seh police ah come an have ganja in ah them pocket. Fi me pickney nah goh duh dat.

You see, two of the things my parents always encouraged us children to do was to think for ourselves and watch out for people 'wid dutty ways'; that is, those deceivers who seek to place you at a disadvantage. This meant that my mother and father knew that 'the Brain of Britain', which is what they called any of us who thought we were too clever whilst being devious, would never allow such a thing to happen. To them, the mere suggestion that any of their children would place themselves in such a vulnerable position was an insult to their intelligence and they just weren't having it. They knew that I occasionally smoked weed, but knew that there was no way 'me wouldn't dash weh that before Babylon come'. Moreover, when I was paraded in front of the lady who they told me I had robbed, Ivy (I never found out whether this was actually her name), she stunned them exclaiming, "I know him, that's one of Mrs Henry's boys!" Ivy worked next door to the Newsagent for whom my twin brother and I delivered newspapers and we would often run little errands for her, which is the main reason why she knew I was not the 'black youth' in question. Furthermore, there were no other black twins that lived locally and, as such, my brother and I stood out like the proverbial sore thumbs, which obviously worked for and against us, depending on the circumstances.

The underlying seriousness of this incident cannot be overstated as it relates directly to the focus of this book, which will use a Deejay perspective to tell a story about the black British experience, adding another dimension to our tales of living in Babylon. An experience that has been constantly misrepresented, or overlooked, by many who have written about it because they ignore the crucial role the Deejays and

Sound Systems had in the lives of many black youth. At this point I wish to make clear that Sound Systems cannot be reduced to a 'large mobile disco', as there is an aesthetic value that far transcends any such description. They were often a labour of love and deep affection and when the boxes were neatly stacked up and they sounded 'criss an heavy' it was the best they could be. Additionally, a Sound System is also known as a Set, or The Set, probably because you have to 'set-up' and 'string-up' (wire up the speakers etc.) before you can 'play out'. Another reason for this could be that in Jamaica they differentiate between a Component Set (Rack System), which is the type of stereo you would play music on at home, and 'The Set' as the Sound System you would hear in a Reggae dancehall. By focusing on these aspects of the culture I will consider how a section of the community that is supposedly 'voiceless' primarily because they are deemed to lack 'intelligence' articulate their oppression in novel, informative and interesting ways.

The reason why I make such an assertion is that incidents like the above encounter with the police, led me to 'tek up the mic' and present accounts that, whilst drawn largely from my personal experiences, were not by any stretch of the imagination peculiar to me. In fact, once these experiences were lyrically transformed by the Deejays and then delivered 'live an direct' from amplified platforms, as provided by Sound Systems in the Reggae-dancehall, they became the recorded documentation of an alternative living history of the black presence in Britain; a living history that took the harsh realities and ironies of living in Babylon and then told a story of what it is truly like for a community to be on the receiving end of white supremacist thought and action. This, in turn, demonstrates how certain ironies form the basis of some of the most poignant and profound cultural criticism ever to deal with the black experience in Britain. Thus, thinking through such ironies is of utmost relevance here because they exemplify why I feel I must offer a song of 'ourselves' as a counter to the numerous stories that often misrepresent, for one reason or another, a lived black reality. A song that, whilst premised on W.E.B Du Bois comment, 'How does it feel to be a problem?', details how this issue has been tackled by those who have realised that their 'problem status' is largely the product of an oppressive imagination.

Recognising that your downpressor does not provide a platform from which your 'problem status' can be challenged or countered means you have no option other than to use what is available. In other words you, the members of the black community, have to provide a space within from which you can tell anyone who chooses to listen, your version of events. A place where your voice, a black voice, can be heard and appreciated by those who have shared a similar experience, or at least can recognise some truth in the picture that is being painted. That is why I argue here that, although many black people have actively resisted certain overly negative constructs, the spaces in which they 'voice' their alternative opinions are relatively 'hidden' from the oppressor's gaze. This means that, as I demonstrate in the lyrical extract above, the notion of what it means to be 'intelligent' as a Reggae-dancehall performer is determined from within the culture's specific frames of reference 'cos ah street life educate me/we, ah hard life educate me/we'.

The main reason why I am able to make this claim is because I was there, raving and Deejaying in dances from 'them time deh' and, as such, I am using this 'insider' knowledge to present an account of how the Reggae-dancehall became an alternative public arena. Moreover, the documenting of this 'hidden' history has been assisted by the fact that much of it is contained on live Sound System cassette and videotapes that were disseminated across what Gilroy dubs the 'black Atlantic' (Gilroy, 1993a). By using these sources I will demonstrate how British Deejays were involved in a complex system of outernational 'intellectual' exchanges that redefined what it meant to be conscious/intelligent/original. These exchanges were initiated by the Jamaican Deejays who were the first ones to 'chat mic' in this fashion during the early 1960s, followed by 'us' in the Afrikan Diaspora, firstly in the UK and then in the USA and other places.

Of equal importance, my argument will demonstrate how Cooper's (2004) focus on Apache Indian as an exemplar of British Deejaying, whilst noble in its intentions to make the British contribution known, further obscures the voices of those who opened the door for commercially viable, non-threatening, performers of his ilk. This, more so when we consider that pioneers like Tippa Irie, Macka B, Pato Banton, Top Cat and Starkey Banton are still out there touring the world and keeping the faith and the British Deejay perspective alive. To make the point even clearer, I was speaking at a conference in Birmingham, England (June 2005) when a bredrin, 'Chubby', approached me after I had delivered my talk. He remembered me from back in the 1980s and stated that he was glad to see that Lezlee Lyrix was still chanting down Babylon. I then asked him if he had read Cooper's book on 'Sound Clash' and he said he hadn't so I informed him that a Deejay was chosen from his 'manor' (the West Midlands) as the focus for a chapter on British Deejaying I asked him to guess who it was and he instantly suggested it was Macka B, to which I said 'no'. He then said, 'Well, it must be Pato Banton', and I pointed out that he was not even mentioned anywhere in the text. When I told him it was Apache Indian he held his head in his hands and said:

> Ah wah kind ah foolishness is that. No one really rated him around here so where them get that from? He was a wagonist who copied yard (a term of endearment for Jamaica, as in 'back ah yard' or 'back home') tapes and couldn't even chat but we know why them boost him. To them ah Indian looks better on TV than ah Afrikan and it's as simple as that. (Chubby, Personal Communication 2005)

In agreement with Chubby's reasoning I am curious to know exactly how it can be suggested that he 'is still bending the iron over the fire' (Cooper 2004:277), when in reality Apache Indian has for more than a decade successfully distanced himself from the culture that made him 'fat'. But perhaps this explains why it is important that one who knows—the story from this side of the pond—must place this performer in his proper context, that is, as a commercial artist. For to dedicate a whole chapter to Apache Indian and not mention the fact that many of his releases on vinyl, 'Movie over India' = 'Movie over America' for instance, were 'pirated' from Nicodemus and Supercat's Yard-tape performances is incredible. Now, don't get me wrong; I fully appreciate why many producers and performers were keen to work with him, he was a good meal ticket and did raise the profile of British Reggae music. And, in some senses, why not 'bade offah him' in much the same way that he was 'bading offah we', for are we not used to being exploited with little return? So, why not capitalise on such a good opportunity? However, to use him as an exemplar of the contribution British Deejaying has made to outernational Sound System culture, is akin to believing that Elvis was the 'King of Rock 'n' Roll' and Eminem is the first rapper to be 'poetic'. This, a suggestion that was made in 2003 when it was reported that:

> American rap star Eminem has been praised by leading poet Seamus Heaney for his "verbal energy". He made the comments when asked by a journalist if there was a figure in popular culture who aroused interest in poetry and lyrics in the way that Bob Dylan and John Lennon did during the 1960s and 70s. Mr Heaney, former Professor of Poetry at Oxford University, said: "There is this guy Eminem. He has created a sense of what is possible. (http://news.bbc.co.uk/1/hi/entertainment/music)

Think about how ludicrous it is for this 'expert' to make such a statement about a white boy whose 'verbal energy' comes from using an identifiably black cultural form, to express his opinions about living in a white world. Herein we find the key to what makes my contribution profoundly different from any other thus far, as I am fully conversant, in much the same way as Chubby, with the hidden aspects of Deejay culture and need not rely solely on recorded releases or commercially viable performers to make my case. For, unless you were of the culture and privy to these cassette recordings, you would not appreciate that many of the lyrics and performers that dominated the Reggae-dancehall scene were not featured on vinyl, much less the TV. To emphasise this key point and give an insight into my love of this culture and why it is so important that one who is of it best represents it, consider the following extract that I performed on a Reggae Sound System:

> Me never start MC till the end ah 81, me never start MC till the end ah 81, the first Sound me chat pon was Saxon, in ah 51 Storm down in ah Lewisham, is I daddy Rankin an ah next bredder-man, ah Mello an Levi at the microphone stand, Rankin ask D Rowe fi mek me ride the version, pon 'Shank I Shek' me put the mic in ah me hand, me start chat lyrics in ah different fashion, me look pon Levi face ah bare confusion, is like him couldn't understand what's going on, seh when me mash it up ah bear congratulation, an Levi ask me one question, Lezlee which Yard-tape you get them lyrics from, me seh move pirate that's origination, happy an you love it say murdee. (Lezlee Lyrix, Ghettotone 1983)

The lyric provides an insight into why December 31st 1981 was one of the most memorable moments in my life and details my concerns over how the culture has been known up to this point. This was because it was the first time I performed on a Reggae Sound System and it is a moment I often relive in that space where *re-memories* and revisiting taped sessions allow me to do so. The notion of using 'rememory' was introduced by Toni Morrison in 'Beloved' (1987) and explained by Gordon (1998:164/9) to denote a 'deeply social memory', that is not just 'history, but haunting' as if you experience the memories of someone else. However, what is significant about this moment is that to Deejay on a Sound System was something I had dreamt of doing and, although lyrically prepared for at least a year before this time, a lack of courage had prevented me from fulfilling this dream. That night caught up in the raptures of New Year festivities, sufficiently plied with the necessary and encouraged by my bredrin, I stepped across that invisible barrier that 'separates' audience from performer and chatted some of my lyrics. As suggested above, the response of the audience to my lyricism was immediate and overwhelmingly favourable and that I performed on the most popular Sound System in south-east London, Saxon, sweetened the moment even more. Crucially in the lyric I speak of the difference between myself as an 'originator' and those who are content to 'pirate', when asked by (Papa) Levi 'which Yard-tape you get them lyrics from'.

These taped sessions are, as suggested above, generally recorded on cassettes and have since the late 1970s been commonly known as 'Yard (Jamaican) Tapes'. However, from the early 1980s other points in the Afrikan Diaspora began to partake in these exchanges, which by this time also included video cassettes as well, most notably from Britain, the USA and Canada. These recordings are known as 'Session-tapes' within the culture as they do not come from Yard and we shall use this definition in this book. Appreciating the relevance of these terms in the Reggae-dancehall is central to this discussion, as their usage makes known how black youth articulated their thoughts on various issues in a 'conscious', articulate and highly inventive fashion. My greatest claim then is that an exposure to the lyricism contained in Yard-tapes provided many British-born blacks with alternative sets of knowledge, which assisted our struggles in racist Britain as outernational Afrikans. Afrikan when spelt this way, as argued by numerous Africentric scholars, is reclamation of a self that is freed from the racist depictions of the African/inferior as the antithesis of the European/superior. This notion is premised on the Afrikan as a central historical presence that subverts the notion that we made no meaningful contribution to 'world history' or civilisation before the chattel slave era. Similarly, I use Africentric and not Afrocentric as an Afro was a powerful aesthetic, political statement, linked to the poignancy of the 'Black Power /Panther' movement of the 1960s and 1970s. As such, if we are to challenge the assumptions that an 'enemy language' like English is premised upon, then we as Afrikans must determine how such challenges are made.

These are crucial aspects of rethinking the self, autonomously, in much the same way as other words that are used within the culture such as 'Soundman' are often pluralized and used instead of 'Soundmen', because of the negative association that 'men' have within the culture. For instance, when Rastafari employ the notion of 'men' it generally signifies the difference between Rastafari as 'man' and therefore of God, and 'men', as corrupted by the Devil, which is why I have often heard Rastafari refer to an individual male that they regard in this fashion as a 'little men'. And because of the profound influence Rastafari culture and speech has on all aspects of this verbal art form, this notion of 'men' like many other semantically realigned terms, is widely used and recognised within the Reggae-dancehall arena. Therefore, whether a certain word is used to denote the singular or plural will be evidenced by the context it is used in throughout this work, for we are considering how a particular usage of language empowers and uplifts.

I argue here that this type of language use explains how the British Born Deejays used Patwa, Jamaican language, to express an alternative perception of self, as contained in the Session-tapes that document the lesser-known dimensions of Reggae-dancehall culture. One such dimension is that the venue for my primary venture into the world on the other side of the Set was '51 Storm down in ah Lewisham', which was in fact number 51 Lewisham Way. Interestingly enough, the naming of the venue as '51 Storm' is a good example of how this alternative 'education' manifests in the concrete, because the name was coined from 'Hurricane Charlie' which devastated the Island of Jamaica in 1951. Consequently, the very naming of this site linked those in

London across time and space with the History of Jamaica, and demonstrating how this aspect of the culture is important to those who wish to retain a sense of 'home from home'. However, what is supremely ironic and overly significant is that the venue was two doors away from Goldsmiths College Sociology Department (until it moved in 1997) and directly opposite the Anthropology Department. These departments have played a major role in my academic orientation; as they provided the intellectual frameworks and conceptual tools that formed the basis of my first joint honours degree. Seriously, I doubt that the staff and faculty at Goldsmiths College were aware of what transpired on a Saturday night in this alternative public arena, where the seminary was more organic in its orientation to a collective learning process. Learning that was based on countering much that was taught in formal institutions like Goldsmiths College, where black people learn little or nothing positive about themselves as Afrikans. This means that there was a physical and an intellectual closeness between these valuable sites of learning that perfectly captures why I chose to write this book on the black experience in Britain; a closeness that will be evidenced throughout this journey and mediated through both cultural lenses, for as the Jamaican Deejay, Capleton, suggests:

> Them call it University, but I an I call it You-never-see, cau you never see you self in ah fi them story an is time black people know these tings or we nah goh reach no-weh. (Capleton, 1999)

Therefore, if the fact of black peoples' 'education' is that 'You-never-see' yourself in the 'story' then this needs to be made known to the wider black community who need to 'know these tings' otherwise 'we nah goh reach no-weh'. In Capleton's opinion, the task of the Deejay (as educator) is to uplift the people by providing the types of knowledge that demonstrate an Africentric approach to the black experience. This entails making the necessary claims, historically, culturally, spiritually and politically, in a manner that fills many significant gaps in our 'education'. Hence the 'voice' is a current manifestation of traditional types of Afrikan resistance to European cultural hegemony, 'in which music and song are conceived as ideological weaponry for survival' (Cooper 2000). My unveiling of this alternative 'hidden' voice makes known a perspective that counters the myriad racist distortions that othered blacks in the white imagination and alienated many of us in the land of our birth. The suggestion is that as a Deejay I am uniquely positioned to offer a more personal insight into the relation between theory and practice based on my grounded and lived experience. However, and paradoxically, whilst I also recognise that I am an academic whose task is to make this counter-culture known, my perspective is constantly checked by my otherness as an 'outsider' within an institution where blackness is far from valued. An 'otherness' I re-experience in the physical moments when I stand in Lewisham Way and reflect on the duality of my 'education' as student/observer/participant/listener/tutor in the academic arena that is Goldsmiths College and in the Reggae-dancehall arena symbolically represented in '51 Storm' where I was Deejay/student/participant /listener. Therefore, Reggae-dancehall music becomes the cultural template through which performers consciously and intelligently express their innermost concerns, because:

> We must not underestimate the ways in which our own experiences have generated ways of seeing the world that are insightful, innovative and more relevant to the challenges that we face based on our own experiences. Therefore, we need to be more confident when we deploy these self-generated concepts as they particularly speak to our own experiences. That does not mean that we accept our own categories without interrogation. What it means is that we recognise what it is they are trying to capture which has not been, in my opinion, accurately defined before. The Deejays are giving us the functioning word, which we need to make flesh and give expression to; as we come out of an era of cultural reflection and analysis. (Rupert Lewis, Personal Communication 2001)

It will be through an evaluation and subsequent rendering of the 'functioning word which we need to make flesh' that I will present an 'insider' account on the validity of the Deejay's lyricism that has not been 'accurately defined before'. The manner in which this will be achieved will be to employ a methodological approach that will regard the biographical information I have collated from recorded reasonings and Yard/Session-tapes as viable sources of information. The inference then is that to fully appreciate the culture we need to consider these 'self-generated concepts' as the modes we use to define and record our own experiences. Therefore, the story will be one in which the performers present their own arguments, in their own words and on their own terms, in a 'commonly agreed language' (Small 1987: 290). By doing so I will tell our story in a more informed manner than has been achieved before, because as the Jamaican journalist, Basil Walters, states:

> The commonly held view is that dancehall Deejays are semi-literate at best, uneducated and unsophisticated...Well, Henry whose stage name is Lezlee Lyrix, is on the threshold of opening new frontiers of respectability to the way people view dancehall Deejays...So far the plumbing engineer of 20 years has already broken new ground, being the first Deejay to venture into the realms of academia. This British based "thoughtist" (thinker) who through his music is eloquently articulating the conditions of disaffected youth in Britain. (The Sunday Observer, 29/4/2001)

The most significant aspect of Walters' commentary, which makes known the ethos behind this discussion for a more profound appreciation of pro-black expressive cultures, is captured in the word "thoughtist". In this respect "thoughtist" is synonymous with 'lyrics', a term that Jamaicans often use to describe a person who is deemed to be intellectually engaging and highly proficient in their usage of language. In fact my becoming known as Lezlee Lyrix in the Reggae-dancehalls was by virtue of an impromptu naming ceremony, early in my career, where three of my bredrin, Basher, Loosh and Jackson announced to all in attendance that, 'ah Lezlee Lyrix we ah goh call you cau you have the most brain food'. Hence, by providing a space in this book, within which the British born "thoughtists" will speak with their own 'voice', I will document a 'hidden' history of black Britain from a novel evaluation of Deejay lyricism. This which led to many of the 'street styles' popularised in contemporary British pop music that are being collapsed under the misnomer of 'urban' music.

Structure of the book

I have opted to utilise the metaphor of the 45 rpm single (we still use the format in the Reggae-dancehall) to present this 'hidden' oral/aural history. The main reason for this is that without the 45 single there would have been no subject for this work, because as Deejays we are reliant on the rhythms contained on these recordings to construct and deliver our lyrics, which are chosen by the 'Selector' and played by the 'Operator'. Of even more relevance is the fact that the A-Side would generally contain the performance of another artiste, the 'vocal', and thus you were exposed to their 'story' before you had the opportunity to tell your own. As Deejays, we were free to 'bubble' (vocally interject) alongside their vocal by making the odd comment or harmonising to 'build up the vibes', but our account would have to wait for the 'version', the B-side. Our moment came when the record was 'pull up', and then 'tun over' onto the B-Side, allowing the Deejay to present their lyrical take on social realism and this is how I would like this account to be read. Therefore, the A~SIDE of the study will contain my engagements (bubbling) with the 'vocals' of other commentators and the B~SIDE will present a Deejay 'version' based on the lyrics and reasoning one would encounter within the Reggae-dancehalls.

In chapters 1 – 3 of the *A~SIDE,* **Overstanding blak cultural expression**, I will present the history behind the ideas that have influenced the outcome of this book by engaging with the literature that I believe opens a space for me in which to argue my case most effectively. This details and challenges the manner in which black experiences of racial exclusion/oppression have been documented in social theory, given that many of the black folk about whom this stuff was written have never read it. I make this point because I have taught numerous courses at degree level on race and racism in Britain and have found that some of the most pernicious material is omitted. When I do include a fraction of it, many of the students are in shock and cannot believe that social researchers made such overtly racist comments about black people in the name of 'scientific objectivity'.

This book is aimed at as wide an audience as possible and so I think it necessary for me to engage with some of what was suggested about us black folk, in order for the reader to better understand the historical context that gave birth to this form of social commentary. Similarly, it is my wish to present an investigation and interpretation of counter-cultural forms that cannot, and should not, be reduced to any form of 'sub' categorisation. I am detailing how black youth had palpable control over the Reggae dancehalls, where they overstood and therefore managed, aesthetically, culturally and politically these spaces that were 'owned' by blacks in urban Britain.

In chapter 1, I present the historical rationale behind my opting to use blak without the 'c' as denoting a particular orientation within the black British community. I argue that although there were many similarities in the racialised experiences of black people in Britain during the 1970s and 1980s, there were also significant differences on a 'conscious' level. These differences tend to be obscured in the many theories of the black presence in Britain, especially those that un-problematically regard black communities as a 'social problem' or 'settled' where the inference is almost one of contentment. As a counter to this type of 'outsider' account, I will in Chapter 2 present in detail how I have come to recognise myself as the 'outsider' academic/ethnographer who is 'inside' the culture in question composing a song of 'self'. One overarching concern with this position has been coping with the realisation that the ethnographic gaze was/is largely responsible for the construction of its research object and subject. Hence the power the ethnographer/writer has over the 'folk' or culture under scrutiny needs to be considered, for what is often deemed to be 'their' reality, is often that aspect of their social world that is deemed 'worthy' of study. This is a serious concern for me because I know that many who write about the 'black experience' only do so to achieve their post graduate qualifications and then move on to the next piece of 'exotica'.

In Chapter 3, the final chapter of the A~SIDE, I argue for the recognition of an entity called 'black music' that resists various over-intellectualised notions of whether or not there can be such a thing. I do so by evaluating much that has been written about why 'black youth' in urban Britain embraced Reggae-dancehall music, which fails to consider 'black music' as a site for the outernational exchanging of alternative social, cultural, political and historical knowledge. I therefore highlight the flaws in the types of analysis that do not overstand how to live and breathe in Babylon through conscious thought and action. Equally I will claim that without this type of consideration such theorisations all too often erroneously cite the supposed 'rap influence' on the British Deejays, as the most crucial factor in our lyrical development. A view that has somewhat obscured the seminal role Jamaican Reggae musicians/performers played in the 'creation' of the British Deejay. This means that I necessarily engage with much that was written about black people in Britain; because I want to prepare the reader for my argument which will, in the B~SIDE, demonstrate why overstanding the Deejay contribution is crucial to documenting the hidden experience of living in Babylon.

The *B~SIDE,* **Drama On Plastic: The critique from the street!,** consists of four empirical chapters in which I focus on the lyricism of the Deejays to demonstrate how Reggae-dancehall music is a vehicle for resisting and transcending racial oppression/exclusion. This means I will provide an insight into the motivation behind black youth in Britain becoming Deejays and, by doing so, demonstrate their unique take on social realism. It needs to be noted that for various reasons the notion of 'black youth', who were the prime targets of social research, became synonymous with a hypermasculinity because:

> In sociological and cultural research, it is the forms of subcultural resistances by black male youth that are analysed...Black women are seldom recognized as a particular socio-cultural entity, nor as important enough to merit serious academic consideration. (Carby, 1999:226)

The accuracy of Carby's trenchant commentary is telling, for it demonstrates the lopsided nature of the type of academic enterprise that largely obscured the black female presence in these endeavours to understand this highly visible 'social problem'. This can be partially explained by the predominance of males in these forms of expressive culture as noted by Noble who suggests:

> As in many forms of black popular music, the main producers of Ragga have tended to be male, expressing through the lyrics and the DJ sound systems - exemplary forms of musical production and

distribution - a strongly urbanized working-class male culture...The prime exponents of Ragga lyrics are male, with only a few female DJs gaining Diasporic attention in the 1990s (namely Lady Saw and Patra). (2000: 150)

As noted by Noble, female representation 'up-front' in Sound System culture as Selectors or Operators was low, as was the number of female Deejays, yet the female presence was high with regard to sheer numbers of those who frequented Reggae-dancehalls. This obvious imbalance will be reflected in this account as the focus is on Deejaying, which to this day remains a male dominated enterprise. However, the mere fact that many theorists focused their 'knowing' gaze in this myopic fashion meant that the 'voices' of 'black male youth' were also 'hidden' in many respects for:

> In this sense young black men like myself in the 70's were associated with the dangers of the future; pessimism, dirt and noise and therefore had to be controlled by those who muted the voices of young black women, which was also a way of controlling the thoughts and actions of the black communities in Britain whose parents, we are told, failed to control their children. (Ronnie McGrath, Personal Communication 2002)

McGrath's argument is relevant because by analysing the narratives contained in these 'hidden voices', we, the objects of this type of social research, quite often present an alternative account of what it meant to be a black youth, both male and female, in Britain during this moment. It is for this reason that in Chapter 4, I will pick up on the themes discussed in the A~SIDE and present an argument that counters the negative depictions of black youth, with which we are still faced with, as a means of 'promoting the youts' (Champion, 1983).

In Chapter 5 I take this crucial notion of 'promoting the youts' a stage further as I focus on how 'conscious' thought and action are determined by the 'choices' the Deejays make to challenge the downpressor on the terrain of language. This is because any consideration of the form must note the significance of the Jamaican Deejays and the seminal role they played in our embracing of the culture. Furthermore, I will demonstrate the complexity behind the notion of 'consciousness', for many 'conscious Deejays' are proficient 'burial' artists. What then becomes a crucial consideration of this idea of 'consciousness' is how the Deejay determines the moments when a particular style will be most appreciated because, as will become evident, true 'originators' must have within their repertoire 'all kindah style'.

Chapter 6 will focus on the internal registers that determine 'originality' as opposed to 'piracy', that which was regarded as antithetical to the originator's position within the culture, as the 'pirate' was 'ah lyrics thief'. This theme will be expanded in Chapter 7, the final chapter, where I focus on a shift in Deejay consciousness that led many Deejays to aspire to a level of professionalism, which was a consequence of the form becoming commercially viable. However what became a major issue was who the form was representing with regard to the effectiveness of its libratory potential as the 'hidden voice of blak British urban expression'. The main concern was twofold: firstly, the 'pirate' Deejays, who had access to recording studios or record companies, were in a position to earn from the products of another performer's mind. Secondly, the mainly white owned record companies and other forms of white minded involvement seemed to be more interested in promoting the gimmicky side of the culture, which meant that the blak/conscious side became subsumed under the weight of this type of expectation. For these main reasons, I will argue that when an identifiably black cultural form becomes appropriated, much of its potency as a resistant and transcendental force is lost and, as such, it becomes regarded as unrepresentative of those who use it to chant down Babylon.

Conclusion: Future Prospects

Summarising the main points of discussion will allow me to conclude the book with a statement on the worth of resistant forms of cultural expression, which enable the downpressed to resist and transcend the myriad forms of white racism. This is because my argument clearly demonstrates that it is imperative to rethink the worth of 'insider' accounts that give 'voice' to the 'voiceless' in a manner that more accurately reflects what it is like to be on the receiving end of racist exclusionary practices in contemporary British society. I will then present a proviso for future studies of this nature that seek to increase our appreciation of the black presence in Britain in a more inclusive manner.

Run Di Riddim

WHAT THE DEEJAY SAID

WHAT THE DEEJAY SAID

Chapter 1

'Black youth', whose truth? The redefining of difference

Introduction

Scientific objectivity cannot mean the denial by deafening silence the true record of oppressed people, and it is only human and realistic to be emotional about facts and realities which are truly moving in their cruel and inhuman impact. It is part of the condition of the civilized mind to raise an aware and moral voice in righteous indignation; to push the pen more furiously and sensitively to historical records which define our universal humanity or inhumanity. When we do this we are not simply moralizing and condemning evils. More than that as Herbert Aptheker has written it is: "because struggling against them educates and unites people. (Prah, 1992:15)

Language is a marvellous thing. It both mirrors and leads our collective thinking, changing to reflect changes in our culture and at the same time nudging those changes forward. (Roosevelt Thomas. Jr, 1996:xi)

In this opening chapter I present an argument for the recognition of 'adaptive responses' (Troyna, 1979) to racial oppression by black people in Britain, which are not reliant on various pathological explanations that largely view these responses as types of instinctive or deviant behaviour. This entails an evaluation of the 'scientific objectivity' of certain social theorists who sought to explain the behavioural patterns of black people in general, and black youth in particular, during the 'crisis' periods of the 1970s and 1980s. What is crucial to my argument is that this was the historical moment when Deejaying was at its most forceful, pushing the 'pen furiously' to create tales of 'rejection' that gave a voice to the voiceless, whilst 'educating and uniting people'. I will therefore offer an evaluation of how the notions of 'rejection' as forwarded by many social theorists, failed to recognise 'rejection' as an 'adaptive response' to a real social predicament. More so when it is the language of 'collective thinking', written or spoken, that is adapted as in the case of blak, which is a 'self-generated concept'. Such concepts, I will argue, represent the real need to embrace a more positive notion of an Afrikan/blak self as a tool for negotiating a sane path through a hostile, racist, environment.

To assist my argument I will begin by presenting an alternative view of 'black' consciousness; demonstrating how the ideal 'black', as posited by the 'Black Power Movement' of the 1960s, has become confused with various generalised notions of 'oppression'. This will clearly demonstrate how a fuller appreciation of Deejay lyricism, as part of an outernational system of knowledge exchanges across the 'black Atlantic' (Gilroy, 1993a), details how the 'hidden voice' countered many of the established theories/views/opinions that categorised black youth as unintelligent and uneducable. I am therefore arguing for the recognition of a more complex pattern of conscious thought behind specified usages of Jamaican language (Patwa), within the alternative public arena that is the Reggae-dancehall.

1.1   Redefining difference: UK Blak

Be natural be proud you were born that way, be natural be proud you were born that way, say it loud, I'm black and I'm proud, believe me say it loud, just a little louder. (Dandy, 1969)

The word in language is half someone else's. It becomes "one's own" only when the speaker populates it with his own intention, his own accent, when he appropriates the word, adapting it to his own semantic and expressive intention. Prior to this moment of appropriation, the word does not exist in a neutral or impersonal language...but rather it exists in other people's mouths, serving other people's intentions: it is from there that one must take the word and make it one's own. (Bakhtin, 1981:293/4)

In society you can find me, if you stop living life so blindly, Daddy says we'll never change things, but I have faith in the African abroad. UK Blak, ending the silence now, UK Blak letting you know that we're about. (Wheeler and Macintosh, 1991)

The usage of 'blak' emerged in urban London during the late 1980s and when Caron Wheeler of 'Soul to Soul' fame, released an album entitled 'UK BLAK' for EMI records, the word became known in mainstream British society. By omitting the letter 'c', Wheeler was making a profound Africentric political statement that reflected a conscious move by certain members of the black community to distance themselves from the negative connotations of black as the colour of doom, oppression, bad luck etc. This meant that the term blak, which was created within the counter cultures of the Afrikan Diaspora, had much currency and signified an alternative way of thinking about the black presence in Britain. By using the term blak, the British born of Afrikan descent expressed a defiant attitude that questioned and challenged the seeming acceptance of their lot by the parental generation. This is a crucial aspect of black youth culture that I consider here as representative of an intellectual engagement with a dominant society, which largely fails to consider or represent your lived reality. Therefore, in the first instance, the positing of blak is a way of expressing how it was not enough for certain black youth to physically populate the British isles as the silent unwanted other, which for many is what their parental generation were seemingly contented to do. Rather for these youth, who often knew no other place as 'home', a conscious decision was made on the terrain of language to stake a claim for 'belonging' that required using our own 'accent' to 'populate' the words of the dominant culture; thus 'appropriating' them and making them our 'own' as we were not content to be the 'passive receptacles of the will of the enslaving other' (Cooper, 1993:174). Therefore the fact that 'Daddy says we'll never change things' did not deter blak youth like Wheeler and Macintosh who had, through their exposure to an outernational system of alternative knowledge, 'faith in the African abroad'.

Rendering the true significance of this moment will be one my of major concerns as it demonstrated that within these counter cultures, the taking of 'your' words and making them 'our' own refigured what it meant to be 'black' in the urban British context. I am arguing that the redefined word was a semantic and expressive declaration and that, by 'ending the silence', 'we' (blaks) were letting 'you' (mainstream white society) know 'that we're about' and, in this way, thus challenging and disrupting Britishness as an exclusively white domain. We need only to think about the replacement of 'Afro-Caribbean' with 'Black Caribbean' or 'black' with 'urban'—in contemporary Britain—to understand how Afrikans are constantly being 'played' by those in power in a game that often results in a loss of historical memory. In fact, Gilroy, from another cultural and political perspective, arrives at more or less the same conclusion in a section of his book 'The Black Atlantic', entitled 'UK Blak'. Gilroy failed to provide an actual definition of 'blak' throughout this section but nevertheless suggested that:

> The issue of identity and non-identity of black cultures has acquired a special historical and political significance in Britain. Black settlement in that country goes back many centuries, and affirming its continuity has become an important part of the politics that strive to answer contemporary British racism. However, the bulk of today's black communities are of relatively recent origin, dating only from the post-World War II period. If these populations are unified at all, it is more the experience of migration than by the memory of slavery and the residues of plantation society. (1993a:81)

The major point seems to be that the blacks in Britain, in a relatively short space of time, were losing a crucial part of their historical memory that would obviously root them back to Afrika. And of equal importance, they were also distancing themselves from a black historical presence in Britain that dates back 'many centuries', well before the chattel slave era (Fryer 1984, Bygott 1992, Okokon 1998, Henry 2002). For an affirmation of the historical continuity of this black presence to be truly effective against 'contemporary British racism', it had to counter the view that blacks were recent arrivals, bereft of a valid history and only 'unified' through the 'experience of migration'. What then becomes crucial is how to achieve this goal when faced with a 'history' that excludes any meaningful Afrikan involvement in the global arena as anything other than chattels, because not many are aware that:

> There is nothing inevitable about history. History consists of those bits of the past that someone had the knowledge, interest, foresight and ability to record for future generations. The telling of the black history of London, ancient and modern, is more flawed than most

historical narratives for several reasons, some personal and individual, others institutional and cultural. (Okokon, 1998:7)

What is of primary interest here is Okokon's suggestion that there are 'institutional and cultural' factors that obscure a more meaningful black historical presence, which is quite different from a suggestion that blacks achieved nothing of historical note. Furthermore, by stating that many had the 'foresight' to 'record for future generations' that which obviously they wished to be known and transmitted is dependent upon having the 'ability' to achieve these ends in certain spaces. It is imperative we consider how within the Reggae-dancehall, a system of knowledge exchange was created that enabled many blacks in the UK to pass on this knowledge to 'future generations'. Therefore, the Reggae-dancehall became a site where notions of history and belonging could be aired and discussed, by those who had the ability to transform their everyday experiences into a lyrical form of recorded documentation. Consequently many blacks became exposed to the Deejay lyricism that featured the 'telling of black history in London', as part of a series of ongoing negotiations in the Reggae-dancehalls. Thereby offering a more realistic appraisal of what it meant to be regarded and treated as the unwanted nigger/wog/spade/coon 'other' in the 'mother country'. Furthermore, this would mean that for many Afrikans an exposure to a more positive notion of self (in this instance via an exposure to Deejay lyricism) strengthened black communities by offering them a tangible source of self-empowerment that was controlled from within.

It was out of these strivings for a more positive notion of self that blak emerged as a counter to the 'history' that placed the Afrikan, and those of Afrikan descent, as Europe's antithesis. Hence the conceptualisation of what it meant to be blak became part of an ongoing quest for the reclamation of a more positive self, free from the biases of the types of European history that turns my-story, as an Afrikan, into a mystery. The main point is that blak has a historical, cultural and political worth that needs to be fully appreciated, as it speaks out of that space where people know and live (experience) something, articulate the concept as part of an ongoing reality (voice it), and then coin a word to facilitate the concept. Conceptualisations like blak, therefore, speak to a particular take on reality based on conscious thought and action and cannot be separated from the social conditions, or the cultural communities, from which they emanate. This must be understood as a reflection of the mood of a community that recognises the reality of their structural position as 'other', who then choose to use whatever tools they have at their disposal to resist and transcend racialised oppression. Many who are not familiar with the history that led to the usage of particular words (that trigger concepts), often dismiss their usage as mere 'code switching' forms of 'wordplay' that lack significant depth. In fact in agreement with Sebba's (1993) findings on the role and purpose of 'black language' use by the generations who were born in post-war Britain, Mühleisen, argues that:

> Sebba's study also illustrates that for most of these second-to third-generation speakers, a form of British English (here London English) is their first language. Their uses of Creoles/patois are often quite restricted and London Jamaican is always used in conjunction with British English in a code-switching style. The functions of Creole are therefore limited: its communicative purpose is not as important as its symbolic identity as a marker of black identity. Sebba identifies the use of Creole, or 'talking black' as a social rather than informational activity. (2002:43)

This type of analysis denies the fact that in all languages there exist several words, concepts and phrases, that are not translatable into other languages, which is why you often overhear English examples of this occurrence punctuate the conversations of speakers of other languages. The point is that I have never heard this type of language use described as 'code switching' or 'wordplay', which means the perception of English words and phrases are somehow regarded as different when used in this fashion. Therefore, to suggest that 'talking black' is 'a social rather than informational activity', denies the practicality of using language to state an alternative position/perspective, because it relegates such usage solely to the realms of the 'symbolic'. There is a failure to recognise the profundity of staking alternative claims in a language that you command, where a clear-cut distinction between the 'social' and the 'informational' cannot be justified, as exemplified in the Reggae-dancehall when the Deejay is most definitely 'talking black'. It is for this reason that during the 1980s there was a spate of British Deejay lyrics that solely dealt with what it meant to be blak in Britain as I conceptualise it here, which is a critical part of what is in essence an 'informational activity'. For example, two of the most popular were entitled 'Proud To Be Black': the first recorded by Crucial Robbie (1985) and the second by Macka B (1988). Both performers 'chatted' the lyrics on Sound Systems before they were recorded and, so, the content was known within the culture before they were 'put on plastic' (recorded). Crucial Robbie presented a scenario in which a 'black sister' was ashamed of her appearance and did her best to destroy 'the African' within her. Ultimately she self-destructed in her endeavours to 'bleach her skin', 'twang an gwaan stoosh', which is Jamaican for acting stuck-up, posh, and such like, because she constantly compared herself to her white friend's Eurocentric ideals therefore operating out of an aesthetic that was anti-Afrikan; whereas in Macka B's lyric, he suggested through an exemplary usage of 'black talk':

> Even though I might be subject to racial attack, even though certain people see me as second class, even though it might be harder to reach to the top, I would never want to change the fact that I'm black, cau me love how we walk an me love how we chat, love we culture, love we music, yes me love all ah that, an me love how we cook spicy food in ah pot, an the rhythm in ah me a supn that me nah swap, cau me proud that me black, yes me proud that me black, an why not. (Macka B, 1988)

Both performers deal with many of the issues that still impact upon the lives and perceptions of peoples of Afrikan descent who are afflicted with western-eyes-ation and aesthetically, culturally, spiritually and politically, view being Afrikan as negative. For this reason, Macka B presents an ontological take on being Afrikan that places an aesthetic worth on the very things that many believe are the marks of our supposed inferiority. So, whereas the sister in Crucial Robbie's lyric 'twangs' and acts 'stoosh', Macka B states that 'me love how we walk an me love how we chat', which for him is due to being Afrikan in Europe's New World. A 'New World' that was fashioned upon a notion of whiteness by murderous, racist Europeans, driven by white supremacist thought and action, to the detriment of the human family, especially those who, like Afrikans, are classified as non-white. In this context the 'rhythm in ah me a supn that me nah swap' is the knowledge of yourself as Afrikan, for when I reasoned with him about this lyric, he stated, 'check what I say in the 'Them Kinda Blackman' tune on the 'Global Messenger' (2000) album, cau is just Afrikan roots every-time' (Personal Communication 2001). I also asked Macka B why the emphasis was on 'man' and he informed me that 'when I an I use man I am speaking of the male and female principle, because it is impossible for I to separate woman from I self'. This will in fact be, unless otherwise stated, the way in which the term will be generically employed in this study for reasons that will become apparent as we journey through this cultural form. Hence:

> The negative stereotype of the Blackman is something that must be challenged at all times. In this time of increasing knowledge and truth, a more positive and powerful Blackman is emerging from the mental chains. A man who knows why things are the way they are and what must be done to redress the balance. (Macka B, 2000)

Macka B clearly states that black people need to realise that the way we conceptualise self through 'negative stereotypes' can only be countered by an increase in 'knowledge and truth'. By doing so, in this instance via the social-'informational activity' that is Deejaying, we will then be in a position to 'know why things are the way they are' and more importantly do 'what needs to be done to redress the balance'. It is this type of awareness that fuelled the cultural and political sensibilities that generated the concept blak as a form of 'ideological weaponry' (Cooper, 2000) in the battle to slip the yoke of 'the mental chains'. Hence, blak has a political dimension that arguably mirrors the sensibilities behind the usage of 'black' as put forward by the authors of 'Black Power' during the mid-1960s. They argued that black power 'called for black people to consolidate behind their own, so that they can bargain from a position of strength' (Ture and Hamilton, 1992:47). The suggestion was that until black people 'close ranks' and reappraise the reality of their oppressed social status, from their own racial and cultural perspective, they would continuously be politically neutered within the 'open (white) society'. Simply put, 'those who have the right to define are the masters of the situation' (Ture and Hamilton, 1992:36), and so to alter the situation, there is a need to discover knowledge that enables you to define reality in your own words, on your own terms. The onus was firmly placed on black people to rediscover their African heritage, to counter the 'white lies' that robbed them of knowledge of self, because our history is 'not taught in the standard textbooks of this country' (1992: 38). Moreover, the fact that our history is not found in 'standard textbooks' meant that the spaces and places that this could be corrected would have to come from within the black community, because:

> If black people are not represented as grotesque caricatures then they are ignored and it is as if...white people construct the world and are the makers and doers, the creators of culture and societies, and 'we're just here'. (Scafe, 1989:17)

As a counter to this distorted view of the black presence, recognition of an Afrika before the chattel slave era was imperative; otherwise, there would not have been any meaningful historical referent from which to stake your alternative claims. The seriousness of this perspective cannot be overstated as the alternative claims are derived from an exposure to different ideas, from which these Africentric positive self-concepts are generated. Therefore, black had to become synonymous and demonstrative of:

> A culture and identity that is rooted in the Caribbean and Africa, that continues to grow and absorb other influences into its original cultural matrix. The term must be understood in this context. (Sutcliffe, 1986:2)

British Deejaying is demonstrative of the manner in which this 'original cultural matrix' has grown by absorbing and synthesising various elements that once sewn together, became a potent voice in the quest for real social change across the urban landscape. Hence, a more positive identity was freely articulated within the Reggae-dancehall arena, because it was dependent upon making links that do not necessarily seek to prove a purity of origins; rather, it was based upon a similarity of life chances and experiences of racism. Although, as Gilroy states, 'the desire to affirm and celebrate unbroken continuity is clearly a response to racisms that deny any historical currency to black life' (cited in Ugwu, 1995: 23) and I would suggest that it is part of a process of discovering a more rewarding sense of who 'we' are in Europe's New World. Unsurprisingly, this principle that argued for Afrika to be acknowledged as an empowering reference point, for black people, was largely undermined by ludicrous claims that blacks were being 'racist in reverse' or 'black supremacist'. Claims that Ture and Hamilton (1992) rightly dismissed as 'deliberate and absurd lies' that could only detract from what was really at stake, the reclamation of Afrikan humanity. Consequently this type of confusion, as to how the term black should be interpreted/deployed, was never truly resolved and for this reason it can still in one sense be construed as pro-Afrikan, or, in another, as anti any type of oppression. For as Mercer poignantly suggests:

> The radical appropriation of the sign/black in the democratic struggles of the postmodern era disarticulated it out of one signifying chain and rearticulated it into another as an empowering metaphor for political identity. (1990:402)

This is not that surprising when we consider that black struggles for autonomy paved the way for many other 'oppressed' groups to state their alternate claims. For instance according to Edgar (1981):

> Without Black Brotherhood, there would have been no sisterhood; without Black power and Black Pride there would have been no Gay power and Gay Pride. The movement against the abuse of the powers of the state...derived much of its strength and purpose from the exposure of the F.B.I.'s surveillance of the Black Panthers and the Black Muslims. (Cited in Gilroy, 1982:296)

Further endorsement of this crucial argument comes from Lawrence Hayes, a member of the Black Panther Party, who served over twenty years in an American prison, as many others did in the struggle against white racism, he suggests:

> The fact that we gave a platform to many other groups who were fighting for their own civil rights means nothing now, because people have forgotten what we were about. Being black meant being proud of your Afrikan heritage and trying to make that knowledge count for supn, because we gotta learn to help ourselves first before we can think about helping anyone else. (Personal Communication, 1996)

Hayes crucially states, in much the same way that Malcolm X did, that before we can help others there is a need to reappraise what it means to be 'black' in terms of our own 'civil rights', as unique to peoples of Afrikan descent. This, because past political alliances between various groups and peoples of Afrikan descent are no longer viable under this catch-all category. Therefore, it is prudent for the wider community to recognise that the relationship that was forged between these groups under the banner of 'black', especially in Britain, has always been a tenuous one for various reasons. Some of these concerns are being evidenced nowadays in the confusion surrounding the label BME (Black Minority Ethnic) as it, like 'urban', always seems to denote or relate to peoples of Afrikan descent. Hence the following observation:

> In Britain, where until recently, that was before the Asians courageously, some would say opportunistically, brought a dramatic halt to the farce, it was fashionable for whoever felt that they were 'disadvantaged because of their racial background' to call themselves 'black', even if they were aryan caucasoids. In other words, the term 'black' had ceased to have any discernible cultural or historical reference. (Ekwe-Ekwe, 1994:16)

It is as a reclamation of the 'cultural and historical reference' which places Afrika at the centre of a 'black' worldview, that I stake my claim for the validity of the term 'blak' as demarcating a particular political, cultural, social and racial perspective. This means that the 'c' in 'black' is regarded as a sign of the ongoing 'colonisation' of the black subject/object in the wider public arena, most notably in the language of Eurocentric academic and non-academic writings. Of equal importance this notion of blak distinguishes itself from the pejorative usage of 'black' in its throwaway commonsense everyday usage, which obscures a conscious commitment to an Africentric worldview that challenges the notion of the 'African' other. Furthermore, this highlights how the oppressed recognise and verbalise their lived reality as a means of countering Euro/logo-centrism, by undermining the 'master' (white) narratives that have historically depicted the African-black as the object of history. Therefore, Deejay lyricism offers an alternative pedagogy for much of the Afrikan Diaspora, because the trauma of the injurious middle passage journey across the Atlantic, dispersal, brutal oppression and other such atrocities, act as firm reminders of our shared history of exclusion, domination and cultural genocide at the hands of racist Europeans. Admittedly, there have been certain changes with regard to the blatancy of racist practices in post-war Britain, but racism on an experiential level has always, for me, remained constant. Consequently, within the Deejay community I am indigenous to, it is freely accepted that:

> Me nuh talk fi the Chiney, Syrian or Indian, me nuh know where them going or where them coming from, all me know seh we ah blakman an in the bible Afrika it mention'. (Daddy Colonel, 1998)

Colonel's argument is representative of a form of cultural criticism that views the black/Afrikan struggle as historically unique, because the chattel slave era was an attempt to strip the Afrikan of their status as part of the human family. It pays to remember the 1790 'Naturalisation Law' in America and the ways in which it influenced the global treatment and perception of the African/black/negro, stating that only 'whites' could be granted 'full citizenship'. Add to this the impact of the 'Dred Scott Judgement' of 1857, which stated that we (blacks) were not human but 'merely articles of commerce' and 'were so far inferior that they had no rights that a white man was bound to respect' (Mullane, 1993:132). Our struggles, therefore, have been premised on a uniquely constructed notion of difference, sanctioned by laws that equated the African to three-fifths of a human being (Anderson, 1997:47) and no other group has had to combat this 'mathematical equation' (Hampton and Fayer, 1990). Therefore those who have this awareness will seek to redefine the terms that perpetuate their oppressed status, both literally and psychologically, and equally refuse to accept that our battle for self can be confused with other struggles against oppression. For:

> In the 1860s the 14th Amendment was enacted to give blacks due process rights. Yet, for nearly a century afterwards, the U.S. Supreme Court ruled against every due process rights case involving blacks. (Anderson, 1997:41)

Armed with this knowledge of black reality is it any wonder that Deejays like Daddy Colonel have no desire to speak for any other oppressed group as 'me nuh know where them going or where them coming from'?. His argument centres on being conscious of the historical differences in our ongoing downpression, then using this 'knowledge' and making 'it count'. For this reason, I will expand upon this aspect of my argument in the next section by evaluating the forms of consciousness that drive these types of commitment to spreading blak awareness in urban Britain.

1.2 'Black' like you or 'blak' like me? The language of consciousness!

It has been said that the slaves who came here from Africa came here speaking a savage gibberish. Slowly they began to acquire a civilized form of communication, but because of their intellectual inferiority or physiological differences they failed to acquire the language properly. Their thick lips and oversized tongues got into the way of English and murdered it...These myths are rooted not only in a profound prejudice against black people, but in a profound ignorance about Africa and its contribution to the world of science. (Van Sertima, 1986)

In agreement with Van Sertima's argument, I am suggesting that this notion of blak is informed by an exposure to alternative ways of viewing the black subject—socially, culturally, historically and politically—that refute 'myths' that perpetuate 'a profound ignorance about Africa'. Therefore, by drawing on a more positive idea of our Afrikan heritage, black people in Britain have a means to empower themselves by challenging these insidious 'myths' about our 'savage' past. Moreover, an exposure to this culture of the written and spoken word, demonstrates how intelligent and profound social commentary is often presented by those whose decision to use non-standard English has nothing to do with the size of their 'lips and tongues'. This means that I embrace Mintz's view that the legacy of slave 'institutions' is embedded within the 'social forms and perceptions of New World peoples' (1989: 62), as witnessed *par excellence* in the diverse musical cultures of the Afrikan Diaspora. A view that assists an outernational Africentric orientation as problems that many would have us believe are localised, and particular to the British context, are put in a global perspective and disseminated through identifiably 'black talk'. In fact, nonsensical definitions that obscure an Afrikan heritage like 'black Caribbean', 'black British', 'coloured', 'peoples of colour', 'urban' etc. are interrogated for their cultural relevance and political substance. The basis for this claim is obvious in light of the fact that many blacks in Britain regard themselves as 'Afro-Caribbean', yet interestingly enough this categorisation is no longer featured on many of the forms that request this type of 'ethnic' identification/information. For instance, the 'Count Me In Census 2001' has no such categorisation, which means that there is obviously something amiss when 'legally' a 'definition' of self obscures the Afrikan aspect of your identity. Therefore, your 'ethnic origin' is determined by those who are in a position to define, or redefine, this aspect of your everyday 'reality', which makes them 'the masters of the situation' (Ture and Hamilton 1992). In this way they are no different from the white masters who convinced many of us that we were niggers, thereby accepting that we were indeed less human than our white counterparts. Without consciously being aware of these factors that are chief determinants in the politics of identification, is it any wonder that many blacks in Britain display the types of confused public behaviour that borders on the insane? For example, consider the comments of the Tory enlisted Patti Boulaye, a black singer and supposed spokesperson for the black British, who seriously suggested that:

> Stephen Lawrence's killers were obviously Labour voters... Prejudice is what makes black footballers as good as they are...A good economy stops black people from feeling so black. (The Mirror, 12/11/1998)

Whilst the comments of the 'vacuous' Boulaye are astounding in their insensitivity and lack of meaningful intellectual engagement with the lived reality of many black people in a racist society, they do highlight a major problem in contemporary Britain. That is, how can the notion of black as an oppressive sign in the English language be countered by those who are largely bound, whether they like it or not, by its negative signification? For it is one thing to suggest, as Hall (cited in Back 1996: 4) does, that a positive notion of black within the sphere of 'representation' can effectively 'unsettle' the 'reified images' of blacks that dominate popular culture. It is quite another thing to see how this manifests in the concrete, where a cursory glance at any 'authoritative' source, i.e. your television set, handy dictionary, encyclopedia, or your average textbook presents quite another story. I would suggest that, far from furnishing the black person with a source of empowerment that would basically equip them to counter/unsettle these 'reified images', these sources quite often compound a sense of black inferiority. To make the point clearer, in an edition of the Jamaican daily newspaper 'The Gleaner' (16/3/01), it was reported that a group of West Indian cricketers were attacked by 'Aussie racists' during their Australian tour. One of the victims, the ironically named, Marlon Black, who was injured after being hit with various projectiles, suffering multiple wounds to the body, suggested, 'it was really unfortunate, it was just a little misunderstanding...I think they might have mistaken us for African people'. I am led to wonder if the outcome of this 'unfortunate...little misunderstanding' would have been more amicable had Mr Black been given the time to brandish his Trinidadian passport, thus demonstrating to the 'Aussie racists' how un-African he was! This somewhat distorted perspective on what it is to be African perfectly captures how the logic/rationale behind Black's, and Boulaye's, comments can be accessed through an analysis of Deejay lyricism. More importantly, it will also demonstrate how these depictions of black/African as inferior are consciously countered in alternative blak cultural spaces, for as Papa Levi suggests:

> Everytime that I clip on the TV and I see three or four black celebrity, them always seem to hitch-up with cokey, children what are they trying to tell we? Nuff black them a lust, fame an status, when them get rich them own people them dust, but hear me, everytime me clip on the damn TV, as far as me two bullfrog eyes can see, nuff blackman with little popularity, whether in ah sport music or movie, as them get a little success financially, them draw fi Caucasian automatically, faster dan a speeding Lamborghini, them run gaan ah church immediately...nuff ah the bride relatives ah call him darky, who nuh call him darky ah call him monkey, but darky don't mind darky deh with whitey...nuff ah fi we people get brainwash, them drink dutty water fi reach the top, an me think that wrong an me know that slack, you know wot I mean arry, friggin eediot, dah one deh want kick in ah him damn neckback, karen will you marry me? Karen caan wash me socks, me nuh eat the bacon neither porkchops, blackman you fi do better dan that. (Papa Levi, 1994)

The reasoning behind Papa Levi's sentiments is obvious in light of Boulaye's and Black's comments, because for them to be recognised as black/African is to accept that they are less than their white/European counterparts. Hence, being successful, as in directly benefiting from a 'good economy', according to Boulaye's rationale, 'stops black people from feeling so black'. What may we ask is it to feel 'so black' that a modicum of economic well-being can so successfully offset? The answer I would suggest lies in how we are socialised into accepting that 'the whiteness of whiteness is the blindness of wilful innocence' (Lazarre, 1997: 49). It therefore comes as no great surprise that much that is associated with being white/European is deemed to be good/human/superior, whereas black/African is to be bad/inhuman/inferior. This said, should we be shocked by statements such as the above, uttered in my opinion by very 'un-well-beings, that are the symptoms of the menticide that was a consequence of the chattel-slave era and continues to this day in the form of 'Post Traumatic Slave Syndrome' (Leary, 2004)? Hence:

> Even with the passage of the civil rights acts of the 1960s, Leary explained, no measures were put in place to help African Americans cope with all they had suffered, and to rectify the damage that the maltreatment had done to them mentally, spiritually and physically over many generations. Plus, today Blacks in America still face racism, oppression and societal inequality. "There was never a period of time when Africans in this nation were given the permission or the wherewithal to heal from our injury, so the trauma has continued," she stated. (Lamb, 2004)

To paraphrase, the damage to the Afrikan psyche as a consequence of chattel enslavement is seldom acknowledged in the wider public arena, with the ongoing fight for fiscal and psychological reparations a testimony to this reality. As such, many 'successful blacks' believe that white acceptance is based on denial and 'playing the whiteman' to the detriment of their own humanity. For them, there is no visible sense of loss or healing forthcoming as the trauma of the enslaved past is not a consideration. Thus, the way to deal with contemporary racism is to consume your way through it, covetousness for them becomes a viable coping mechanism. Is it not any wonder, then, that Levi would suggest that as soon as these 'brainwashed blackman' become financially successful, 'them draw fi Caucasian automatically', because by doing so they will obviously not 'feel so black'. Moreover, in his opinion, this is a deliberate ploy of a dominant white culture that encourages black people to 'drink dutty water fi reach the top'; in other words, act the 'darky', clown or buffoon like the 'friggin eediot' Frank Bruno, if 'you know wot I mean arry'? Considering the overwhelming 'popularity' of this black 'personality' and his ilk, it is important for us to realise that these struggles over language, as they affect black representation in mainstream society, are far from being resolved, although many would have us believe it. In fact, take a passing glance at any of the recent publications on race and ethnicity and see if they have even begun to acknowledge the fact that Africans are still at the bottom of the human chain, irrespective of what we are led to believe. This is a fact mirrored in the amounts of negative press that Afrikans are receiving from the global media powerhouses who attack our cultures from every conceivable angle, always suggesting we need to be saved by the benevolent white man. To this, Amos Wilson suggests that it fits into the pattern that suits white supremacist thought and action where black people are 'used to being saved by Europeans' (Wilson, 1994); from Tarzan to white Jesus I might add. For this reason, Levi suggests that 'everytime' black people 'clip on the TV', they need to seriously consider the types of messages that are being disseminated by a dominant culture by continuously asking ourselves, 'what are they trying to tell we'?

Seeking to answer such a question led to the usage of 'blak' as a counter to 'black' as a negative sign, which spoke to the condition of those who are enwrapped in its negative signification with regard to their mental/physical placement in a white racist society. I am speaking of a practical knowledge, which is intrinsically linked to a practical consciousness that challenges the notion of 'black' as a banner for almost any oppressed cultural/racial/social group. Therefore, the suggestion is that the systems of oppression that presently render the blak voice 'hidden', represent a continuum first utilised to exploit, subjugate and control the chattel slaves, during that which Khalid Muhammad has dubbed the:

> Afrikan hellocaust, because we paid and continue to pay a hell-of-a-cost, and will continue to do so until we realise that we cannot allow our enemy to control what we say, when we say it and how we say it…we must learn to define ourselves from our own perspective based on blak culture, consciousness and commitment. (1997)

To identify yourself as blak means that you see a clear link between your current predicaments, as a person of Afrikan descent and the treatment meted out to your chattel slave forebears at the hands of racist Europeans. Hence this notion of blak is a mark of conscious self-empowerment, based on recognising the historical oppression Afrikan people have faced, premised on a simple truth that best demonstrates Hall's idea of the politicised nature of 'struggles over language'. This simple truth argues that without the power to define your own subjectivity on your own terms, through a particular usage of language drawn from within your own cultural 'frames of reference', you will constantly be defined/redefined from without by those who do not have your best interests at heart. Therefore the sensibilities behind Muhammad's usage of 'hellocaust' as a description of the 'price' the Afrikan has paid, and continues to pay, for their exploitation as a marker of 'inclusion' in Europe's New World, transcends a simplistic notion of rhetorical 'wordplay'.

I must state at this point that my perspective on 'struggles over language', with regard to the dissemination of a specific type of worldview, is only concerned here with how Deejays counter the English language as an agent for the maintenance of white supremacy. For whilst constructing lyrics and exploring various types of word/sound, the 'conscious' Deejay realises that white supremacist thinking permeates the culture of the English language, thus perpetuating black inferiority as natural. In a nutshell British born Deejays, who we can safely assume have a competent command of their mother tongue (Standard English), make a conscious decision to express themselves in another linguistic form, Patwa. By doing so they challenge the assimilatory force of Standardised English, which, when fully embraced, often erases all traces of an autonomous self that seeks edification from an Afrikan centre. This occurs because the language that identifies the ultimate form of belonging for us 'others'—our status as British subjects—is paradoxically determined by a rhetorical notion of citizenship that appears to be neutral when in reality it is ever beyond our grasp. Wong (1986) addressed this issue when arguing that black youths resisted the detrimental nature of their mother tongue's 'alphabet of terror', by embracing Rastafari language and symbolism as a part of a British counterculture. Furthermore, many of the Deejays whose lyrics are featured in this study have, according to Kimani Nehusi, been 'highly educated and certified by the dominant white society, yet choose to express themselves in their own language'

(Personal Communication 2000). As I will demonstrate below to use language in this way means that you fully recognise that:

> The language of instruction and literature is saturated with words, concepts, idioms, sayings that have strong and loaded values and nuances that suggest, directly or indirectly, notions of racial superiority, inferiority and suppression...These notions of racial dominance and superiority were formerly reinforced in schools, where the languages of Third World peoples were denigrated and marginalized. (Wong, 1986:118)

As a Deejay one of the strongest ways to counter the legitimacy of the 'language of instruction' is by demonstrating how the enemy distorts 'truth' in your own usage and manipulations of words and sounds. For instance, the Deejay can take a word like 'education', explain what it should be based on, our commonsense assumptions of a meritocratic 'learning' process, then provide what they deem to be a more accurate description of this process from a blak perspective: 'head-decay-shun'. By doing so, the Deejay draws on cultural resources that purposefully challenge the neutrality of the English language. In this case the term 'head-decay-shun' stems from a Rastafari notion of the 'brainwash education' we received from the savage white master that made us 'good' and 'obedient' chattel slaves and now seeks to 'turn Afrikan in ah robot' (Papa Levi, 1994). This means that Rastafari has evaluated the notion of what it is to be 'educated' by your enemy and concluded that what occurs is decadent and something to be shunned. It is imperative that we appreciate black language as a counter-hegemonic force from this perspective, because it provides the tangible links between resistance, survival and transcendence that are necessary to the promotion of an Afrikan-centred aesthetic/perspective. That is why in this context 'for a black writer to be born into the English language, is to realise that the assumptions on which the language operates are his enemy' (Cited in Gilroy, 1987).

Baldwin states that we are in fact 'born into' a language and suggests that being 'born into the English language' is, in the case of the black subject, synonymous with being nurtured by an enemy. For if like Baldwin you (a black person) are highly proficient in the 'correct' usage of Standard English, written and spoken, yet still find that you cannot measure-up to the 'English Standard', another set of issues are raised with regard to the links between, history, language, culture and identity. This is wrapped up in the English language is a heritage that projects a white/racial/cultural national identity that, by its very nature, excludes non-white peoples. For this reason we need to be aware of an enemy language that has tampered with our minds for many centuries and consequently erased/distorted/ destroyed much of our historical, cultural, and spiritual memories. Therefore, redefining and reconstructing the dominant language can only become a form of self-empowerment when the historical necessity is known. For as Bolinger suggests, much consideration is needed when evaluating the role of language in our contemporary societies because:

> The influences of language on thinking and behaviour must be everywhere pretty much the same. The manifestations will reflect social differences more than fundamental linguistic ones. (1990:ix)

What I am advocating is a fuller appreciation of how the differences between groups that evidently share the same 'language' are social/cultural constructs, which subsequently become racialized and politicised. In other words, you cannot stake your alternative claims through the language of your oppressor, unless you recognise the role that language has played in your historical oppression. Therefore, the perspectives offered by myself and the other performers who are the focal point of this work provide tangible and workable solutions to those who can identify with their reality because as an:

> Ideology for liberation must find its existence in ourselves, it cannot be external to us, and it cannot be imposed by those other than ourselves; it must be derived from our particular historical and cultural experience. Our liberation from the captivity of racist language is the first order of the intellectual. *There can be no freedom until there is a freedom of the mind.*[His emphasis] (Asante, 1995:31)

Asante's suggestion demonstrates that for many black people a process needs to be undertaken, which seeks salvation from the shackles that Europe has placed on the Afrikan mind, based on the forms of self-help that are determined from within the cultural milieu as advocated by the 'Black Power Movement'. I am suggesting that the tools, 'self-generated concepts', that are used to free 'the mind' are located within

44

blak libratory cultures and are coping and transcendental mechanisms in a racist society. Therefore, these 'self-generated concepts' have a history of furnishing the downpressed with an alternative worldview, especially when presented through language which promotes a blak aesthetic that is not reliant on European notions of acceptable forms of cultural expression. For what is being described is conducive to a re-figuring of the 'black' self by freeing it 'from the captivity of racist language', because 'words may obscure as much as illuminate that which they are meant to signify' (Tilley, 1990:284). For as Wheeler and Macintosh suggest, we are now 'opening our eyes and ears, allowing us to save our day, no more frustration, pushed back in isolation, positive creativity, aching to be set free' (UK Blak, 1991). Their perspective is representative of the ever-present blak 'voice' that critiques from the streets and ultimately disrupts the façade of a black British 'settled' community because:

> The black presence ruins the representative narrative of western personhood: its past tethered to treacherous stereotypes of primitivism and degeneracy will not produce a history of civil progress, a space for *socius*: its present, dismembered and dislocated, will not contain the image of identity that is questioned in the dialectic of mind/body and resolved in the epistemology of 'appearance and reality'. (Bhabha, 1993:114)

Blak is an example of how 'black' needed to be redefined and therefore partially resolves Bhabha's epistemological concern that the 'appearance and reality' of the 'black presence', in the grand narratives of Europe, obscures a positive historical presence. Therefore, in order to ruin 'the representative narrative system' we have to be clear about what type of 'black presence' can achieve this end. This is where the importance of defining your own reality is crucial, for any investment in the 'treacherous stereotypes' of the African, as espoused by Eurocentric miseducation, will subsequently undermine your position. Thus it is pointless calling yourself 'black', which is steeped in confusion and negative connotations, unless you are in a position to stipulate what is meant by the term from within your own cultural frames of reference. When this is not the case, it is unlikely that a viable 'history' based upon any type of 'process', 'civil' or otherwise, will be 'produced'. Furthermore, to successfully combat the absence of a positive black historical presence, it is necessary to overstand the 'language' your oppressor utilises to perpetuate your oppression; thus keeping you in the dark. Once this is achieved, you will—as a collective—be in a stronger position to counter white downpression by seeking an alternative education that convincingly refutes Eurocentric 'head-decay-shun', which is why there is a need to:

> Conceptualise black self-esteem or self-acceptance in part as a reaction to white attitudes toward blacks. Some blacks maintain positive self-esteem regardless of what the white man thinks of them. Others turn their anger at negative white attitudes inward toward themselves and their ethnic group. (Saunders, 1998:389)

It is the conceptualising of 'black self-acceptance' that is crucial to the argument I am forwarding, because the manner in which this can be achieved is by experiencing the counter-cultures that promote a positive notion of a blak-self, 'regardless of what the white man thinks'. Therefore, much that is expressed in Deejay lyricism, such as Levi's assertion that 'me nuh eat the bacon neither porkchops, blackman you fi do better dan that', clearly states that there are many who do not believe that you need to 'play the white man' (in this case having a white partner on public display) to be regarded as 'successful' in a racist society. For this reason, I will engage with the negative usage of black as constructed within the sociological imagination, which became instrumental in labelling a certain section of British society pathologically deviant.

1.3   De-constructing 'black youth'

> For all his efforts, indeed his achievements, he knows he is black: that colour is part of his identity and he knows that this will ultimately affect his life chances. And this gives him a sort of unity even if he does not wish to acknowledge it. (Cashmore and Troyna, 1982:28)

> Youth Deejays like Smiley Culture, Papa Levi, Asher Senator and many more exhibit well, in my view, the real meaning of black youths in Britain, who are ambitious creative and willing to achieve. These black youths have extended cultural strongholds that are normally well fortified. (Jah Bones, 1986:65)

What? While I was forgetting, forgiving, and wanting only to love, my message was flung back in my face like a slap. The white world the only honourable one, barred me from all participation. A man was expected to behave like a man. I was expected to behave like a black man-or at least like a nigger...When people like me, they tell me it is in spite of my colour. When they dislike me, they point out that it is not because of my colour. Either way I am locked into the infernal circle. (Fanon 1986:114/6)

Despite its ubiquity and constant invocation the meanings of 'black', as highlighted above, are as contested now as they were during the moment Fanon was postulating on his seeming entrapment within his 'infernal circle'. The circle representing the bounded definitions that apparently provided access to an-'other' world (the white world), whose idea of the 'black' subject is mediated by a notion of colour, which depends on denying phenotypic difference. Thus the sign (a non-white complexion) becomes an essentialist double negative, a Catch-22 situation that on the surface leaves the black subject, 'for all his efforts', in a no-win situation. The reason why I suggest that this 'infernal circle' is merely an illusory surface is because the 'white world' does not bar blacks from 'all participation'; rather it attempts to dictate where and how that 'participation' will be tolerated/included, as highlighted in Levi's 'Nuff Black' lyric. For, as Jah Bones suggested, black youths were 'ambitious, creative, positive and willing to achieve', but because their chosen mode of expression was 'culturally fortified' it remained 'hidden' from the general public gaze. There was an awareness amongst black youth 'that colour is part of' the manner in which we identify ourselves as a collective, realising that in a racist society our colour 'ultimately affects' the 'life chances' of the black community. This fundamental point is critical to my revaluation of the pathological explanations of black cultural forms, resistant or otherwise, that led to the 'social construction of black youth as a social problem' (Solomos. 1988: 2). Such 'constructs' led to a pathological notion of what it meant to be 'black' becoming a 'commonsense' explanation for all the ill that was attributed to the black community in Britain during the 'crisis' period of the 1970s and 1980s. Markedly so when we consider the blanket condemnation of the black community after the 1981 riots because, according to Gilroy:

Lord Scarman's report in the first phase of the riots in Brixton is a crucial document in the history of this discourse on the black community. It set the official seal on a definition of black crime and tied these to what were felt to be distinct patterns of politics and family life, characteristic of black culture. (1987:104)

Gilroy suggests that although it was 'black youth' that were regarded as the 'problem', it was the parents or guardians who lost 'control' of their offspring, due to the 'weakness of Afro-Caribbean communities' (Lawrence 1982:100) that were to blame. This notion of the characteristic (*read weaknesses*) of black culture fed directly into what Willis described as 'patterns of racial culture' (1977:47), which represent the blurring of the distinctions between 'formal' (the State) and 'informal' (commonsense) ideas on racialized attitudes. Crucially, the blurring of the distinctions between formal and informal racism assisted the ideological incorporation of the black youth 'problem' into 'state policy' (Amos et al, 1981, Solomos 1988) whilst sanctioning 'race relations' research. Therefore, the depiction of black youth as deviant, and their parental generations as weak, had much currency:

> Within the practical ideologies of a whole number of state institutions. Policing is perhaps the best example of how such images of black criminality have legitimised forms of repressive control which affect whole communities of black people. In addition to the police, agencies such as the CRE, the health service, the education department and social services are all state bodies whose policies find theoretical justification in race relations research. (S. Jones, 1986:71)

As Jones rightly suggests the 'theoretical justifications' that are so crucial to this type of 'repressive control' had far reaching consequences for the black community, especially black youth, because, as Fisher and Joshua argue:

> As with so many other aspects of British domestic race relations, the emergence of 'black youth' as a discrete 'social category' has been a piecemeal, disjointed affair, clouded in competing ideologies and explanations, and steeped in crisis. (1982:129)

In order to evaluate this notion of 'black youth as a discrete social category' we must cast a critical gaze over the highly influential work of certain British 'race relations' sociologists, who, Bourne (1980) argues, responded to the 'problems' Britain was facing from its immigrant population during this particular moment. These theoretical responses created their own specific types of 'problem' as they sought to decipher the unwanted and highly visible presence of black youth in Britain. Consequently the conceptualisations of race and ethnicity that emerged out of these theories often mirrored commonsense notions of what it apparently meant to be black/male/problem, or black/female/ invisible, in Britain during the 1970s and 1980s. These pathological 'miss'-conceptions have had a major influence on the manner in which black youths in particular, and black people in general, are still perceived in the popular imagination. In fact according to Gandy:

> We see that the media are charged with continuing to rely upon racist stereotypes, emphasizing negative aspects of behaviour, and suggesting deficiencies in morality and intelligence that stigmatise an entire population. At the same time the media are seen to ignore available evidence and examples of the highest levels of discipline, achievement, and commitment that have sustained these communities through centuries of oppression. (1998:157)

Gandy suggests a reliance on 'racist stereotypes', then 'emphasizing negative aspects of behaviour', goes hand in hand with a denial of the subjectivity of Britain's black community that would be gleaned from an impartial approach to the 'available evidence'. Moreover, when this is not forthcoming, the 'racist stereotypes' have a truth like quality bestowed upon them by virtue of being validated by social 'scientific' researchers and thus gain much currency in the popular/public imagination. This is because many who sought to interpret the behaviour of 'black youth' during the 1970s viewed their actions as primarily negative, without placing them in the context of how one resists or reacts to exclusionary practices in an overtly racist society. Thus, their immediate concern was how to render an account of this 'alien' presence, based on interpretations of how black behavioural patterns reflected a failure to adapt to British society. A focal point was the 'moral panics' caused by the black youths' seeming propensity toward various types of 'violent' criminal behaviour, especially 'mugging', during the late 1960s and 1970s; 'with the victim typified by the media as white and often helpless, mugging heralded an era of racially directed crime' (Fisher and Joshua, 1982:130).

Theorists like Jefferson and Clarke (1973) argued that the 'over-representation' of 'Afro-Caribbean youth' in the crime statistics was due to their 'structural placement' within British society. For instance, by being located at the social margins they were likely to experience higher levels of disillusionment with the educational system, which would obviously limit their employment opportunities. Naturally, this would lead to higher levels of unemployment, which in turn exacerbated the intergenerational conflicts with their largely 'conformist parents'. The 'historical accuracy of this view of Afro-Caribbean culture' (S. Jones, 1986:52) was questioned by Hall et al (1978), as it tended to reinforce the notion that black criminality was a type of pseudo 'political negotiation' of the oppression young blacks experienced due to their 'structural placement' within British society. These issues posited by an increasingly more visible black youth presence, especially during the 1970s, prompted a number of sociological studies aiming to explain their 'cultural and political disposition' (S. Jones 1986: 54). What is even more important to my argument is that by detailing a sample of these accounts, makes it known why black youths sought to counter such gross distortions, lyrically, within the Reggae dancehalls. For this truly contends the notion that black youth did nothing to counter the manner in which their presence was portrayed and managed in the wider public arena. That is why I feel it is prudent, at risk of being branded parochial or anachronistic, to present the type of sociological enquiry that, whilst now being regarded as myopic (hindsight is a fine thing) and dated, was nevertheless a major problem for those of us - black youth - who bore the brunt of its negativity during this historical moment.

The fact is that a major concern for these theorists was to detail/comprehend the relationship between the first and second-generation black British population (Jefferson and Clarke 1973, Hall et al 1978, Cashmore and Troyna 1982). Basically, this relationship was deemed to be the result of a conflict that arose out of a parent culture whose 'values and morals' were formed in the rural settings of close knit 'religious' Caribbean communities, contrasted with the more 'secular urban industrial environment of Britain in which they (black youth) have grown up' (Garrison 1979:11). This view largely suggested that black youth had something of an 'identity crisis', as they could not access their parents' 'religious culture' and thus sought solace in 'youth cultures' that were based on rejection. The major impact of the rejection of parental values by black youth was that it allegedly caused a 'generational breach' (Cashmore, 1979), out of which came the identification of black youth with the escapist ideologies that are contained within 'sub-cultural' forms. Therefore, if this relationship, which arguably manifested in various types of intergenerational conflict, was to be understood the sub-cultures that were so alluring to black youth would have to be investigated. Consequently, the conflict situations black youth were experiencing at home supposedly spilled over into the wider community, which led to the 'generational breach' causing a 'disjunction' in their relationships with 'young whites' (Cashmore and Troyna, 1982:7). One explanation for this 'disjunction was the popular assumption that white youth were viewed as being 'more stable', thus explanations of the unstable behaviour associated with being a black youth were based, according to Cashmore (1979), on 'truculence'. Accordingly it was argued that:

> This group has made it quite clear that it does not intend to succumb to any attempt to integrate it into the mainstream of the society. Black youths are in the process of cultivating their own distinct values, interests, meanings and ambitions; they reject efforts to solve their problems as inapposite. Accounts of their dishonesty and arrogance are not uncommon and they themselves do nothing to suggest that the accounts are inaccurate. Thus follows the possibility that when such a problem becomes recalcitrant, we ignore it; the feeling amongst young blacks is that they want to be left to such devices. (Cashmore and Troyna, 1982:3)

Stating that black youths were 'recalcitrant' to the point where they would 'cultivate' their own 'distinct values' intimates that there was a blanket rejection of any type of 'integration' into mainstream society. For Cashmore and Troyna, this is exemplified in their 'arrogance' and 'dishonesty', which 'they' endorse by their unwillingness to adhere to socially acceptable behaviour. The 'fact' that black youth do not challenge the 'inaccuracy' of these 'accounts' will be evaluated and refuted in the B~SIDE, which gives voice to the voiceless. However, of immediate concern is that Cashmore and Troyna present various arguments to support this notion because 'we all know there is a problem surrounding young blacks' (1982:18). They argue that by 'linking social conditions to such responses' they will provide an insight into the black youth 'problem' that 'we all know' about and suggest:

> We choose to see insecurely rooted black youths, prematurely matured and sprouting in a cultural marshland of well-daubed tower blocks and inner-city areas, educated on words which they find irrelevant – and do not know how to spell anyway. Occasionally they are stimulated by images and strike up postures, often as sudden violence. (1982:18)

Obviously this insight is based on the understanding that black youths are like weeds or fungus, that which is 'insecurely rooted' and grows wildly 'in a cultural marshland' and just require removal from the urban landscape, once their unwanted presence is acknowledged. The seriousness of such statements needs to be appreciated, as we know how the views of social scientists often influence policy and other forms of public and private practice. With no need for cultivation, care or attention, 'prematurely matured' black youth were a blight on the white working-class inner city areas. Given that they reject formal education, their 'social condition' worsens and acts of 'sudden violence' are their only means of dealing with their unseemly predicament. Logically, then, their actions justified the undivided attention they received from the likes of the Special Patrol Group (SPG), whose role in this instance was to uproot, remove and dispose of these unwanted black growths that sullied the white English Garden. The above argument, that even these theorists suggested was theoretically and empirically 'inadequate' (1982:6), nevertheless mirrored the idea of a 'discrete social category' which became synonymous with the young black men who McGrath (2002) suggested were wrongfully 'associated with the dangers of the future'. But how can we explain the oxy-'moronic' statement, 'prematurely matured'? One possible explanation that comes to mind is that the pre-pubescent black youth of the 1960s were easily managed, being physically smaller than the adult white population. In fact, it was not uncommon for white people in general, during this moment, to treat black children as less than human in much the same way as they treated their pets:

I remember when we were little kids and white people would rub their hands in our hair for luck, like if we was some type of black puss, saying stuff like alright sambo alright chalkie, as if they were terms of endearment. When I show this to young people they laugh but it wasn't funny for us and that is why people need to understand the measures that were used to downpress us in ah dem shitstem. (Christine Asher, Personal Communication 2001)

As I too experienced this type of treatment and much worse at the hands of ordinary white folk, I make it my duty to let those who are coming behind me understand how constructs, such as 'black youth' influenced these forms of 'unwittingly' racist behaviour and practice. A point that is endorsed by Allen as she argues:

The category 'black youth' is a construction which either facilitates or hinders the analysis…such a category oversimplifies the structure of a class society and the relations of the culture within it which function to reproduce the social relations between classes, generations, genders, and ethnic groups. Scholars of race relations have been engaged for a quarter of a century or more in Britain in attempts to come to terms with the problems created by disciplines firmly based in Eurocentric and ethnocentric assumptions. (1982:144)

What is interesting about Cashmore and Troyna's 'chosen' viewpoint is that it is premised on the 'Eurocentric/ethnocentric' assumptions, which Allen suggested we should be mindful of as they often 'hinder' our analysis. For the suggestion that 'black youths' are illiterate, because they cannot respond to formal 'education', is countered in Coard's (1971, 2005), 'How the West Indian Child is Made Educationally Sub-Normal in the British School System'. In his argument Coard made many recommendations; one such recommendation was that curricula which teaches 'all children black and white' a more inclusive history of non-European peoples, especially those that constitute the ethnic minorities or migrant communities in Britain in the 'educational sphere', is a viable way to 'break the vicious circle of self-contempt' (1971: 43/44). My argument is that if such a study was readily available detailing an analysis of socio-cultural factors that perhaps explain 'educational underachievement'—that which is still the bane of our contemporary, Eurocentric, educational system in Britain—then why did these theorists invoke the pathological as the answer to black youths' seeming uneducatedness? For to state that black youth only respond to images echoes the pathological and overly racist psychoanalytic hypothesis that Africans (blacks) operate solely on the 'pleasure principle', have no 'work ethic' and are 'incapable of guilt' (Bulham 1985:84). This viewpoint is endorsed by their 'research' findings, as they locate the potential sources that are perhaps the required 'stimulant' for the belligerent, illiterate and uneducable black youth. The most obvious is that their 'fascination for violence' stems from their 'incredible enthusiasm for movies in the *Kung Fu* idiom', coupled with their 'celebration of a range of archetypal violent anti-heroes, Dirty Harry, Chuck Norris and the late Bruce Lee' (Cashmore and Troyna 1982:33). As if this mixture of the fictitious with the actual was not enough - Clint Eastwood is Dirty Harry - they conveniently forget who produces these images, primarily white owned Hollywood and, what is the history behind such images? More often than not, the celebration/commemoration of the violent, murderous 'heroes' and 'heroines' of the American dream, acted out in the wild west, Vietnam, Pearl Harbour et al. This said, for these theorists 'incredible enthusiasm' that leads black youth to explode in 'sudden violence', is traced back to their Caribbean ancestry because there is said to be:

> A penchant for violence within the West Indian culture, possibly stemming from the days of slavery when the only method of retaliation was doing physical damage to the overseer, agent or even the slave-master. (Cashmore and Troyna, 1982:33)

What this type of investment in the pathological black subject does, is limit the scope of these 'adaptive responses' to an overly deterministic notion of full compliance or rejection based on 'sudden violence'. The suggestion is that the slaves who did not 'retaliate' are representative of the 'parent culture', whose 'West Indian culture' is based on capitulation and deference. Whereon 'black youth', according to their rationale, display the disposition of the rebellious slaves who totally rejected the ways of the master class and that this explains the conflict situation they find themselves in with their parental generation. However, these restricted theorisations do not recognise the cognitive strategies the oppressed employ to resist their 'structural placement' in a racist society, because:

In order to comprehend what made up resistance, it is essential to set aside a variety of preconceptions about the nature of resistance. The real point here may be to spare the past the need to live up to the interpretations we impose upon it—at least long enough for us to try seriously to discover what, indeed, did happen. (Mintz, 1989:50)

Mintz' suggestion is that there are in the 'nature of resistance' factors that certain 'preconceptions' about 'past' events only serve to obscure, and therefore limit, our comprehension of the worth and nature of these cultural forms. For this reason, 'what made up resistance' is often overlooked in the context of peoples of Afrikan descent, a factor that was dealt with by Spencer (1995) in his reinterpretation of Baker's (1987) concept, which argues that within Afrikan cultures of resistance there is a 'mastery of form' and a 'deformation of mastery'. The argument details how the Afrikan competently mastered the outer form of much European expressionism, but chose to cloak their mastery in conscious acts of deformation, which the master obviously misread as signs of their inferiority. Therefore, when applying this argument to how black youth 'resisted' racist exclusionary practices in Britain, we can dispense with staid accounts that are limited by negative 'preconceptions' that overlook the significant role of countercultural forms. This is because, by using Jamaican language (Patwa) as the primary form of expression, black youth were consciously cloaking their resistance and 'retaliated' in ways other than to 'explode in sudden violence'. Hence limiting an understanding of 'retaliation' to a simple dichotomy between overt displays of violence/non-violence is unrealistic, as it denies the cognitive strategies the oppressed will employ to combat and transcend their overall oppression. Furthermore, black countercultures have a history/tradition of direct defiance and resistance that refute those theories which limit the understanding of black cultural expression to the 'reactive behaviour' of mindless youth.

Conclusion

I have argued that the 'popular' notion of 'black youth' was a construct that had serious consequences for those who were deemed to be members of this 'discrete social category'. The main contention is that we cannot begin to discuss the cultural expression of black youth, 'deviant' or otherwise, without firstly grasping why these forms were necessary in the context of a racist society like Great Britain. For this reason, I began this discussion with the practicalities behind the need to define your own reality, arguing for the usage of 'blak' as denoting a specific type of consciousness that emerged from a British based counter-culture. The point I am making, is that more consideration is needed when 'interpreting' resistant cultures, due to the manner in which past experiences are appropriated and passed on in a 'performance' that outwardly masks an inner reality. These outernational appropriations within the confines of the Fanon's 'white world' ensure that a space is created for alternative ideas of being Afrikan. By voicing these alternatives in Patwa, the Deejay becomes the 'mouthpiece' of these 'interpretive communities', where a positive Afrikan humanity can be reclaimed. Of equal importance, by using orality in this fashion, the Deejay continues a tradition of thinking yourself into being, which is beyond the hegemonic scope of a dominant society as it 'resists' in ways that are not generally recognised as resistence. In concordance with this line of reasoning I have stressed the need to consider the notion of 'rejection' as an 'adaptive response' that cannot be reduced to mindless criminality, or a reaction to a 'generational' or 'psychological breach' caused by the pathological black familial structure.

Building on this discussion I will, in the next chapter, present a synthesised account that best demonstrates the links between theory and practice, which will endorse my claims about the inadequacy of certain interpretations of black cultures. This will be argued from the standpoint of an ethnographer concerned that the story of 'real people' (Rigby, 1996) must dominate this type of discussion.

Chapter 2

The colouring of ethnography

Introduction

I try to find some meaning among the mass of the population who are daily performing a miracle, they continue to survive! Walter Rodney

In this chapter I will demonstrate how I have reasoned through many of the practical problems I have encountered whilst composing and giving 'meaning' to this miraculous song of self and community. These problems have been approached thematically, with a focus on three main areas of specific concern: firstly, a consideration of the 'power' that the ethnographer/writer has to redefine the subject/object through the notion of 'ethnographic inscription' (Bourdieu, 1989). This represents a continuation of the theme outlined above where I argued that the idea of 'black youth' as a 'discrete social category' was a construct, evidenced in a particular style of social theory. Secondly, I develop this argument by engaging my own socio-cultural and political sensibilities as a means to establish a greater overstanding of the 'outsider within'. That is to say, what issues the black researcher faces upon realising that the relationship between the 'observer' and the 'observed' is 'coloured' through the author's power to 'write' the reality. In point of fact, those I reason with here are familiar with my Africentric stance, which garners a level of trust because they realise that I will not betray them or the culture that we represent. Therefore, when we reason, our mutual understanding is derived from a similar worldview, which basically regards the black/African as the 'constructed' antithesis of the white/European. It, in turn, becomes our duty to do something about this situation in our own works/writings, given that many who have black faces seem to endorse the views of our oppressors, to our collective detriment.

Finally, I explain my necessity to provide bridges of meaning; this, due to an obligation to make the essence of the culture known, as accurately as I possibly can, in the form of a written document. I therefore find it hard to consider myself as the detached, impartial, objective observer and indeed suggest that the use of a strategic notion of bias is necessary to the kind of 'hidden' history which I present. For as long as I participate 'within' the culture (I still Deejay), I am constantly in the 'field' gathering data by reasoning with the various people I encounter. As will become clear, a crucial part of being a Deejay is remaining circumspect, always seeking to be inspired to write a new lyric through constant reasoning, which is why my antennae are always up. The suggestion is that knowledge of your situation increases with every conversation/reasoning and it is this, in turn, which inspires the Deejay to write. Thus, any telling of the story of 'real people' (Rigby, 1996) must reflect this sense of an ongoing relationship with the self and the community you represent, for they are ultimately your judge, jury and executioner.

2.1 Knowledge, power and the 'politics of location'

The way in which questions are put, the points of view assumed, presupposes a relativity of interest; all characteristics imply values, and every objective description, so called, implies an ethical background.
(De Beauvoir, 1972:28)

Unlike the majority of ethnographic/academic writing, which arguably focuses on the abstracted object of study, my considerations are based on how to interpret and theorise a project that is far more visceral than the usual academic enterprise. It is for this reason that, in the previous chapter I offered an intervention into the theorisation of black youth, like myself, during the so-called 'crisis' periods of the 1970s and 1980s. The emphasis was on how these theories on notions of black culture and identity need to be situated in 'self-generated concepts' (R. Lewis,

2001), like 'blak' and then interrogated from an Afrikan centre. Otherwise, counter-'public spheres' like the Reggae-dancehall will not be recognised as viable sites of alternative learning, where debates around ontology - in the sense of what it means to be/exist as blak/Afrikan - and cultural identification are freely aired and discussed through a 'relativity of interest'. Therefore, the manner in which I 'understand Black reality and responses to injustice' (Thompson, 1998: After word) will be used as a conceptual tool to consider how ethnographers have misrepresented this 'Black reality'.

Unsurprisingly, then, the positions that I consider here 'imply values', that the researcher needs to be aware of, which affect how 'reality' is rendered as a textual analysis, because there are various ethical problems that I have faced, and continue to face, as an Africentric researcher. In many cases, as soon as the suggestion is uttered or committed to paper, I hear the gasps of disbelief, see the barriers come up and the shutters go down. On that account, I feel it prudent to evaluate these problems in a manner that clearly states how my insider analysis differs from many that are considered here. Thence, the A~SIDE becomes the site for critically assessing how the 'mystery', my-story, has been told from the outside; this, to counter much that been written about the black presence in Britain because:

> Concern about the ways in which anthropological scholarship achieves its effects as 'knowledge of others' is manifest as an explicit epistemological concern for the ways in which interpretations are constructed and represented as objective discourse about subjects on (or among) whom research is conducted. (Woolgar, 1990:24)

Any attempt to interpret social phenomena has to grasp the meaning the actors place on their actions, in concordance with the 'cultural identities' that are a necessary aspect of any alternative worldview. In this sense, 'cultural identities' are complexly linked to the strategies that the downpressed devise and develop through a direct engagement with the racist system that 'excludes' them, thereby countering its adverse effects through pragmatic and practical communal action. My appreciation of this type of action allows me to provide 'knowledge of others', in this case the black community I am indigenous to, by thinking through certain aspects of 'our culture' that have led us to this point. It is important for me to make known what 'our culture' means from an insider perspective. Because, as Gates (1992) reminds us, the mechanisms and strategies we employ to resist and transcend oppression, have 'histories' that have 'sustained these communities through centuries of oppression' (cited in Gandy, 1998:157). Therefore, the 'histories' that are drawn upon within the black community, that not only 'sustain' us but also give much meaning to our lived reality, are presented throughout this discussion as thoughtfully as possible. Hence there is no attempt in my work to separate the Deejay's lyricism from the worldview that spawned charges of 'you're too close to the subject to be objective' do not faze me in the slightest. This charge was levelled against me by an eminent, white, professor on race, who got upset when I suggested that, 'as we say in Jamaica, who feels it knows it'. I am not interested in spurious claims for objectivity, because often the best way to truly appreciate something is often to have the lived experience.

I use the lens of academia, coupled with my insider perspective/ position, to make these conscious reflections on 'black reality' known. The suggestion is that the messages contained within Deejay lyricism have much currency in the black community, because they give primacy to the personal, and quite often contradictory, racialised experience. An experience that does not impartially affect one section of the 'black' community and, therefore, I must be wary of levelling the differences I have highlighted between a 'black' or 'blak' consciousness. This, more so, 'when internal differences around gender, sexuality, and class, begin to weaken or unsettle 'Black' as a composite racial category' (Noble, 2005:134). By doing so I recognise fully that 'it is doubtless impossible to approach any human problem with a mind free from bias' (De Beauvoir, 1972). I would add that this is based on the knowledge which you bring to the academic table. Clearly, the main reason for staking this claim is that much of the ethnographic literature, which seeks to interpret black expressive cultures, Hebdige 1977, Cashmore, 1979/1997, Hewitt 1986, S. Jones 1986, Sebba 1986, Back 1996, Foster 1999, Stolzoff 2000, was not written from 'within' but from 'without' the cultures that are under scrutiny. Therefore, it is reasonable to assume that they may lack 'some of the insights that a member of the community might have' (Sebba, 1986:150). I am not suggesting that 'insider' accounts will always be more 'valid' or 'authentic', as the notions of insider/outsider are highly problematic; this, a point that will be clarified momentarily in my critique of the Jamaican Ken Pryce's

'Endless Pressure' (1979/1986), which was regarded as an 'insider account' on the black community during the moment in question. My argument, conversely, centres on the notion that:

> No one has ever devised a method for detaching the scholar from the circumstances of life, from the fact of his involvement (conscious or unconscious) with a class, a set of beliefs, a social position, or from the mere activity of being a member of society. (Said, 1978:8)

My claim here is that a similar cultural experience, a shared social position with its own 'set of beliefs', can inform an alternative moral/ethical standpoint with regard to the 'position' that the ethnographer assumes within the field. And so, to aim towards some type of 'scholarly detachment' is unrealistic to say the least; I would then be devaluing that which has allowed me to recognise myself as the object/recipient of racist exclusionary practices in the real world. In fact:

> The objects of anthropological discourse cease to be real peoples, the production and reproduction of their social life and communities, their exploitation and suffering, and their attempts to fight back: they become the producers of texts, which it is the anthropologist's job to "interpret." Knowledge and the ontology of "facts" becomes the privileged domain of expert discourse, totally divorced from the social, intellectual, and discursive space occupied by real people; it becomes the property of those who would wield power. As a result, social facts no longer need to attain or demonstrate authenticity; their authority derives from their status as an emanation of assumed intellectual, and actual political, power. (Rigby, 1996:89/90)

Taking a lead from Rigby's poignant critique means that, as a blak scholar, I must remain circumspect when confronted with interpretations of racialised patterns of behaviour, because these are often subject to the influence and manipulation of the 'outsider' looking in. Therefore, my interpretation of 'knowledge and the ontology of facts' will evidently differ from many who theorise black culture; I have been totally immersed in it and so regard it as a natural part of self. I am arguing that the interpreter's theorisation of the culture in question is part of a process of academic scrutiny, out of which only relative 'truth' claims can be made. The suggestion is that:

> Even the best ethnographic texts – serious true fictions – are systems or economies of truth. Power and history work through them, in ways their authors cannot fully control. Ethnographic truths are thus inherently partial – committed and incomplete. (Clifford, 1986:7)

Thus, although the 'texts' people 'produce' may well become 'the property of those who would wield power' over them, perhaps the 'truth' in what is being described should be tempered by our knowledge of the ethnographer as author. If this is so, then it is the 'politics of location' that needs to be considered, because how you locate yourself in relation to the culture in question impacts on your final analysis. Therefore, the researcher, who is not familiar with the 'systems of values' that are 'inherited' from within the 'moral culture', can easily miss the cognisance readily taken for granted which is an important part of how 'culture' is transmitted across time and space. However, to ground this aspect of my analysis in the concrete, and thereby making this critical point clearer, I will demonstrate in the next section why my argument from an 'insider' perspective is necessary to facilitate a fuller appreciation of the potency of blak counter-cultures.

2.2 Paying the 'Pryce'

> Rastafarianism and rudyism have had the most direct impact on the attitudes of teenyboppers. But their influence cannot be understood except in relation to the significance of Reggae and the part it plays in the life-style of teenyboppers and West Indian young people in general. (Pryce, 1979:143)

In a major study on the effects of West Indian culture on black youths in Britain, during the 'crisis' period of the 1970s, the Jamaican Ken Pryce offered an 'insider' perspective entitled <u>Endless Pressure</u> (1979/1986). Pryce's work was lauded and more importantly validated by orthodox social theorists like Cohen who suggested, in the foreword to the second edition of <u>Endless Pressure</u> (1986), that:

> It is doubtful that the finer prism of differentiation through which Pryce observed the black community could have been cut and polished as well by a white sociologist. Being black and from the

West Indies (Pryce is Jamaican, but lives and works in Trinidad) meant that he was both accepted by the community, yet stood somewhat outside it…I have rarely seen this difficulty resolved so well as in Pryce's study, where he carefully combines the access granted to the insider with the analytical distance possible for the outsider. (Pryce, 1986:xvi/xvii)

The relevance of Cohen's endorsement of Pryce's account is critical to my idea of the 'colouring of ethnography' because it perfectly captures how the social theorist is expected to distance the communities they study. Now lest we begin to believe that, in this time of the 'reflexive turn' in academic/ethnographic writings, things have really changed since Pryce's work was published and given that we are in the time of giving the 'native' the camera and tape recorder so they can 'document' their own realities, consider the following. I was involved in a debate about a leaked Scotland Yard report on 'child sacrificing in London' in the 'African community' and got into a discussion on BBC Radio 4 and in various newspapers with Dr. Hoskins, an 'expert' in the field. I suggested that I would not comment on the report as I had not read it, but would discuss the issue of how the Afrikan is invariably misrepresented and demonised in the western imagination. I took this viewpoint because we can see the same kind of patterns of behaviour in European cultures, but they are interpreted in completely different ways' (The Evening Standard, 16/06/05). This comment was followed by:

Experts differ on the merits of the Scotland Yard report.
Dr William Les [sic] Henry, a lecturer in sociology at Goldsmiths College, said aspects of the reports were pigeonholing crimes together and were patronising and racist. He said: "This is one of the crises with social sciences anyway, when they are supposedly interpreting the folk ways or cultural habits of alien cultures." He said that the models such reports are based on are that "Africans are less civilised, less rational."

But Dr Hoskins said: "This is very detailed, qualitative report that actually comes out of the communities. This is not white people saying this. This has actually come from the communities, authored by people in the community and that really stymies the racist line." He added: "We are dealing with real cases here. When you actually talk to them, these are hard and fast facts." (The Evening Standard, 16/06/05)

Does this mean that we are to believe that the 'community', in this case the 'Africans' in question 'authored' this document, in the sense that they wrote and prepared it for publication? Of course they didn't and that is my point. You can talk about 'hard and fast facts' but just who is responsible for determining what a 'fact' is and how it will be represented in the final analysis? In this case, it is misleading to state that 'this is not white people saying this; Of course it is-Hoskins himself is white. It is he and his team of 'experts' who determine the final product and control what will be ultimately included and excluded as forms of knowledge in the written document. For this reason, we need to be mindful when listening to these 'experts', myself included, who try to convince others that things have changed because people nowadays 'author' their own accounts and this 'stymies the racist line'. I am suggesting that we need to be careful when reading anything that is based on some type of expertise supposedly representing a 'qualitative' account, and then in turn claims to be an ultimate or authentic 'truth' based on analytical 'distance' because:

> Institutionalised by university seals of approval, such knowledges impact on the life chances of people who find themselves measured, not only by the abuses of overt racism but also by the insidious cultural orthodoxies of the academic imagination. (Keith, 1992:551)

It was through his investment in this 'culturally orthodox' orientation that the 'academically distanced' Pryce explained the black youth presence as an 'expert' in the field and like Hoskins only dealt with 'hard and fast facts'. These 'facts' were founded in relation to the 'six lifestyles' he observed as key to interpreting the behavioural patterns of members of the the first and second generation West Indian community in Britain. The six types were 'hustlers, teenyboppers, proletarian respectables, saints, mainliners and inbetweeners'; adherents to each 'lifestyle' were recognised by either their 'expressive-disreputable' or 'stable law-abiding' (Pryce 271:1986) social conduct. These 'six lifestyles' were subsequently dichotomised into distinct 'walks of life', which separated the 'proletarian respectables' and 'mainliners' from the 'work refusers', who consisted of first generation 'hustlers' and the so-called 'teenyboppers' (which I find to be a clumsy and highly inappropriate term for black youth). Now, what is of real interest here is that Pryce attributes the differences in these 'lifestyles' to the instability of the West Indian family structure, out of which it is the 'young who invariably suffer' as:

> The fragmented social framework in which West Indian family life takes place means that the individual is instantly spat out onto the street whenever a family crisis occurs. This happens because West Indians lack a group identity and a tight, communal form of group life based on a sense of collective interdependence and mutual obligation among kinsmen. (Pryce, 1979:119)

Pryce forcefully argues throughout his text that the 'culture' of 'teenyboppers' (black youth), which is of primary interest here, is spawned from their precarious positioning within this 'fragmented social framework'. Even more perniciously, he argues in 'West Indian family life' there is a 'lack of group identity' and no 'communal form of group life based on a sense of collective interdependence and mutual obligation among kinsmen' (Pryce, 1979:119). These claims, devoid of any sense of what occurred historically in the Caribbean with regard to the formulation of complex patterns of kinship etc, are as outrageous as they are untenable and need not overly concern us here. However, according to Pryce, this was a firm enough basis from which to claim that this 'fragmented social framework' ensures that 'West Indian family life' cannot hope to cater for its young people, whether in Britain or the Caribbean. Consequently, to alleviate their suffering, black British youth invariably partake in a 'culture' of street crime, which can be rooted back to 'a minority and deviant subculture within the West Indies itself' (Lea and Young, 1984:127).

> Thus England's black settlers are forever locked in the bastard culture of their enslaved ancestors, unable to break out into the 'mainstream' alternative. Their presence in the ancient territory of the 'island race' becomes a problem precisely because of their difference and distance from the standards of civilised behaviour which are second nature to authentic (white) Britons. (Gilroy, 1993b:25)

Gilroy's critique was an attempt to counter the residue left by theorists like Pryce, Cashmore and Troyna, who premised their pathological explanations on the difference between white/English/British and black/African/West Indian forms of social conduct and public behaviour. A perspective that was obviously influenced by the position of those earlier theorists who regarded black/African cultures of the 'New World' as 'distorted imitations of European-American culture' (Maultsby 1991:185). Undoubtably such explanations fit neatly into 'sub' types of cultural theory that measure black 'settlement' or discontentment according to an idealised white 'standard of civilised behaviour'. The suggestion there is that an attempt is made by the parental generation to embrace or aspire to these 'standards' of Britishness because this represents for them the culture of their 'mother country'. Importantly, they expect their children, especially the British born, to 'naturally' do the same and more so upon considering that they are being socialised and educated in a dominant culture wherein these 'standards' are the norm. When this is not forthcoming it can result in intergenerational conflicts that have dire consequences for black youth, due to their supposed blanket rejection of recognised 'standards of civilised behaviour'. This 'failure' on the part of black youth culminates in the inevitable scenario because they are, according to Pryce, 'instantly spat out onto the street whenever a family crisis occurs'. In addition, due to this 'failure' to do what is 'second nature to authentic Britons', Pryce further suggests that 'teenyboppers' responded to familial and white 'rejection with rejection'. Consequently, this form of 'rejection' led to the embracing of Reggae music and Rastafari because 'Reggae has decidedly criminal connotations' (S. Jones, 1986:56), epitomised in the notion of a 'Rasta-rudie black oriented counter-culture' (Pryce 1979:156). Thus:

> Teenyboppers were identified with Reggae in the first place mainly through their involvement in the expressive-disreputable orientation; this was the social opening through which the music gained entry into Britain. The production of music in the black community is and always has been the exclusive business of hustlers (and now teenyboppers): Reggae was first played in Britain in black discos and blues dances, etc....Members from the other West Indian life-styles play no part in the music business. (1979:154)

The accuracy of this perspective on Reggae music and black youth has been challenged and subsequently refuted elsewhere: Lawrence 1982, S.

Jones 1986, Gilroy 1987, Back 1996. However, what is of interest is the manner in which Pryce grafts his dichotomous view onto the musical habits of the West Indian community, where he once again invokes this notion of distinctive 'life-styles'. In fact, to bolster this 'authentic' claim, he further suggests that:

> This indicates where in the West Indian social structure the music comes from. Almost all the Reggae singers in Britain (and in Jamaica) have either been delinquents or ex-hustlers or have come from particularly impoverished backgrounds. This is mainly how Reggae – already mixed up with crime and rebellion before it came to Britain – was incorporated into the life-style of the expressive-disreputable orientation. (1979:154)

Musical affiliation is understood as a consequence of (your) class position within the West Indian social structure, which is then used to validate the idea that poverty and rebellion are synonymous with criminality. There is no place in his narrow 'class [criminal]-based' perspective for Reggae music as serving:

> A multiple role in relation to the community: it provides at once an opportunity for sharing in creative experience, for participating in music as a form of community experience, and for using music as an avenue for the expression of group sentiments. (Nketia, 1974:22)

Ignoring how ludicrous it is to relegate musical production of an entire generation to a community's 'criminal' element, there is a more pressing twofold concern with Pryce's 'academically-imagined' irrational rationale. Firstly, his failure to recognise Reggae music as anything other than the 'expressive-disreputable orientation' in the 'black community' denies the historical worth and necessity of these expressions of oppressed 'group sentiments' as coping and transcendental mechanisms. The second concern is based on Pryce's confusing idea of the links between poverty, crime and rebellion that created this 'social opening' for the 'teenyboppers' to, I suppose, 'teenybop' in. This, logically, would mean that the only black people who feel the need to embrace music as a means to offset this 'endless pressure' are the ones who create their own 'problems' due to their chosen 'life-style', which naturally results in clashes with white authority figures, especially the police. Furthermore, this choice (if it can be deemed as such) of 'life-style' is a direct consequence of their 'structural placement' in the lower strata of British society. For Pryce, this is determined by their positioning within a West Indian class-based hierarchy that simply manifests, itself intact, in Britain. There is no mention by Pryce of the fact that 'the over-determining salience of race in Britain led many migrants to close ranks regardless of class...as many...felt that all Jamaicans were in the same social class' (James 1993:244). This explains why the migrants from the West Indies chose to 'close ranks' and, because of the Jamaican numerical advantage, many white Britons generally considered all blacks to be Jamaicans, in much the same fashion that all black criminals are now considered to be Yardies; Yardies are Jamaican nationals – they hail from Yard/Jamaica.

However, Pryce's argument that the 'proletarian respectables' and 'mainliners' distanced themselves from the 'lifestyles' of other classes as they were more likely to be 'churchgoers' representative of 'the peak of conventional respectability in the black community' (Pryce 1979:222), can easily be refuted. The keyword here is 'conventional' which, if we follow Pryce's line of argument, means the aforementioned acceptance of 'standards' of Britishness. Thus, for 'mainliners', the only means of achieving 'proletarian respectability' is to adopt a 'lifestyle' that distinguishes and distances them from those who 'choose' to oppose 'conventional' British behaviour. The keeping of Reggae sessions, parties or 'blues' dances was for him a significant sign of this 'unconventional' stance, that was fuelled by 'hustling' or other types of 'delinquent' behaviour. A notion that is rejected by Dirty Desi who argues:

> Me lay down in me bed, Jahman me feel sleepy, me gal seh to me, hey look Desi, me look pon the TV-tell me what did I see-it was ah documentary about the SPG, the special police group in ah Hackney, them interview police about street attacks, them seh 95% is done by blacks, them show how the police patrol in van and them show how them harass the poor blackman, you couldah pickpocket or ah Christian, with you bible in ah you hand, you coming from church, the next ting you know you get stop fi ah search, you coming from school an you on the go, the bull (police) them want to search you from you head to you toe, so go. (Ghettotone, 1983)

Desi's lyric perfectly captures the manner in which Pryce's inadequate theorisations did little justice to those who were on the receiving end of the government's policies to curb the menace that was the unwanted black presence. It is for this reason that why Desi argues that it does not matter which 'lifestyle' you supposedly represent, 'pickpocket/ Christian/schoolchild', the treatment you receive at the hands of certain white authority figures is much the same. Desi's argument demonstrates how as an oppressed community we utilise the medium of 'music as an avenue for the expression of group sentiments' (Nketia, 1974:22), and that cannot be reduced to these distinctive and overly deterministic 'lifestyles'. Moreover, from my own personal experiences and memories, my father (who worked and reared children from the time he arrived in Britain until his retirement) kept parties in our family home and my Baptist 'church-going' mother (who also worked until her retirement as well as bearing and rearing children) shared the responsibilities with him. My memories of these moments and in concordance with other theorists such as Nketia 1974, Davies 1989, Spencer 1995, suggest that:

> Music is integral to all aspects of black community life. It serves many functions and is performed by individuals and groups in both formal and informal settings. The fundamental concept that governs music performance in African and African-derived cultures is that music-making is a participatory group activity that serves to unite black people into a cohesive group for a common purpose. (Maultsby, 1991:187)

Pryce fails to consider this aspect of black musical culture, and so traps himself within the rigidity of his dichotomisation, because he cannot see the value in these types of 'participatory group activity'. In fact, his theorisation of the Caribbean community in Britain will not allow for 'members from the other West Indian 'lifestyles' to 'play' any 'part in the music business'. Therefore, although Pryce considers many of the racial and cultural aspects of the Caribbean community in Bristol, which he argues is 'pretty representative of the experience of most working-class West Indians in Britain' (1986:271), he largely views these 'lifestyles' as types of 'false consciousness'. These are 'lifestyles' that express the 'culture traits' of the 'colonial proletariat' whose relocation in the West Indies, as a result of chattel slavery, had robbed them of their African 'essence'. His view is oppositional to what was, for Nketia, 'the fundamental concept that governs music performance in Afrikan and Afrikan-derived cultures that serves to unite black people into a cohesive group for a common purpose' (1974:22). Unsurprisingly, then, for Pryce the West Indian's:

> Social contact with whites made acculturation on the part of the African descendants possible. The negro came to learn a great deal about his master. Socialization not only taught him what role to play in the society, it now made it possible for him to speak his master's language, and to ape his values and institutions. (1979:3)

He suggests the 'aping' of the master's values and institutions during the colonial era led to the Caribbean migrant having no say in their 'acculturation' and they were thus 'forced into accepting British Culture along with their servitude' (Rex and Tomlinson, 1979:291). On that account, the deviant 'life-style', as embraced by the 'teeny bopping' black youth, is a direct consequence of their 'forced acculturation' and a valid explanation of their negative 'cultural traits'. For as Back and Solomos suggest:

> The unwritten assumption is that minority populations and their children constitute a group which exhibit interesting, problematic and varied identities, while the identities of the majority are viewed as unproblematic. (Back and Solomos, 1996:132)

Back and Solomos make known that the premise upon which this type of social analysis is founded is flawed as it posits a notion of Britishness that is considered stable and 'unproblematic'. Ergo, the differences between 'minority populations' are exaggerated and reified for the purpose of explaining these differences in behavioural patterns noticeable when measured against a 'stable' British culture. This means that the observable differences in 'lifestyles' become the definitive factor in understanding visible conflicts between the generations of West Indians who reside in Britain. However, this position on the nature of the distinct 'lifestyles' which divided the West Indian migrant was questioned because:

The various counter positions of integrationist/separatist, law abiding/disreputable, and compromisers/rejectors, found throughout the sociology of race relations, are categories which neglect the unifying experience of racial domination. That experience is shared by young and old, male and female, dread and non dread alike...To impose a frozen schema onto such dynamic and ongoing political processes is to seriously diminish their impact and significance. (S. Jones, 1986:70)

According to S. Jones, there was a tendency to determine the political positions of the black community along generational and class lines by their musical tastes because theorists, like Pryce, overlooked the manner in which the politics of black music blurs class-based distinctions in this 'frozen schema'. This was because his 'culturally orthodox' account failed to recognise the solidarity provided by a medium that views being black with the reality of being oppressed in a white racist society. Class-based conflicts between the proletarian and the bourgeoisie, which perhaps have currency within a West Indian social milieu do not fit so easily in the context of the black experience in Britain. It is not my concern, whether or not it was Pryce's intention to lend weight to the pathological ideas that sought to explain the musical affiliations of black youth. What is of my concern is that this was how his message was largely received. More importantly, this perspective devalues and distorts the role Reggae music has played, and still plays, in the struggles for liberation from the types of popular racism that affect the black community outernationally. The form, as a tool for liberation, is relatively unknown in his context, and so I will now shift my focus to another explanation of Reggae music's role and purpose.

2.3   Counter cultures as adaptive response

One of the first theorists to evaluate the relationship between Jamaican popular music, its associative cultures, and their effects on the cultural sensibilities of black people in Britain was Hebdige (1977). Hebdige, whose subcultural perspective proved to be highly influential, argued that the embracing of resistant Jamaican cultural forms by the British blacks was linked to a history of colonial oppression and the memory of chattel slavery. Consequently he argues:

The experience of slavery recapitulates itself perpetually in the everyday interactions of the Jamaican black. It is principally responsible for the unstable, familial structure (disrupting the traditionally strong kinship networks which survive among the peoples of West Africa) and obviously goes on determining patterns of work and relations with authority. It remains an invisible shaping presence which haunts the slums of Ghost Town and even now defies exorcism. It is interpolated into every verbal exchange which takes place in every Jamaican slum. (1977:426)

Hebdige, like Pryce, Cashmore, Troyna and many others, invests heavily in the notion of the 'unstable, familial structure' as a causal factor in West Indian orientations to 'work' and 'authority', which is largely responsible for the conceptualisation of their modes of expression as subcultures. However, what Hebdige does more thoughtfully than Pryce and many others is attempt to explain why these forms were so appealing to black youth in Britain without relying on criminality as their sole attraction. This means, ghostly 'haunts' and 'exorcism' aside, resistance is framed in the context of the 'verbal exchanges', which perpetually challenge the authority of the dominant culture 'in the everyday interactions of the Jamaican black'. Hence 'the experience of slavery' remains in the outward expression of Jamaican cultural forms as the 'invisible shaping presence', which enables them to cope with the harsh reality of life in the 'slums'. Furthermore, Hebdige, like many subcultural theorists, saw in the adoption of these Jamaican cultural forms by black youth in Britain, 'a semantic subversion of the dominant white ideology' (S. Jones, 1986:50) due to the emphasis on 'style'. This notion of style was read as a generationally specific response by black British youth to the types of social/cultural/ racial exclusion that underpinned the broader subcultural understandings of youthful deviance in the 1960s. Therefore, their embracing of Jamaican cultural forms, for instance 'verbal exchanges' in Rasta-Rudie language, in tandem with certain dress codes was, for many theorists, akin to the usage of American rock 'n' roll symbolism in 1950s Britain by the 'Teddy Boys' (Brake 1980, Cashmore and Troyna 1982). However it was an attempt to understand the 'white consumption' of black cultural forms, especially in the context of 'Afro-American music as an outside tradition' (S. Jones, 1986: 82), that led to so much interest in West Indian cultural 'style'. Many theories were focused on the manner in which, 'Black idioms of expression provided the means through which various groups of white musicians could share and reflect the experiences of their youthful audiences' (Hebdige, 1977:426).

In consequence this approach with its emphasis on 'style' often muted the history and politics behind the 'adaptive responses' of black youth to a hostile environment as, in this context, they were viewed as a type of symbolic escapism. This was seen as a constant in the history of the 'black Jamaican' experience, which was a direct consequence of their 'expulsion…from the 'wider linguistic community' (Hebdige, 1977:426). As a result the 'black Jamaican' whether young or old who was 'deprived of any legitimate cultural exchange', sought solace in the 'symbolic transactions' that mediated between their 'experience of Jamaica and their memories of Africa' (1977:427). Hence it was a form of escapism reliant on external means to symbolically display disapproval at the oppressive colonial system, for instance 'putting on the covenant' (dreadlocks) as an outer symbol of your Afrikaness that puts fear/dread in the downpressor because:

> In a sense, the transition was never satisfactorily accomplished, and the black Jamaican remains suspended uneasily between two worlds, neither of which commands a total commitment. Unable to repair this cultural and psychological breach, he tends to oscillate violently from one world to the other and ultimately he idealizes them both. Ultimately, indeed, he is exiled from Jamaica, from Africa, from Britain and from Brixton, and sacrifices his place in the real world to occupy an exalted position in some imaginative inner dimension where action dissolves into being, where movement is invalidated and difficult at the best of times, where solutions are religious rather than revolutionary. (1977:427)

For Hebdige, the 'black Jamaican' is constantly in this liminal state, suspended betwixt two worlds that are the product of an irreparable 'cultural and psychological breach', and thus can never truly inhabit the 'real world'. The most the 'black Jamaican' can hope for is an 'exalted position' within a schizophrenic psychodrama that offers 'religious rather than revolutionary' solutions. To understand the embracing of Rasta-rudie 'subculture' by black youth in Britain, the un-'real world' that is a product of this 'psychological breach' needs to be accessed and explained. The manner in which Hebdige sought to do this was by focusing on the external manifestations of this psychodrama, which was witnessed par excellence in the 'symbolic reversal' of Rastafari. This notion of 'symbolic reversal' was explicated through his interpretation of 'style', which proved to be highly influential in the way Rastafari has been understood in subcultural studies of black youth. For instance, Hebdige suggests that the Rastafari 'worldview' was based on a 're-appropriation' of 'Biblical mythology', which entailed the Bible being 'taken, read and flung back rude' (1977:428). Therefore:

> The crucial act of faith constitutes an archetypal technique of appropriation which escaped the traditional religious displacement by grounding God; it entailed a radical reappraisal of the black Jamaican's potential. We need only turn to the Rude Boy to assess the revolutionary significance of the Rasta perspective. For the secularization of the Rasta Godhead coincided with the politicization of the dispossessed Rude Boy, and the new aesthetic which directed and organized the locksman's perceptions, found a perfect form in Reggae. (1977:430)

What is of importance to us, here, is Hebdige's notion of the manner in which Rastafari 'grounded God', as this allowed Rastafari to escape 'traditional religious displacement' and deal with the immediacy of their problems in the here and now. This meant that, for Hebdige, 'Rasta' was conscious of the influential role which the Bible, in its various guises, had on the popular imagination of the Jamaican people. Therefore, by 'secularising' the doctrine, they could make known the crucial historical role that the Bible played in the contemporary plight of the peoples of Afrikan descent. Further, unlike Marxists who would suggest that the Bible is merely a means of maintaining an ideological stranglehold over the masses by promoting 'false consciousness', Rastafari believe that the Bible contains 'truth', but that it has been misused by those who do not know God. Crucially the fact that they chose to reverse Biblical symbolism, through their own hermeneutic of suspicion, is not that surprising when we consider that they were advocating an alternative aesthetic based on blackness/good, negating whiteness/evil. This type of reversal is, according to Spencer, not unusual for peoples of Afrikan descent as it is akin to an Afrikan notion of spreading or transmitting a "social gospel" (1995: 68), which dealt with real earthly problems. That means Rastafari advocated a 'social gospel' based on knowing your enemy; it is not enough to pray to a transcendental being who is portrayed as white and so:

> Don't tell me of yuh white god don't teach me anything wrong, would yuh white god save me from white man oppression, mi nuh want nuh white god, is just a black messiah cau when the white god a bless how him nuh bless Sizzla. I want what is rightfully mine so mi nah stay mute, your system is designed to distract me from the truth, but it will come to pass and known unto the youth and in the process of time we will know the truth, you give we white god to praise in slavery the doctrine carry on into black community. (Sizzla, 1994)

Sizzla unequivocally states that, as a conscious Rastafari, he cannot wait on those whose forbears dehumanised the Afrikan with a system that 'distracts me from the truth', as part of the legacy of chattel enslavement, to then become our saviours. The point is we have to do that for ourselves, and in my opinion one way to do so is to 'make it known to the youth' that we are not 'salt', which in Jamaica means being cursed with misfortune. Rather, we have been, and in many ways still are being, assaulted by racist Europeans who do not wish for us to know that we are still suffering from the historical legacy of chattel enslavement, that which ultimately made 'white right' by holding 'black back'. Hence, it is up to us as Afrikans to 'lick-out against a system that seh white is right, cos from you pro-blak them want give you a fight' (Lezlee Lyrix, 1996) in our daily encounters with white supremacists and black-skinned, Eurocentric downpressors. Especially those who come with a black face and a white mentality, in the guise of preachers, who in one breath say 'Jesus noh have noh colour' and then encourage us to bow to their 'white god' who Sizzla states never 'bless' we, as Afrikans, yet!

Without this type of overstanding of the profundity of Rastafari consciousness, the culture and its advocates will forever be misrepresented by those who fail to appreciate that it is not about escapism. It is actually about learning why as Afrikans we are in this situation, and using that knowledge to determine what can be done on our own terms to transcend a system that is, by its very nature, anti-Afrikan. A perspective that makes perfect sense in light of a call in 1937 by one of the major influences on Rastafari, Marcus Mosiah Garvey for 'black people to emancipate themselves from mental slavery, this being a major responsibility for themselves and themselves alone' (Nettleford, 1999:313). Unsurprisingly, the idea of being responsible for your own destiny, and immediate fate, was missed by many theorists who saw Rastafari as an escapist movement, based on anthropological notions of millenarianism 'where solutions are religious rather than revolutionary' (Hebdige, 1977:426). For instance, Cashmore suggested that, 'Garvey was not interested in modifications of the present society but sought only one objective: the return of black peoples to Africa' (1979:19). This flagrant misrepresentation of Garvey's Pan-Afrikan stance did not end there, for it was further suggested by Cashmore and Troyna:

> What Garvey actually did, however, is less important than the mythology which developed around him. He became elevated to the role of prophet by early Rastafarian leaders who saw him as the harbinger of a new age. The disparity of the man and the myth surrounding him was bridged by the attribution of a single undocumented phrase; 'Look to Africa when a black king shall be crowned, for the day of deliverance is near.' Around this, a total belief system and, indeed, a new conception of reality was created. (1982:72)

Reducing the impact that Garveyite doctrine had on the consciousness of Afrikans worldwide, and Rastafari in particular, to one single—by inference—alleged statement, adds currency to the mythos that denies the practicality of Rastafari, not to mention the profundity and relevance of Garvey's outernational, libratory message for those of Afrikan descent (Lewis and Lewis, 1986). To suggest that a 'total belief system, and indeed a total new conception of reality was created' at this juncture fundamentally denies history. More importantly, it not only denies history, but also the tried and trusted methods the downpressed have employed, historically, to combat their suffering across a range of contexts. This was a main feature in the manner in which Hebdige suggests Rastafari took the Bible and flung it 'back rude', exemplified through their recognition of the power and manipulation of the spoken word. This represents a historical feature of many Africentric cultures of resistance and transcendence in Jamaica and many other black spaces and places, that predated Rastafari. This arose primarily because of the

European's outlawing of the written word to the children of Afrika and their chattel slave descendants. Furthermore, what Cashmore and Troyna's position does is make it easier to argue for the relevance of the 'generational/psychological breach' in the black British population, especially with regard to religious beliefs. This is exemplified in the idea that whilst the parental generation sought to 'improve conditions through involvement with local churches' (Cashmore and Troyna, 1982:73), for black youth:

> The concomitant realisation that conventional Christianity was a masquerade perpetrated by the white man to expedite his total domination, both physically and mentally, bred new feelings of resentment and antagonism amongst a sizeable number of black youths. As the 1970s progressed, more and more young blacks immersed themselves in the movement and simultaneously broadened the virtually unbridgeable chasm between the first-and second-generation migrants. (1982:73)

Cashmore and Troyna argue that rejection of conventional Christianity by the black youth led to 'profound behavioural consequences' evidenced in the embracing of a 'stylised Jamaican patois, a language of fictive kinship', that was transmitted through the culture of Rastafari. They suggest that black youth accessed the Rastafari worldview through the medium of Reggae music, which, as previously suggested by Pryce, provided the 'social opening' that welcomed their 'expressive-disreputable orientation'. The 'new reality' that was promoted by Rastafari through the lyricism of Reggae music appealed to the '1960s' rudie, whose 'nascent gang structures' (S. Jones, 1986), became 'secondary socialising agencies' (Cashmore 1979) for the disaffected black youth. This meant that the black youth in Britain were now 'drifting' under the 'influence' of Reggae into 'Rasta peer groups' with an 'acceptance of Haile Selassie as God' (S. Jones, 1986:61). It follows that this was the basis of Cashmore's notion of the Rasta's 'new reality', based on Garvey's supposed prophesising of the crowning of an Ethiopian King.

The commonalties in these perspectives is revealing; all are centred upon the embracing of a culture based on a type of 'false consciousness' that always distances the black subject from inhabiting the 'real world' in which they face very real problems. For instance, if there is 'kinship' it must be 'fictive'; if there is a 'new reality', religious or otherwise, it has no political substance or historical precedent as it is based on the 'myth'- making of Marcus Garvey or such like. Of more importance, Cashmore regards these factors as definitive in the self imposed exile of black youth from the wider black community, because usurping the white Jesus of Christian orthodoxy and replacing him with a black godhead only increased the generational gap. Moreover, the conflation of Rasta/rudie /Reggae as 'delinquent subcultural, solutions' (Brake 1980:27) further places an emphasis on external manifestations of style. Thus dreadlocks, the wearing red, gold and green as colour symbolism, specific use of language and listening to Reggae music become the chief determinants in recognising the deviant black youth. Hence 'rebellion has become a solution, a subcultural style stretching from reinterpretation of Rasta, to street crime and 'voluntary unemployment' (Brake, 1980:27).

The emphasis was on the idea that black youths not only render themselves unemployed and thus opt for a life of street crime; they also valorise their difference by openly displaying Rastafari symbolism. Furthermore, Cashmore and Troyna, in agreement with Brake, suggest that 'hustling' and 'pimping' and other forms of 'street crime' are the 'easy options' that black youth employ as their main 'strategies of survival' (1982:32). This meant that there was a tendency in this perspective to reduce the 'political scope of the movement' (Gilroy, 1982) and ignore the consequences of the 'structural placement' of black people in a racist society. With this in mind, Brake's suggestion that black youth are unemployed by choice becomes highly problematic and reinforces the notion of a culture of 'black' street crime. For as Gilroy suggests, 'we must resist the equation of Rasta politics with work refusal' (1982:293) as well as the depiction of Rastafari as an escapist youth cult, which uses Reggae music to maintain its distance from the wider community, because:

> Once dread style has been set aside as the essential qualification for 'cult membership', it becomes clear that many older black people share the movement's pan-Africanist sentiments and take pride in its refusal of racial domination. It is often forgotten that blacks arrived here bearing traditions of anti-colonial struggle wherever they set out from. Older West Indians have encountered the discourse of Rasta before...Their sympathy with the movement should be no surprise;

the solidarity it provides the whole community appears to offer a refuge from the new pressures of *popular* racism. (1982:292)

Understanding Gilroy's perspective is crucial to appreciating the fact that Rastafari and Reggae music came out of Jamaican culture and not vice versa, which means that these forms can only be appreciated as part of a historical continuum that resisted white downpression by promoting black/Afrikan unity. Moreover, it allows us to critique the widely held belief that there was a tendency by people from the West Indies to adhere to these clear cut dichotomous 'lifestyles' as posited by Cashmore, Troyna, Pryce, Brake and many others. This was a dangerous and damaging belief, central to how the black youth presence was depicted and managed during this critical moment in the Afrikan experience in Britain. In addition, it clears a space for a more meaningful discussion as to why these resistant cultural forms were/are so appealing to blacks in Britain and the Caribbean, whilst at the same time rethinking the role of Reggae music as a counter-cultural force. I hold this to be the main conduit for promoting the black 'solidarity' that is central to a discussion of this 'hidden' outernational 'voice'. This aspect of my argument substantiates the use of my knowledge of the culture in question, recognising an 'expertise' that is grounded in a lived experience of being an Afrikan in the united sindom.

2.3 'Epistemological Privilege', who feels it knows it!

Reggae music's purposeful message, which has been a constant since its 'creation', was the foremost reason why blacks in Britain embraced it, as a means of expressing their disapproval at being alienated in the land of their birth. By staking this claim I am clearly challenging how certain narrow perceptions of black youth infiltrated commonsense notions of the black experience and reduced them to so-called 'sub' types of cultural expression. This is the critical point missed in many of the above mentioned accounts I engaged with above that sought to give 'meaning' to the black youth presence in Britain during this historical moment. The point is that the knowledge base, from which that 'meaning' is derived, needs to be made explicit because reflection without a consideration of your own 'truths' is problematic. However, I am not suggesting that as a blak male researcher I am not aware of many of the problems associated with the form with regard to how race, gender and sexuality are constructed and perceived within the cultural milieu. Per contra, on the other hand, I am arguing that because I was socialised as an indigenous member of the black community I have access to, and a greater understanding of, certain 'hidden' aspects that the 'outsider' would not. Ethnographic truths' cannot accurately reflect the reality of a people's lived experiences, given that they are in many cases shackled by a Eurocentric 'academic imagination' that often omits more than it includes. I believe that it was this type of omission with which Hall (1993) grappled with when he suggested that there was a 'oneness' within 'cultural identity', which underlies the 'more superficial differences' of the 'black experience' (1993:393). Hall further suggests that:

> Within the terms of this definition, our cultural identities reflect the common historical experiences and shared cultural codes which provide us, as 'one people', with stable, unchanging and continuous frames of reference and meaning, beneath the shifting divisions and vicissitudes of our actual history. (1993:393)

What then appears to be at stake is how the memory of a common historical experience equips black people with the necessary 'shared cultural codes' (coping mechanisms) by providing 'narratives from the past' (Hall, 1993:394), which deal with everyday life in a racist society. Therefore, that which is often taken for granted remains 'hidden' and (thus) cannot be recovered through a logical process of observation, such as an 'orthodox' empirical/ethnographic study. I am suggesting that historically accepted 'truths' about racism and their relevance to cultural studies, ought to be interrogated from a black perspective for these, like my personal collection of Yard/Session-tapes, are often our 'continuous frames of reference'. This means that I have thought through the ramifications of this type of cultural consideration and (thus) argue for an interpretation, which will offer another type of 'truth' from a blak perspective. In fact Thompson (1998), an advocate of 'epistemological privilege' for black scholars during the 1970s, offers this germane and rather trenchant commentary on why this viewpoint should be recognised:

> Support for an epistemological privilege was a protest call for Black intellectuals to take control of the scholarship and research previously dominated by white people. The application of this ethical principle to sociological research means accepting that Black people are the ones who have the experience and insight needed to understand Black reality and responses to injustice. (Thompson, 1998:After word)

Applying this 'ethical principle' to the 'construction' of the 'racialized subject' (Carby 1999:97) demonstrates the need for 'epistemological privilege' because access to the cultural form under consideration here has been unproblematic I am from the community it represents. Therefore, unlike an ethnographic account of the 'objectified other', I share many of the concerns about how black people are generally rendered 'voiceless' within the discourses of 'racialization'. These concerns are those of 'real people', (like myself) and partially explain why I undertook this work as my 'insights' are grounded in a lived 'black experience'. That is why the 'hidden voice' that describes and documents our experiences of racism, as the 'one people', that is so crucial to how we (blacks) 'are positioned by, and position ourselves within, the narratives of the past' (Hall 1993:394) is often misrepresented in much academic writing. For as Little (1991), citing Taylor (1985), suggests:

> Given that social phenomena are partially constituted by the self-understanding of all participants, a social theory can alter the social arrangements or facts that it describes...the theory is not about an independent object, but one that is partly constituted by self-understanding. (1991:233)

Simply put, it is not enough to recognise the existence of Hall's 'cultural codes' if the necessity for them as anti-hegemonic devices is overlooked, as the messages contained therein contribute to these ongoing histories. These histories contain elements that are in a constant state of flux because a personal narrative becomes something else once it is shared in a particular type of 'social arrangement'. In fact it is during these moments of sharing our 'self-understanding', Deejays telling life-stories in the Reggae-dancehall, that the oppressed can recognise themselves within the grand narratives of the Afrikan Diaspora. For the overall message is one of a commonality of condition

81

with regard to the positioning of the black 'other' in a white-dominated racialised arena, which has gained most of its currency by devaluing the 'black experience'. This means that explanations that are too reliant on 'symbolic escapism' or 'lifestyles' foster 'false consciousness', which further mute the lived reality of black people, are untenable as they deny the history of resisting and transcending white racism. I would suggest that utilising this history, based upon 'self-understanding' in its most practical sense, is paramount for a researcher who is endeavouring to ethically represent a cultural form, which is in essence a song of himself. This becomes a serious epistemological and ontological concern because my worldview—the locus of my self-understanding—based on this alternative notion of a blak self, has influenced the manner in which I negotiate this ethnographic journey. In other words, I am simultaneously using my 'insider' knowledge base, and position within the culture, to assess the 'validity' of the 'outsider' accounts I contend in order to substantiate my alternative interpretation. I am suggesting that there is a difference between using knowledge to access and theorise a perceived sociological problem, the abstracted academic enterprise, and using knowledge pragmatically to overcome the actual 'social problem' that affects everyday livity. Therefore, my methodological approach considers the practical worth of knowledges that are generated within the culture, for instance the notions of 'blak' and 'outernational', and uses them as conceptual tools to create bridges of meaning that enable me to stake my alternative claims.

Once this fundamental is appreciated we can comprehend why the Deejay consciously chose to participate in the outernational musical and cultural exchanges of the 'black Atlantic' that sought to resist and transcend white racism. That is why Jah Bones' observation has such validity; he recognised that the Deejays were extending 'cultural strongholds that are normally well fortified' (1985: 65), which means that access was largely denied to 'outsiders'. Of equal importance is the notion of access, in the context of the Reggae-dancehall, which needs much consideration because the performers and their audiences are invariably accessible to each other. This is a fact that has been well documented as there is said to be no physical distance in Afrikan musical cultures, between audience and performer (Gilroy 1986, Back 1987, 1996, Stolzoff 2000, Bradley 2001, Liverpool 2001). The ethos, being one of collective representation which blurs the distinctions between the partakers in the culture, which has been dubbed 'musicking' by Small (1987) when he argued:

> My first assumption is that *music is not primarily a thing or a collection of things, but an activity in which we engage.* One might say that it is not properly a noun at all, but a verb; the absence of a verb in English, as in most European languages, to express this activity is significant, and may point towards the European attitude to the making of music...certainly the conceptual gap is interesting. I intend using...from now on the verb *'to music'*, (after all one can say 'to dance' so why not?) and especially its present participle, 'musicking', to express the act of taking part in a musical performance. In order to narrow the gap that is assumed to exist between performers and listeners in European musicking, I define the word to include not only performing and composing (what is composition but the preparation of material for performance) but also listening and even dancing to music; all those involved in any way in a musical performance can be thought of as musicking. (Small, 1987:50)

We can clearly see the idea of how a lack of distance, 'narrowing the gap', represents the 'one people' mentality because there are certain sensibilities shared by all concerned, which implies that there is closeness in the mental distance (cognitive structures) that makes the Deejay's lyric culturally relevant. By using self-reflection as a conceptual tool to assess the validity of these moments of closeness, which occur when Afrikan communities partake in that which Small dubs *'to music'*, I am able to state that this outernational worldview is dependent on recognising what Levine has termed a 'similar life style' (1977:3/4). This 'similar life style' unifies the downpressed in ways that have maintained black/Afrikan communities throughout our sojourn in Europe's 'New World'. However, this type of self-reflection throws up an ethical problem, which is how to justify my rendering of a form that is regarded as a 'cultural stronghold' and is still used to edify and counter discrimination and various types of racist exclusionary practices across the social landscape. Consequently, ethically and morally, how much of what I know should I make known, in light of the manner in which white-dominated social theory has been used to the detriment of black people as argued throughout this study? As a consequence of these considerations, whilst reasoning with the British Deejays, Asher Senator and Papa Benji, I asked them how they felt about an enterprise that used Reggae-dancehall music to detail and counter various misrepresentations of our experiences as black youth in a racist society:

> **Asher:** How you mean, Lez! Only we can deal with Reggae because we are what the music is about and I am writing a book on it myself, cos when I read some of the stuff that has been written, choh! Bout we ah criminal weh nuh do nut'n but beat up an disrespect we woman. Them ting deh just cause division with I an the daughtah them, an is why when we were out there chatting all over the place, trying to uplift the youts, the press and them people deh was not interested in what we had to say. In fact nuff of them were fraid fi come ah dance fi see what did ah gwaan an is why them write and chat so much rubbish bout we.

> **Benji:** It's like when I read that thing (undergraduate dissertation) that you wrote and you was talking about San's (Jamaican Deejay Papa San) 'Longest Lyric' when he mentioned things like Echo having a diploma and Trees (Jamaican Deejay General Trees) being a shoemaker and one whole heapah tings that people who didn't listen to Yard-tapes would never have known. It's true when you check it, what Senny (Asher Senator) just said because the reason we know was because we were chatting and used to listen to them man deh and get nuff vibes from them as well.

> **Asher:** Yeh but it was the same way how they got nuff vibes from us because nuff of what we were chatting went over there (Jamaica) and came back in ah different style. What about King's (British Deejay Peterkin's) 'fast style', all of them were on it, even Briggy who was one of the most original of the yard man them. Nuff nuh know them ting deh Lyrix bout the youth them aanyah. (Personal Communication, 1999)

Asher Senator's notion of 'nuff nuh know them ting deh' presents an insight into the epistemological problem I face as a blak scholar; I am in fact one who does 'know'. But how do I make what I 'know', known, in a way that does justice to the potency of a form that is constantly under attack from the 'outsiders' it was designed to chant down in the first place? For, as I argued above, we were aware of what 'the press and them people deh', "foreign enthusiasts" (Stolzoff 2000), were saying about black youths in Britain, based on the aforementioned propensity toward crime and other types of deviant behaviour. This was borne out in the above where Benji mentions that in Papa San's 'Longest Lyric' he informs the audience of aspects of the Deejay's lifestyles that few would have associated with artists of this genre of performance. For instance, San states that 'Echo goh to good school an get him diploma', which challenges 'the commonly-held view that dancehall Deejays are semi-literate at best, uneducated and unsophisticated' (Walters 2001). This issue is important because I am also considering how these accounts challenge the popular view that 'the lyrics of the Deejay define the furthest extreme of the scribal/oral literary continuum' (Cooper, 1993:136). Although Cooper's comments were based on Jamaican Deejays, the fact that Deejaying was perceived as an 'oral' art form makes it easier for this type of overly misrepresentative argument to be forwarded. This argument is countered by the types of lyricism that are featured in this study, which are composed (as will be demonstrated in Chapter 6) for (the) live performance and therefore straddle the oral/scribal continuum in a fashion that has not been adequately theorised in the Reggae-dancehall context.

In concordance with the above I believe that each generation builds on previous knowledge to construct their epistemological reserve, that which gives cultural relationships social and historical meaning in the present as part of a 'common fund of urban experiences' (Gilroy, 1993a:83). That is why in the B~SIDE I have included two *re-memories* to demonstrate on a practical level how notions of biography, history and memory can be deployed as philosophical tools in an endeavour to make the significance of the traffic (ideas) that cross the divide between the 'public' and 'alternative public' spheres of representation known. Furthermore, by using these descriptive accounts in this manner, I practically demonstrate how lyrics become the type of 'hidden' narrative that is central to a rethinking of the black experience in Britain, for by taking memories and re-using them in this fashion the Deejay transforms personal reflections into collective social documents.

In order to create a lyric that speaks to your 'structural placement' in the present, personal comparisons need to be made with past experiences of your social condition in the 'real world'. For this is what gives the 'hidden voice' the type of substance that impersonal outsider accounts generally lack and why Asher stated 'them chat so much rubbish bout we'. Therefore culture, as patterns of behaviour, continuously moulds, transforms and develops the available raw materials as each generation makes their contribution to this 'common fund' of experiences. In this case it is the Deejays who lyrically contribute to this ongoing history in a language that is representative of the black cultural politics of their time. Thus their *re-memories* are in essence representational devices that in this context become descriptive tools for documenting our lived experiences across the generations, via bridges of meaning, in lyrical form. As a matter of fact, many of these lyrics document stories told to my respondents by various older members of the black community, including parents and other relatives. Similarly, many are based on intergenerational discussions about what it means to be an Afrikan in the Diaspora, often detailing the types of cultural concern that question the role of aesthetics in modern forms of black identity:

> Me granny seh ah weh yuh from, ah which country? Me show her seh
> ah Afrika, definitely. She seh which part yuh favour Kunta Kente?
> Cut yuh dread an dress decently. (Papa Levi, Ghettotone 1983)

The British born Deejay Papa Levi demonstrates how the shift in the perception of what it means to be Afrikan is based on challenging the idea that our identity can be reduced to where we were born, how we dress and how we wear our hair. This aesthetic argument is as important now as it was then and we only need to consider the affliction of skin bleaching and other forms of racial suicide to appreciate its relevance from within. But too often these discussions are muted in the wider public arena, for various reasons, which explains why the counter-cultures that deal with these issues in plain and simple terms are critically important to maintaining this form of dialogue. The Deejay is still largely regarded as a mouthpiece for particular sections of the black community and to this end generally echoes their overall sentiments and sensibilities on the issues that are regarded as the most important at any given time. Drawing together my above views regarding the autonomy of this space and its dependence on self-regulation given that it is the pooling of ideas as a community that most inspires the Deejay to write; this is where the skills of the various types of Deejay come to the fore because your reputation often hangs on the poignancy and overall relevance of your contribution, a factor that I will expand upon in detail in the B~SIDE of this study.

Conclusion

In this chapter I have engaged the most thought-provoking issues that have arisen whilst undertaking this research project as a blak researcher endeavouring to tell the story of 'real people'. I opened with a consideration of the 'power' of the ethnographer and painted a picture of how 'ethnographic inscription' can actually distort the reality it supposedly represents. For this reason I have argued that there is an element of misrepresentation of the black subject in many of the texts I have featured. Therefore, I had to confront my own ontological and epistemological concerns as sources of 'truth' to provide a type of 'status' to my accounts and those of my respondents. Consequently I gave much consideration to the ethical and moral obligations that I have to those who are under scrutiny, including myself, with regard to the manner in which I make this 'hidden voice' heard. What I find to be at stake here is an epistemological problem that hinges on recognising the power your position as an academic has on the 'object/s' of your study and, ultimately, how it affects the way you render an account of 'real people'. For it is commonly understood that the relationship between the 'observer' and the 'observed' should be as 'objective' as possible (Woolgar's notion of 'objective discourse'). However, more realistically, the most 'objective' methodological approach is informed by the researcher's theoretical position, which in turn is informed by their particular political concerns. Hence, what I present here is a counter to the power of 'ethnographic inscription', that seeks to obscure the 'reality' of those it purports to study by recognising my position within the textual analysis as both 'outsider' and 'insider'. This will be evidenced in the final chapter of the A~SIDE where I convey a sense of the worth of black music in general, and Reggae-dancehall music in particular, to explain their importance to my Africentric worldview.

Chapter 3

Black music and the Jamaican cultural influence on black youth in Britain

Introduction

> Music a de beat of the ghetto, me no matter what yuh want seh
> Beenie Man seh so, music a de beat ah we heart so who no know
> bout the music please no bother talk. (Beenie Man, 1997)

I now wish to consider the merits of black music from an 'insider' perspective as I am in total agreement with Beenie Man's argument and will 'talk' from my 'heart' as one who does know and, more importantly, overstands from the inside. Contained within the notion of 'black music', as a concept, there is a constant re-presentation of the history of black/Afrikan suffering at the hands of white/racist/Europeans, irrespective of where we physically live in Babylon. When the worth of black music is evaluated from 'inside', especially as a counter-culture, it represents something that many who try to theorise its value totally miss. It is from this premise that I will feature the lyricism of the Deejays that use an enemy language, as the template upon which they engineer their disapproval of British society. Herein lies a fundamental problem when endeavouring to overstand the efficacy of black musical cultures; the key to unlock the rationale behind these cultures is often concealed in the manipulation of ordinary language. I argue that these types of social commentary need to be understood within their own 'frames of reference', which will become apparent in this final chapter of the A~SIDE.

In light of the above I will reappraise what is meant by the term 'black music' by those who regard this as a premier voice in our struggles against white supremacy. This means that I will argue for a notion of black music as an entity that defies 'scientific' or ethnic-absolutist ideas which try to validate/invalidate it according to some type of 'essential' or 'scientific' criteria. Therefore, to assist this aim, the role that black cultural creativity plays in the formation of 'alternative public arenas' (Gilroy 1987), which operate as sites for these 'hidden' transcultural dialogues, will be considered. This will allow me to focus on black music both as a 'popular' cultural form and an ideological vehicle, which assists the black oppressed in their 'winning of cultural spaces' (S. Jones, 1986). Consequently, this will enable me to clear ground for my argument in the B~SIDE of the study about the significant role black music, Rastafari and an Africentric worldview plays in the lives of black people in Britain.

3.2 'Black music': the 'winning of cultural space'

It is the idea of Reggae music as an 'intervening medium' that offers an insight into what is meant by 'black music' and allows us to overstand how it assists the 'winning' of an outernational 'cultural space'. It is often overlooked by cultural critics who, for one reason or another, argue that without certain 'common structural denominators' (Tagg, 1989)-antiphony, polyrhythm etc.-'we' cannot accept any such concept. They do not appreciate that fundamentally:

> Black music is that which is recognized and accepted by its creators, performers and hearers...encompassing the music of those who see themselves as black, and whose musics have unifying characteristics which justify their recognition as specific genres. (Oliver, 1990:8)

Oliver's definition of black music is probably a highly contentious position from which to anchor this discussion given that his claim for the recognition of 'unifying characteristics' is most often construed as generic or essentialist. Nevertheless, it does allow us to seek out the reasons as to why particular types of music are still deemed necessary to the maintenance of autonomous black communities. This is because for many cultural critics there is a romanticised acceptance of 'naturalness' (Frith 1987, Reynolds 1990) in black music that manifests as a black reclamation of their humanity from a hostile, inhuman, white world. Moreover, there is said to be an 'obsession' with 'origins' which, once established, becomes 'an expression of a yearning for a "natural" state of grace' (Frith, 1987:181). This obsession apparently means that black becomes a 'signifier for being more human' (Reynolds, 1990:156) and thus obscures its rather spurious claims to authenticity, especially in the realms of 'popular culture'. Therefore, concepts like 'black music' need to be 'scientifically' interrogated by cultural critics to demonstrate how untenable they are because the 'designations 'black' and 'white' are manifestly inaccurate and scientific nonsense' (Melville, 1997:13).

One such critic who met this challenge was Tagg (1989), who in his 'Open Letter' offered the 'interested' reader, a 'polemical problematisation of terms like 'black music', white music', 'Afro-American music' or 'European music' (1989:285). Tagg suggested that it is difficult to find 'common structural denominators' in what has conventionally been classed as black music. Curiously, Tagg begins his discussion by explaining that his 'Open Letter' is aimed at 'white European or North American students, friends and colleagues'. This confession excludes the main 'object' of his study, those of 'us' whom he would not 'insult' by implying that we 'believe' there is some type of validity in a concept like 'black music'. Tagg's main bone of contention is the fact that discussions about 'black music' are far more common than discussions about 'white music' which, he suggests, is due to narrow essentialism. The inference is clear as it posits that if you are 'black' then you have a 'natural' ability to make music, which reinforces various stereotypes that have been employed by 'cultural' Europeans to subjugate 'natural' Africans. Tagg further suggests that this is often due to our 'acceptance' of these musicological categories, without providing working 'cultural definitions'. Hence:

> It would be restricting the meaning of the term 'black music' quite severely to make it denote the music of dark-skinned people in the USA and nowhere else in the world. However, this is precisely the sort of meaning implied – seldom openly declared and even more rarely defined – on most occasions I have come across the term. This implied meaning of 'black' is not only restrictive; it is ethnocentric. (1989:287)

This undoubtedly implies an investment in the 'racist hypothesis that there are physiological connections between the colour of people's skin and the sort of music people with that colour skin can produce'

(1989:287). I find it interesting and most peculiar for Tagg to emphasise the difficulty in accepting that which represents some type of convention with regard to 'black music' and then wonder why 'white music' is not generally discussed along the lines of essentialism. I make this assertion because 'white' is generally the unspoken qualifier in racist societies and their former colonies; therefore, its 'normalising' effects warrant much consideration. Especially so, when commenting on 'rarely defined' types of 'ethnocentrism' that fail to appreciate the significance of working 'cultural definitions' that seem to take whiteness for granted. Perhaps this is because whiteness is 'a powerful norm that had been so constant and persistent in society that white people never needed to name it' (Berger 2000:204). This point was raised above when Allen suggested that many scholars 'hinder' their analyses because they have not come to terms with the 'problems created by disciplines firmly based in Eurocentric and ethnocentric assumptions' (1982:144). Thus to nitpick at various notions of 'black music' in order to 'discover' whether or not there is any universal 'authenticity' before 'you' can accept its validity (for instance, it must contain antiphonic exchanges or be polyrhythmic) smacks of a Eurocentric bias that denies the realities of the black experience in white societies. Although this experience is often expressed through the medium of music, it is not restricted to dealing with the joys or sorrows one encounters within the realms of music alone. In fact, 'Diaspora challenges us to apprehend mutable itinerant culture. It suggests the complex, dynamic potency of living memory: more embodied than inscribed' (Gilroy, 1994:212).

As Gilroy suggests, what is at stake is a failure to recognise the validity of these musical modes of expression, which in fact represent a counterculture that is intrinsic to the psychological wellbeing of the black downpressed. Moreover, it is the history of resistance against the imposition of European values on non-European peoples that is often the commonality between the supposedly diverse experiences of non-white peoples, as expressed in that which we term 'black music'. In fact it is black music's challenging of the processes of violence and forced dislocation which distorted the African presence by making it 'other' to Europe's 'self', that gives the form its universal appeal. An appeal that was missed by Tagg and yet eloquently posited by Cooper, who captures the essence of how valid black music, is as a song of ourselves, because:

Jimmy Cliff's 'Many Rivers To Cross', one of the most heartrending of the songs from the movie *The harder they Come*, was transposed from its culture-specific Jamaican context to become a praise song for the Free Azania Movement. Like the Atlantic ocean, the many rivers that must be crossed are not only barriers, but routes of cultural exchange. (Cooper, 1993:196)

Cooper's reasoning provides an example of the practicality of black music as a major site of 'cultural exchange' that enables us to move away from staid accounts that seek to impose unrealistic criteria upon its scientific tenability. The fact that those to whom the music speaks outernationally can recognise the message is crucial to my argument about why we used the form in Britain to debate and discuss our own 'problem' status. Therefore, how the music is validated and authenticated is generated from within the culture and, as Cooper suggests it cannot be geographically bound because it is a 'route of cultural exchange'. Thus it is widely accepted from within that:

The preeminence of music within the diverse black communities of the Atlantic Diaspora is itself an important element in their essential connectedness. But the histories of borrowing, displacement, transformation, and continual reinscription that the musical culture encloses are a living legacy that should not be reified in the primary symbol of the Diaspora and then employed as an alternative to the recurrent appeal of fixity and rootedness. (Gilroy, 1991:127)

The suggestion is that black music assists the 'winning of cultural space, in which an alternative black social life could flourish' (S. Jones, 1986:192), whilst warning against those who would 'scientifically' or otherwise, reduce the complexity of this form to a notion of 'ethnic absolutism'. It is the notion of 'winning cultural spaces' that warrants the utmost consideration here as it allows us to access the sites where these 'battles' are won or lost. For the battles are invariably ideological and thus cannot be reduced to the 'scientific' or 'absolutist' whims of cultural theorists or musicologists, who 'seek to "grasp" music…in a manner appropriate for musical production, rather than for musical listening' (Frith, 1996:63). The main reason being that the types of 'musicking' under consideration here, and many of the 'musicians' who partake in these types of artistic expression, operate outside the realm

WHAT THE DEEJAY SAID

of 'formal' musical education. Furthermore, although Frith's insight is useful, these 'musicians' probably would not see the relationship between 'musical production' and 'musical listening' as oppositional. I am particularly commenting on Reggae Sound System culture where the main participants rely on pre-recorded music of some type or other on which to base their performances. Equally, as Gilroy has suggested, black musical cultures 'dissolve the distinctions between art and life, artefact and expression which typify the contrasting traditions of Europe' (1987:164/5). Thus, as Baldwin eloquently posits:

> There is a great deal in the world which Europe does not or cannot see: in the same way that the European musical scale cannot transcribe – cannot write down, does not understand: the notes, or the price of this music. (Cited in Gilroy, 1987:153)

To argue for an acceptance of an entity called 'black music' is not some 'imagined' essentialist somatic reaction, but rather a claim for recognising a 'popular' cultural form that quite often has at its root a critique of European cultural values. This is something that we have always 'recognised' in our experiences of black music', yet it is quite often an 'interior knowledge that we struggle to bring into use' (Dent, 1992:10). Moreover, oftentimes the 'interior knowledge' is exteriorised at various moments during the 'struggle', yet-due to Bones' (1986) notion of 'well-fortified cultural strongholds'-the black 'voice' remains 'hidden'. Therefore, certain types of performance cultures that manifest via black music's 'popular' appeal need to be recognised as the embodiment of a pragmatic historical re-memory because, as Back has suggested:

> Cultural processes themselves confound the idea that cultures exist as hermetically sealed absolute unities. Urban cultures, in particular, are highly promiscuous in their endeavour constantly to remake and invent traditions in the present. (1996:8)

Promiscuity aside, the suggestion here is that black music creates that space in which alternative notions of being black, both positive and negative, can be discursively debated and disseminated across the urban landscape. Therefore, London can be regarded as a nodal point in a multicultural system of creative processes that encompasses Said's

(1993) notion of 'overlapping territories', in which 'ethnic' negotiations are in a constant state of flux. Thus 'new ethnicities' are encoded within, and disseminated via, emergent vernacular cultures as the urban environment becomes the crucible within which these creative/destructive 'multicultural' processes are aired and discussed. These processes exemplify Gilroy's notion of the 'black Atlantic', where the black British equally participate in the outernational musical and cultural exchanges of the Afrikan Diaspora. This viewpoint is crucial to the ethos of this work as I consider notions of inclusion and exclusion for the generations of blacks who were born in Britain and whose very presence challenges hegemonic notions of Britishness as an exclusively white domain. This is because unlike many of their family members, peers or contemporaries, who hail from beyond these shores, many of these blacks feel a rootedness to the land of their birth. A rootedness that often reveals itself as 'hybridised' types of 'underground' music that are both 'us' and 'other', as they claim a cultural space that reflects and caters for lived experiences. For this reason alone we must resist the current trend to reduce black music to the 'urban', for to do so denies the practicality and necessity of the modes of resistance and transcendence that have historically enabled the black Diaspora to re-member the 'Afrikan hellocaust' (Muhammad, 1997). In fact this clamour for the 'urban' to replace 'black', when denoting alternative modes of cultural expression that are created by black/Afrikan people, is nothing less than the latest manifestation of the Eurocentric cultural hegemony, which has sought to elide any identifiably black presence that successfully counters white domination. This viewpoint is shared by Kelly, who is also aware that:

> Black popular music does not rise magically from the souls of black folk but from the struggle itself-the struggle to maintain communities, to fulfil our material, emotional, and spiritual needs, to survive poverty and brutality, to transform this racist, hostile world we've inherited. (Kelly cited in Neal, 1999:Back cover)

3.2   Reggae music and black solidarity

They say when they listen to some of my songs even if they were thinking of picking up a gun they're not gonna do it. So these are the things I am focusing on right now. That's why I sing conscious songs. It doesn't make sense I sing songs without meaning. I have to sing to protect my brothers and sisters. (Admiral Tibet, cited in Foster, 1999:208)

For there is such a thing as knowledge that is less, rather than more, partial than the individual (with his entangling and distracting life circumstances) who produces it. Yet this knowledge is not therefore non-political. (Said, 1978:8)

Admiral Tibet's sentiments about why he has to sing songs with 'meaning' to 'protect his brothers and sisters' mirror my own feelings about how Reggae music, as black music is a vehicle for promoting black solidarity. This perspective runs contrary to the view that Reggae music was a 'Rasta-rudie black oriented counter-culture' (Pryce 1979:156), which had 'decidedly criminal connotations' (S. Jones 1986:56). Clearly this argument meant that any notion of Reggae music promoting positive notions of 'solidarity' across the 'black Atlantic' was hardly recognised. Unless we consider the types of 'solidarity' crucial to maintaining a 'thick as thieves' mentality, which would be the logical outcome of black youths exposure to a 'criminal' culture that acts as a 'secondary socialising agency' (Cashmore, 1979). For, as suggested above, the discursive nature of Rastafari doctrine, as 'religiously' disseminated through the medium of Reggae music, cannot be overlooked in any balanced analysis of black counter-cultures. Cashmore and Troyna shared this opinion, although for quite different reasons, when they suggested that:

Young men (and women) do not normally turn to religious movements for explanations of their rejection and their deviance. If they are to be affected by ideas such as those Rastafarianism has to offer there must be some intervening medium through which ideas are conveyed to them. That medium is provided by Reggae music. Along with the more libidinal ecstatic messages which they receive from the beats and its themes, they also receive a political message which speaks to their condition. (1982:69)

The fact that their point of view is clouded by this lack of understanding about the complexity of the relationship between the generational adherents to 'normal' religious movements needs to be briefly addressed. To do so I must state that the 'young men and women' would arguably have been exposed to orthodox Christian doctrine from numerous sources before their exposure to Rastafari. For instance, Hebdige's notion of the Bible being 'taken, read and flung back rude' hinges itself on the understanding that the raw materials Rastafari would mould to fit their 'radical' and practical 'social gospel' were already culturally known. Pryce recognised this and he suggested:

> The Rastas are commonly regarded by all and sundry as experts on the Bible. They are particularly addicted to apocalyptic concepts of the Old Testament, and their parable like speeches and enunciations generally reverberate with Old Testament images...Like the Pentecostalists they can usually justify and account for every occurrence in terms of their own peculiar interpretation of the Bible. (1986:148)

Appreciating the profundity of Pryce's likening of Rastafari to Pentecostalism argues that the raw (religious) materials were not only culturally known to the young blacks in Britain, but accessed through the infectious oratory of charismatic leaders. Thus any endeavour to ascertain why these youths sought solace in Rastafari's message must take account of the fact that, in many black communities 'religion is a total involvement...not a mental exercise' (Barrett, 1988:27). Therefore, their exposure to black Christian styles of worship provided the template for re-thinking the role of religious belief, when confronted with the 'oral skills' of many advocates of Rastafari, who appeared on the Jamaican Reggae recordings which dominated these shores during that moment, and any Rastafari with whom they had regular contact. It was the cultural knowledge gained from the various types of symbolic (sacred/secular) language to which they were already exposed as members of the black community, that made it easy for Reggae to become this 'intervening medium'. In other words, it provided the locus for an 'adaptive response' to popular racism by grounding religious beliefs, in a most practical way, because the cultural knowledge base was malleable enough to supply the familiarity, which is the key to understanding the narrative form. According to Gilroy:

> The power of music in developing black struggles by communicating information, organising consciousness, and testing out or deploying the forms of subjectivity which are required by political agency,

whether individual or collective, defensive or transformational, demands attention to both the formal attributes of this expressive culture and its distinctive *moral* basis…In the simplest possible terms, by posing the world as it is against the world as the racially subordinated would like it to be, this musical culture supplies a great deal of the courage required to go on living in the present. (1993a:36)

Gilroy demonstrates how the alternative worldview made manifest in the marriage of the Rastafari message and Reggae music, as an 'organiser' of 'consciousness', cannot be separated from a tradition of struggle against oppression, which subsequently promotes black solidarity. Therefore, we cannot overlook the significant role that religious forms play in the formulation and reformulation of the social, cultural and political sensibilities of these young men and women. To do so simplifies the role the Bible has played, and still plays, in the psychological make-up of the generations of peoples of Afrikan descent who are the subjects of this enquiry. This means that we must recognise the manner in which the historical experience of chattel slavery is totally relevant to any understanding of contemporary black musical expression. For as Alleyne suggests, the merging of African and European religious forms with music and dance was a key factor in unifying the slaves in Jamaica, 'because they were major instruments of cohesion and revolt' (1988:118). The religious message has to be conveyed in a manner in which the people could truly recognise their lived reality. That is what is meant by a 'social gospel' that enables active participation as part of a collective effort to remedy the negative aspects of this ongoing reality. Hence, irrespective of age, Afrikans on the continent and their descendants throughout the Diaspora were (and many still are) expected to partake in 'religious ceremonies' because 'African religious traditions take into consideration not only one's intellect, but also one's emotions, the mental and the visceral' (Barrett, 1988:27). Thus:

Music and dance form an instrument for spreading their ideologies, attracting converts and releasing within the people a feeling of power over everyday suffering and poverty and oppression, as well as a physical closeness or even oneness with the great gods or spirits of their religion. (Alleyne, 1988:118/9)

To demonstrate how the 'spreading' of 'their ideologies', in the context of the Deejay, is becoming evidenced in its most practical sense let us consider this notion of the "social gospel" in black music, which draws on the legacy of chattel slavery in an endeavour to empower black people in the present. It is, after all, part of the Deejay's role and purpose as a spokesperson for the community to 'release within the people a feeling of power' over the negative aspects of everyday livity during the cathartic moment that is the Deejay performance. This will also show how black music is a vehicle for the dissemination of these 'hidden voices' as it provides a space for the Deejays to partake in a diasporic system of intellectual exchange thereby placing their lyricism in an outernational context because the language of choice, Patwa, and the Africentric worldview it represents cannot be geographically bound. In this way, the Deejays consciously challenged the notion that they should be expressing themselves in Standard English because this is the language of their formal education. It was this point that I made in chapter 1 when citing Wong's perspective on how black youths resisted their mother tongue's 'alphabet of terror' by embracing Rastafari language and symbolism and as evidenced in the notion of 'head-decay-shun'. Such reasonings are ever present in Reggae music and are demonstrative of the role and purpose of black music as a platform for countering white/European cultural hegemony, especially as our history is not found 'in the standard textbooks'. For this reason Rastafari argue that Afrikan people need to be aware of the need to, as Baldwin suggested, 'excavate their own history' when visiting institutions like a 'you-nevah see' (university), where alternative accounts of the Afrikan are contained in the 'lie-bury' (library). In addition, those who are already 'excavating history' and are therefore tuned into such knowledge, often demonstrate how 'the aftermaths of slavery still endure in the social forms and perceptions of New World peoples' (Mintz, 1989:62), evidenced in the following extract from 'African Slavery', where it is argued:

> Some people nah go like weh me say, but me a go say it anyway, me a go talk about slavery and the effects of it today, some people just don't want to know, about four hundred years ago, but the thing about slavery it's affecting people now…what about all the lives that were lost, what about the black holocaust, what about African slavery and what its done to you and me…Oh I can see the effects of slavery

still in ah the community, no identity suffering from amnesia, a case of lost memory, Black man and woman can't you see your history never start on the plantation...Holocaust is a word they use for what the Nazis did to the Jews, compensation was never refused, their own land they even got to choose. So what's wrong with us? Was the Black holocaust not so serious? (Macka B, 2000)

Macka B clearly states that as peoples of Afrikan descent we are still affected by the legacy of chattel slavery—'Post Traumatic Slave Syndrome' (Leary, 2004)—especially those suffering from a type of 'amnesia' and have no awareness that their 'history never start on the plantation'. This line of argument is the contemporary manifestation of a historical 'mode of response/resistance' to, and rejection of, the imposition of European cultural values on non-European peoples. In other words, the countering of whiteness as an ethnocentric paradigm for the global maintenance of white supremacist thinking by a blackness which is dependent on 'making connections with the entire Diaspora' (Back, 1996:145). Making these connections includes a re-linking with a more positive sense of a historical Afrikan presence that did not begin 'on the plantation'. Thus the role of the Deejay as educator is exemplified in Macka B's account, as he seeks to promote awareness of how the legacy of chattel slavery impacts on the way we perceive ourselves in the present. Of equal importance by making connections between the Afrikan and the Jewish holocausts, he highlights the manner in which the Afrikan has been historically miseducated; many people have no idea of the true extent of the destruction meted out on the Afrikan by racist Europeans. In the case of Reggae-dancehall music, these 'connections' are maintained because it was/is 'protected' by a 'language, a colour and by a culture which had been forced to cultivate secrecy against the intrusions of the Master Class' (Hebdige, 1979:434). This is why these cultures often resist the 'outsider's' gaze because, as I specified above, this is an aspect of how black music creates an alternative space for those who view their ongoing oppression as a consequence of the colonisation of Afrika by racist Europeans. Hence they recognise, in line with Du Bois (1919), that:

The methods by which this continent has been stolen have been contemptible and dishonest beyond expression. Lying treaties, rivers of rum, murder, assassination, mutilation, rape, and torture have marked the progress of the Englishman, German, Frenchman, and Belgian, on the Dark Continent. The only way in which the world has been able to endure the horrible tale is by deliberately stopping its ears and changing the subject of conversation while the devilry went on. (Du Bois, cited in Prah, 1992:14)

In a time when music is used to 'distract us from our mission' (Capleton, 1999) in the guise of Geldof's 'Live 8' (July 2nd 2005), for example, which definitely 'changes the conversation'. The real 'devilry' that decimates the Afrikan continent to this day is never addressed; the focus is always on 'debt relief', 'fair trade' and 'corrupt leaders', but never on the historical role that white supremacists played in the utilisation of the continent, and its peoples, as a veritable scaffold to build the edifice that we call the western world. It is therefore prudent to appreciate that those who acknowledge this reality utilise black music as a conduit for presenting counter-ideologies to white domination because, 'many don't want to know, about four hundred years ago, but the thing about slavery it's affecting people now'. To consider the ways in which these effects are countered, I will in the final section of this chapter concentrate on black music as it manifests as Deejay culture and provide a fresh insight into the significance of the 'verbal exchanges' (Hebdige, 1977) in Reggae music's message/medium.

3.3 'One hand wash the other': libratory language across the 'black Atlantic'!

Black youth in Britain, by way of the Deejay performance, created a living history that challenged their negative depiction across a range of contexts, and because of the spaces in which it was articulated, it remained 'hidden' from the wider public gaze. This, a factor that was missed by many of the theorists who sought to explain their affiliations to Reggae music and its concomitant cultures without a consideration of what actually transpired in these alternative public spaces. One obvious reason for this approach is that many commentators who have written about the history of Deejaying, especially during this moment, were not active participants in the culture because:

Them never go ah dance, so how could them know what was going on around the Set or even what influenced how and why we did what we were doing. The only way to know the reality of certain things is to ask and not pretend you know when it is obvious to those of us who were there, that you most obviously were not. Most of the stuff I have read that was written about Sound Systems, during them time deh, acts as if we were part of the 'Two-tone' scene that was nothing to do with us. Remember Frontline started copying the Yard-tape style and that's what we turned into our own style, so what they listened to and played could never be played in our dances; imagine if you played Selector or Clash in a session you wouldah get bottle to raas. (Dr Vibes, Personal Communication 2004)

As Dr Vibes comments, these accounts of the British Reggae-dancehall scene are incomplete due to a failure to consider the central role of Yard/Session-tapes, which were the main conduits for the 'interior knowledges' (Dent, 1992) contained in the Deejay message. By drawing on my firsthand experiences of this cultural form I will demonstrate how the genesis of the form has often been misinterpreted. For instance, let us consider Gilroy's (1987) suggestion that during the early 1980s the British Deejays:

> took the confidence of the Jamaican slackness toasters but from the rap MCs they took a refined fascination with the power of language, with the potency of words rather than rhymes. In the oral style of the south Bronx, they found a language which allowed them to speak directly about the social and political contradictions generated in the urban crises of the overdeveloped world. (1987:190)

Gilroy's argument more or less reduces the Jamaican influence to 'slackness', which in this sense is in opposition to 'culture' (this dichotomy will be contended in Chapter 5) and a consequence of the 'dissolving' of Rastafari 'cultural and political hegemony' (1987:190). This argument overlooks the profound influence of the lyricism of the Yard-tape performers such as, Brigadier Jerry, Early B, Charlie Chaplin, Josey Wales, Sassa Frass, Junior Reed, U Brown, Barry Brown, Tony Tuff, Icho Candy, Puddy Roots and Sugar Minott, et al, who played a seminal role in the 'creation' of the 'British Deejay'. All were in fact open advocates of Rastafari and black consciousness and were the backbone of the Reggae-dancehall scene in Jamaica during this moment. For instance, Puddy Roots who performed one of the most poignant and popular lyrics on the importance of Rastafari in the Reggae-dancehall, during this moment, argued:

> Sleeping one night when the father vision I, said, you wanna be another follower of I dread, nat-up you hair youth come livah righteous life son, you will be blessed as a Rastafari. I had to make a living cos I had a family, eh, clothes we must wear an food we must eat, never had a bus fare not a red cent around, me come ah dancehall fi represent Jaro Sound. Seh long haired freaky people need not apply, nuh want nuh old nagah, strictly Rastafari, so, tek off you Tam come hear the champion, along with Puddy Roots at the microphone stand, so run missah wicked yeh run like you mad, Jaro family represent the almighty god, equality an Justice stand for all, so discrimination gainst Rasta must fall. (Kilamanjaro Sound System, 1982)

This extract is representative of how Rastafari philosophy featured heavily in the Reggae-dancehalls during this time; notably when Puddy Roots asserts 'long haired freaky people need not apply, nuh want nuh old nagah, strictly Rastafari', who are expected to 'livah righteous life'. The profound lyricism in this extract should also be noted as an exemplar of the levels of thought and articulation that were a constant feature in these Yard-tapes and their influence on our lyricism in Britain. Let it be made clear that it was not until the mid 1980s that there was a large influx of American rap, which was not 'party' oriented, and by this time (as will be argued in the B~SIDE) British Deejaying was already firmly established. In fact, according to Mikey Reds:

> I was juggling between Yard and the Apple (New York) from the mid-1970s and I know for a fact that when we started chatting, me and Benj (Papa Benji) were chatting in 1980/81, we were chatting more constructively than most of the Deejays and rappers, no matter where they came from. Name me one rap tune that influenced the way you wrote lyrics in the early 1980s. Choh, before KRS-One dissed LL (Cool J) and Marley Marl in 'The Bridge Is Over', most of what we got was wack and that was 1985. (Personal Communication 1998)

In agreement with Mikey Reds I am at pains to recollect any rap records that had an influence on my Deejay style or lyrical content during this moment, a point I will return to in Chapter 6. However, what is critical about his mentioning of KRS-One's 'The Bridge Is Over' is that it was a verbal assault on the 'party party' rappers and, according to KRS-One, is one of the reasons why he began to rap during the mid 1980s. KRS-One argued that 'rap needed a teacher so I became it' (1991) because, for him, lyrics like 'Mary Mary quite contrary, doesn't make sense in my vocabulary'. This view challenges the genesis of the form with regard to how British Deejays were influenced by American rappers who KRS-One himself states, were singing nursery rhymes like 'Mary Mary' (which was the title of a popular tune by Run DMC during this moment). Hence, to suggest that the British Deejay needed rap to introduce them to the potency of 'words rather than rhymes', or that they 'found in the oral style of the south Bronx' a 'language' within which to articulate their oppression, somewhat diminishes the significant contribution of the Jamaican pioneers and the creativity of the British Deejays (that I) featured here. More importantly, subsequent research has unproblematically used this alleged American influence to reproduce the same line of argument (S. Jones 1988, Toop 1992, Back 1996, Sewell 1997). This line of argument limits the scope of 'cultural production' (Hall, 1996) at a localised level as it de-historicizes, and therefore naturalises, the black British experience, which becomes a palatable offshoot of the well-researched African American experience-the yardstick that is often used to measure the worth of the cultures of the Afrikan Diaspora. An exposure to the history contained within the Yard/Session-tapes under scrutiny here is so crucial because the factual accounts (Deejay lyricism) were 'hidden' from many who sought to interpret the culture. In light of these types of analysis it is useful to consider that, in the first comprehensive ethnographic study of 'Dancehall Culture in Jamaica', Stolzoff (2000) argues that an analysis of this form is:

> limited by a perspective that uses records as its central interpretive framework and privileges the role of producers and musicians as autonomous creative artists. I have come to call this perspective the records-artists-producers (RAP) paradigm. It is not surprising that foreign journalists would use this lens to interpret dancehall, because it is the way they have come to know the music, that is, as consumers

of records and concert-goers. I am not suggesting that we completely discount the perspective of foreign enthusiasts, who have been critical to the worldwide popularity of dancehall music, but that we become aware of dancehall's global/local intersections. This perspective remains sensitive to both the Jamaican context of production, performance, and politics as well as the "foreign" (transnational) influences. (2000:xxi)

Stolzoff quite correctly locates a major problem with any perspective that is not familiar with the 'hidden' aspects of a cultural form, that which he calls the '(RAP) paradigm', as it typifies the 'lens' through which an outsider ('foreign enthusiast') would view the culture. My own perspective as a "thoughtist" (Walters 2001) mirrors this argument in some respects although many differences will be made known in our theorisations of its 'transnational influence'. In the context of the author as the wielder of the 'power' to ethnographically inscribe reality, however, certain aspects of his perspective need immediate consideration. For instance, the fact that he too admits to being a 'foreign enthusiast' (2000:xix) is revealing as the above extract suggests that his 'insider' knowledge as an ethnographer is what made him 'become aware of dancehall's global/local intersections'. This awareness came out of a 'primary field site' that provided 'the best of both worlds', which allowed him to meet 'a lot of different players in the field'. By doing so, he and his respondents could discuss 'the dancehall scene not only in the abstract or ideal terms...but also as they were moving through it' (2000:128/9). Consequently he overcame certain problems associated with interviewing 'participants' in a 'formal' setting because 'I could ask them questions about aspects of their activities that I didn't understand'. He therefore confronted 'issues' that otherwise:

> would never have come up had I merely interviewed them or observed them at the Dub Store, nor would their explanations have made much sense without my having the chance to witness their practice. It is through making connections between the daily routine of cultural production and what ultimately gets produced that one begins to understand the significance of dancehall culture. (2000:189)

This observation bestows more credence on his account because it is not based in the 'abstract'; it comes as a result of his participation in the culture as part of 'a daily routine' that provided a greater 'understanding' of the 'significance' of dancehall in Jamaica. This in turn allowed him to consider the role the ethnographer plays in the rendering of the culture under scrutiny, in light of 'the "foreign" influences' that he too would have brought into the field. Crucially the manner in which 'foreign enthusiasts' have previously understood the culture could be reappraised in light of the 'issues' that he faced, which enabled him to give 'hidden' aspects of the culture due consideration.

> In fact, the hardcore Reggae that was popular in Jamaica's dancehalls was difficult to hear outside the dancehall…As a result a distinction arose between dancehall style Reggae, which could be heard only in the dancehall and on limited-circulation cassette recordings of dancehall events, and international style Reggae that was "fit for radio play" and appealed to the world music market. (2000:98)

Stolzoff draws our attention to an aspect of the culture that could 'only be heard in the dancehall' or on what he dubs 'limited-circulation cassette recordings of dancehall events', that which as I suggested above is known within the culture as Yard-tapes. Yet the distinction he makes between these aspects of the culture is in many ways overly simplistic and fails to account for 'hardcore Reggae' as an outernational conduit, which 'appealed' to a specific 'world music market'. This 'music market' consists of those, who, like me who seek the types of knowledge and upliftment, that one only encounters in the black music that contains these 'hidden voices'. Nevertheless the fact that he recognises this distinction is crucial to this discussion as it emphasises why the 'voice' was 'hidden' from many who believed they 'knew' Reggae music and its associated cultures. Equally Stolzoff makes known where 'hardcore Reggae' was more likely to be heard by those who were familiar with its existence, and the manner in which it was disseminated via 'cassette recordings of dancehall events' (2000:98). However, what becomes problematic is his notion of the 'limited-circulation' of these Yard-tapes because, in one sense, their distribution was 'limited' in respect of sheer numbers when compared to recorded releases. But with regard to their 'circulation' according to the British Deejay Tippa Irie:

> They went everywhere. I did a show in Australia in the 1980s and after the show this Australian youth invited us back to his gaff, and

trust me, he had nuff tapes with the whole ah the Set them. Saxon, Coxone, Frontline, Jack Ruby, Gemini, Volcano, Metromedia, Jamdown Rockers, Ghettotone, Downbeat, Third World, Unity, Jaro (Killamajaro), Jammys, I could go on forever. Macka B showed me that he met the youth as well one time when he was out there. (Personal Communication 1998)

Tippa's reasoning demonstrates how this insider perspective works and the Sets that he names are, interestingly enough, not just from the UK and Jamaica, for Downbeat and Third World were two of New York's most popular Sets during the 1980s. Hence although Stolzoff makes this distinction between how the culture was received and perceived through various lenses, his awareness of 'dancehall's global/local intersections' is restricted as there is no significant discussion of its outernational resonance in the alternative 'world music market'. The main reason for this glaring omission is that he fails to consider the seminal role that Yard-tapes played in the transmission across time and space of Jamaica's 'dancehall culture'. Nowhere more so than when he attributes the 'breaking of genre conventions' to Jamaica's first superstar Deejay, the albino 'Yellowman', with regard to how 'slackness' supposedly displaced 'culture'. Stolzoff would have been aware, if he had been part of the Yard-tape system of exchange during the late 1970s to early 1980s, that Yellowman was renowned as a 'pirate' (an imitator) who built his repertoire and reputation from the lyrics of other performers especially General Echo (aka Rankin Slackness). The same Deejay that Stolzoff dismisses in one sentence when suggesting 'there were popular slack DJs before him (Yellowman), such as General Echo' and then, ironically, goes on to cite one of Echo's most popular Yard-tape lyrics "Bedroom Bazooka" as an exemplar of Yellow Man's creativity. In fact, it was suggested by many including Dirty Desi, a British born Deejay who was residing between London and Jamaica at the time of Yellowman's immense popularity during the early 1980s, that if Echo had not been brutally slain by Jamaican police officers in November 1980, 'Yellowman wouldah dead fi hungry'. This was because:

General Echo, The Teacher Fi The Class, has come along way in a short time. The Year 1976 brought about a revolutionary change in D.J. Music. The General's Disco Sound "Echo Tone Hi FI" stopped playing soul music and started to play strictly Rockers. At this time the General decided to D.J. the rhythm tracks at Dance Halls all over Jamaica. This was the beginning of the road to success...By 1977 the General Sound became the No. 1 Sound in Jamaica. General Echo was now on top of the Dance Hall scene. Everywhere he played the crowd followed...The Sound was playing every night and most times the crowd was so large that patrons had to fight to get inside. Others simply stayed outside and enjoy 'The General sound'. (Manzie, 1979)

The above extract was lifted from the sleeve notes of General Echo's debut album entitled 'Rocking And Swing', and provides an insight as to why, even after his untimely death in 1980, he is to this day regarded by many Reggae-dancehall fans as the 'Teacher Fi The Class'. It should also be noted that according to Manzie, who produced the album, Echo revolutionised the genre of dancehall Deejaying in '1976', five years before the date Stolzoff attributes this shift to Yellowman. My own *re-memories* of these events are in line with Manzie's because, as will be demonstrated in the next chapter, many British Deejays were pirating these performances during the late 1970s to mid 1980s. Moreover, Champion, Asher Senator and his 'sparring partner' Smiley Culture, were chatting on a Set called 'Bucanon' during the same moment and the staple of many British pirate Deejays was Echo's Yard-tapes. Many of the British Deejays featured in this study, Papa Benji, Macka B, Papa Levi, Lana G, Tippa Irie, Cinderella, Peterkin, Dirty Desi, Asher Senator and Reds, all cite Echo's originality as a major source of their inspiration to 'tek up the mic an chat lyrics'. On the contrary I have not met anyone, who was into Yard-tapes at that time and would have therefore been familiar with this alternative perspective, who regards Yellowman as an originator of anything noteworthy. However, what Yellowman was recognised and highly respected for was his ability to entertain, which is why Papa San suggested 'Yellowman slack an Yellowman vulgar, Yellowman mek nuff Deejay get wiser, how fi mek money an nuh rob by promoter' (Saxon, 1986). This demonstrates aspects of the history of Deejay culture only known to insiders who were immersed in Yard-tape culture and that we were able to outernationally exchange these types of 'interior knowledges'.

After seeing Yellowman live in London in 1983, I was so impressed that I wrote a lyric about his performance and 'chatted it' on Ghettotone, as well as other Sound Systems, within days of the event.

By presenting this lyric I will provide the best example of 'dancehall's global/local intersections', thereby demonstrating (in a practical fashion) the significant role that Jamaican culture played in the formulation of this 'hidden voice', which documents an alternative black British experience. More importantly it will demonstrate just how this alternative culture works and why the role of the Jamaican Deejays must take primacy over other supposed influences on the lyricism of the British Deejay. Hence:

Spoken intro: Tek in them style yah, special to the man call Mr Dirty an all MC in ah the vicinity, Murder. Well hear comes I play counteraction two happens to be the musical ting call the Johnny Dollar, as I Lezlee ah goh throw it to them collar puppah ghetto you must haffi follah, hear me now supe.

Deejaying: Well ich ni san is how them count in Japan, well ich ni san is how them count in Japan, fling weh the vocal me ah goh ride the version, seh people gather round me have the mic in ah me hand, come listen puppah Lezlee in origination, the other day me tek ah trip, goh over Edmonton, me Lana, Muscle (Musclehead the co-owner of Saxon Sound System), Cookie was the carman (driver), we reach ah Picketts Lock fi ah dancehall session, featuring Aswad an the great Yellowman, organise by Capital an David Rodigan, when we reach on deh, outside ram, man ah snatch ticket out ah next man hand, ah sell them fi forty pound to the whiteman, me see security with dawg, an nuff Babylon, but them couldn't stop the raiders from Brixton, them rush the gate kick down gateman an get ah free entry to the session, when we reach inside we hear the Aswad Band, ah flash down music like the 'Promise Land', well you know Aswad them well dangerous, seh after them came the Band Sagittarius, an up pon the stage jump David Rodigan an ask if we ready fi tek in Yellowman, seh by this time the dance was super jam, when Yellowman appear it was ah eruption, him dress up in ah white fi match him complexion, him chat slackness him sing church song, an bring entertainment to each an everyone, him seh them free Gregory (Gregory Isaacs a Jamaican singer) an shame Babylon, him ah the first Deejay fi come ah England, an really live up to him reputation, Yellowman him ah the one in ah one million, an puppah Lezlee ah him number one fan, Jahdaman Jahdaman Jahdaman me at the microphone stand, if you happy an you love it just lift up you hand. (Ghettotone, 1983)

The lyric amply demonstrates how highly Yellowman was rated by me, and the masses that came out to support his live performance, but it is noticeable that my emphasis is on how well he was received as an entertainer and not on his lyrical content. This is because the Jamaican Deejay Brigadier Jerry (Briggy) was the yardstick by which I measured my own levels of 'originality'; he has always been regarded as one of the most inventive 'cultural' performers. He was so highly rated in Britain was because of our exposure to Yard-tapes and as the Jamaican Deejay Tony Rebel states, 'cassette would circulate and people would hear it' (Stolzoff, 2000:160). Furthermore the profound nature of the 'rhyming skills' and intellectualised rendering of various social, cultural and political events, such as those featured in the extract above, is seldom acknowledged in the accounts that seek to understand this verbal art form. This is the critical role that Yard/Session-tapes play in a truer appreciation of Reggae-dancehall culture; these recordings represent the 'undocumented' side that can fill in many significant gaps in the documenting of black cultural history. For instance when Echo was murdered, there was a series of reflections and tributes speaking of the pivotal role he played in this performance genre. I, too, wrote a lyric about his murder during the period when I still lacked the courage to perform. One such reflection came from Briggy on Echo's murder and using the melody from Queen's 'Another One Bites The Dust', he lamented:

> Uh uh uh slackness (Echo) bite the dust, uh uh uh culture must come fuss, I used to walk with them, I used to taak to them, but culture must come fuss, I used to eat with them I used to reason with them but culture must come fust, I seh uh uh uh slackness bite the dust, I seh uh uh uh slackness bite the dust. I don't know if it's Big John, Echo, or Flux, they was going in ah car man it wasn't ah truck, when all of ah sudden man them run out ah luck, last ting me hear is that them life mash-up, uh uh uh another one bite the dust, uh uh uh I tell them culture must come fuss. (Black Star, 1980)

You will notice that Briggy suggests that there was a closeness between himself as a 'cultural', and Echo as a 'slackness' performer when stating that he used to 'eat' and 'reason with them'. Anyone who is familiar with Jamaican culture will be aware that we do not generally 'reason' with, much less 'eat' with, people we do not respect, which is why this is a profound statement for Briggy to make about a Deejay who should have been his antithesis. The reasoning behind this will become clearer in the B~SIDE, because although Echo was known as 'Rankin Slackness', the first album he released, 'Rocking and Swing' (featured above), was a 'cultural' album. In this album Echo addressed issues like the global oil crisis, religious intolerance and the 'International Year of The Child'. However, I recall that after hearing Briggy's lyric on a Yard-tape within weeks of Echo's death, I was inspired to pen my own tribute because Echo's murder was a particular massive blow to Deejay fans in Britain; he was due to 'fly-out' and tour here the same week he was killed. For this reason I suggested:

> Them (Jamaican police) kill Papa Echo in ah Half Way Tree, them murder Papa Echo in ah Half Way Tree, them kill Big John and them murder fluxy, me never know the breddah them personally, me used to hear them pon the tapes weh me breddah give me an when me listen them me feel Irie. Me hear bout Echo from me bredrin Everton, him seh him used to cork dance in ah Skateland, him seh there was ten woman to each an every man, Papa Echo was a champion. (Ghettotone, 1982)

That I actually went on to pen these lyrics speaks volumes about the profound influence that Jamaican Deejays had on their British counterparts, although you will note that I clearly state that 'me never know the breddah them personally, as I was introduced to them by my 'bredrin Everton'. Everton was an entrepreneurial character who was born in Jamaica, came to live in London during the 1970s, and would often fly back and forth to Jamaica as part of his involvement in the Sound System business. As a result of his constant travelling, he was like a living library stacked with knowledge about the shifts in the culture and, more importantly, he was initially the main source of our exposure to the 'freshest' Yard-tapes. It was Everton who informed us during the mid 1970s about a Deejay called General Echo/Rankin Slackness, whose Sound System 'Echotone' (the name inspired me to call our set Ghettotone) was redefining Deejay performance in the Jamaican Reggae-dancehalls. By providing Yard-tapes Everton enabled us to experience the 'live' Reggae-dancehall Deejay performance that was unlike anything we had previously encountered on vinyl.

It was during this moment that Yard-tapes became the main source of entertainment for many blacks in Britain and their immediate circulation kept us up to date with what was happening in Jamaica's dancehall scene. For this reason, we were aware of the moment when 'Echotone' was not a large enough Set to cater for Echo's immense following and so during 1979 he began to perform on 'Stereophonic Sound System', the owner (Big John) and the Selector (Fluxy) who were also murdered in the said Half Way Tree incident. Equally we were made aware of when new releases or 'dub plates' were likely to be forthcoming from the performers we came to know via Yard-tapes and the reason that I have in my possession a collector's item like Echo's debut. Thus, I feel able to clearly state how the significance of the cultural identification with Jamaican music, which in the context of black communities in Britain was directly responsible for the British Deejay style, is missing from Stolzoff's account. As I will go on to prove in the B~SIDE, it is impossible to map 'dancehall culture in Jamaica' accurately with such an omission because British Deejays played a major role in this system of outernational cultural exchange.

Conclusion

In this chapter I considered how access to an alternative worldview, as provided through the medium of black music, provides a space in which the Afrikan Diaspora can think themselves into being in a more conscious fashion than has been previously recognised. This was demonstrated by describing that, in the history of Deejaying in Britain a struggle, to maintain communities', which not only transcends but also transforms, their racist 'host' communities by bringing certain aspects of the struggle to the fore. Moreover, as was suggested by Gilroy, the transformation of host communities by their exposure to black forms of popular culture is a consequence of how a 'musical culture supplies a great deal of the courage required to go on living in the present' (1993a:36). This is based on a shared sense of oppression/exclusion, because 'our imaginations are conditioned by an enduring proximity to regimes of racial terror' (Gilroy 1993a:103). Therefore, black music often speaks to the experiences of non-white peoples in a racist society, furnishing a site for various types of inter/intra-cultural exchange. For this reason Gilroy puts forward that it is the 'moral aspects' of black music that need to be considered, especially with regard to 'the ethical value of the music and its status as an ethnic sign' (1993a:36). Thus, as Fanon suggested, in cases like these the 'process of identification is automatic' and this is why it was logical for the black youth in Britain to recognise our condition in the lyrics we were exposed to via Yard-tapes. Stolzoff's mapping of the social, cultural and political worth of Reggae-dancehall music is therefore flawed; the aspects of the culture that are dependent on the outernational exchange of ideas were overlooked. So, despite his acknowledgement of the 'outsider' perspective and how it is coloured by the lens through which the "foreign enthusiast" gazes at the culture, his account still lacked the insider perspective of which only one (such as myself) who has lived and breathed the culture would truly be aware.

Pull-up! Summarising the A~SIDE

In the A~SIDE I have extensively argued, by broadening the scope of analysis on the black British experience, that many of the recognised subcultural and sociological accounts misrepresent the manner in which black youth countered, resisted and transcended racism in the land of their birth. These theorisations of what exactly motivated black youth to embrace many aspects of Reggae-dancehall culture, especially the usage of Patwa as a 'commonly agreed language', were largely inadequate as they failed to recognise the history behind these types of 'directed defiance' and thus lacked epistemological rigour and empirical depth. For this reason they often affixed a rigidity to black cultures that did not reflect the lived reality of 'real people', who had a history of countering white racism across a range of contexts. This means that these analyses are unable to present a more complete understanding of the pragmatic nature of black countercultural forms as historical sites of transcendence and resistance. Above all, they fail to consider the 'historical and political continuities in black cultural struggles' (S. Jones 1986:92) against exclusionary and divisive practices in an outernational context.

One reason for this occurrence is that academic interpretation /explanation/expectation tries to rid itself of the problems associated with representation by questioning how it can more accurately represent the 'other's' 'social reality' through freeing itself from the bias of 'ethnographic inscription'. Yet it cannot; the 'social reality' that it ultimately portrays is subject to the epistemological biases of the interpreter/author and can only be accessed/understood via the academic interlocutor, 'as a result, social facts no longer need to attain or demonstrate authenticity; their authority derives from their status as an emanation of assumed intellectual, and actual political, power' (Rigby, 1996:89/90). It is for this reason that I consider myself able to more accurately (in the culture and my exposure to the Yard/Session-tapes, that are used to substantiate my alternative claims, able to) detail the culture's outernational resonance and overall significance to the black British experience; In much the same way as the 'sounds' of the performance are 'hidden' once the lyrics become 'text', the more inclusive tales of 'real people' are hidden in these lopsided accounts of the black experience in Britain. These accounts gave little consideration to the value of an insider perspective which relocates the Afrikan as a conscious being 'in time and across time' (Gordon, 1998:140) and also, I find, in place and across place. I am suggesting that by presenting Deejay lyricism as an exemplar of the practical nature of 'black music', which gives a focus where alternative worldviews can be exchanged, I have highlighted questions in the types of analysis that do not consider these 'interior knowledges' as forms of 'ideological weaponry'.

What occurs in these alternative public arenas are not merely gestures to be reduced to the rhetorical or symbolic, even though these elements are fundamental to the manner in which the culture is 'accessed' and 'known'. In doing so, the cultural matrix in which these alternative views are fashioned and performed is overlooked, any tale of their worth, to those whom the form serves best, will be constantly misrepresented by outsiders looking in. Therefore I wish the above arguments to be appreciated as a substantive contribution to the literatures that denote the validity, role and purpose of countercultural forms that act as coping and transcendental mechanisms for the black downpressed in racist Britain. This type of historical process, out of which a 'self-generated concept' like blak emerged, posits a black presence that uses a common pool of experiences to uplift by voicing approval or disapproval in a racist society. This, in turn, forms part of the internal register by which an Africentric 'consciousness' is assessed along the lines of 'original lyrics' and these discussions make major contributions to the ongoing debate about 'adaptive responses' to downpression and the racist exclusionary practices that need to be considered in any meaningful account of black subjectivities.

In the B~SIDE I will substantiate my claims for a new reading of the role and purpose of black cultural forms based on the empirical data that proves how 'the Deejays are giving us the functioning word which we need to make flesh and give expression to' (Lewis, 2001). Furthermore, by presenting examples of Deejay lyricism, I will counter and correct much that has been suggested about Sound System culture and detail the central role that it played in the black British experience.

Tun it over

WHAT THE DEEJAY SAID

****

Re-memories

I was sitting in my car becoming more and more impatient with every passing moment as I waited for Dirty Desi to come down from the third floor flat where he lived off St Norberts Road, Brockley, London, SE4. I hated that part of south-east London as it backed onto Honor Oak Estate, which was then one of those old grey social dumping grounds that are generally deemed to be suitable council housing for working class folk. I have many vivid and especially chilling memories of this area as it lay in the middle of a shortcut between Samuel (sambo) Pepys, the secondary school I attended during the late 1960s to early 1970s, and Honor Oak Park, which is the part of Forest Hill I grew up in. Sambo Pepys was the nickname given to this school due to its high percentage of black pupils and meant that our school badge, as featured on our blazers, was a magnet for attracting the attention of racists, rife at the time. This was a consequence of the belief that the vast majority of students were black when, of course, this was not the case however it appeared. Nonetheless, this did nothing to deter the ongoing battles between black and white pupils, which often spilled over from our school into surrounding areas like Honor Oak Estate. These-battle driven memories include the numerous occasions my twin brother, myself and a few black friends had to fight, or were chased by, various racists on our way home from school (when you decide to spend your bus fare on other things you tend to make your way home via the quickest route). The shortcut via these flats was a dangerous one, as Honor Oak Estate was a notorious 'white man area' during the 1960s, 1970s and 1980s.

For many of us this and other 'no go' areas represented the stark reality of what it was like to be raised in Britain as a black youth at this time. Now, although we fully expected to be verbally abused on a regular basis by white racists of all ages and sizes in our daily interactions with white society (the school librarian once called me an 'uncivilised savage' for no apparent reason), Honor Oak Estate was one of those areas where as a black youth you would get 'done', if you were not careful. In fact my wife speaks of the same experiences at the Secondary Modern she attended. Sedgehill School is in what was then a notoriously racist part of Catford, south-east London and she speaks of the regular abuse that she suffered on her journeys to and from school. As a consequence, she has always maintained that this is where the notion of black kids going around in large groups comes from - safety in numbers - and is why she and several other black female friends adopted this strategy: their lives were replete with tales and examples of being attacked, physically and verbally, by various white racists. After all, at this time we were dealing with the emergent 'skinhead' phenomenon as well as the anachronistic remnants of the 1950s 'rock n roll' era: the 'mods', 'rockers', 'greasers' and quiff-sporting 'teddy boys'. In many ways, these dregs from another era represented a different type of threat to black youth, because not only were they generally older than us (late teens to early 40s), they were also mobile-especially the 'greasers' and 'rockers' with their motor bikes and the 'mods' with their motor scooters. This meant that the neutral spaces we expected to be safe from attack were collapsed into 'their' space whenever we encountered their racist presence, as dangerous as it was mobile.

This is why I have never been truly comfortable in this type of space and on a warm night during the summer of 1983, sitting in this area around midnight with the roof down in an orange convertible Triumph Stag, less so. I remember that it was around this time that a racist killed my bredrin 'Booky' on his own doorstep (in the infamous Honor Oak Estate) repeatedly stabbing him in the chest during an argument about how loud he was playing that 'fucking jungle music' (Reggae). At last I heard 'me deh yah' as Desi arrived. I fired up the engine and we made our way towards the 'Temple', which was slap bang in the middle of the 'Frontline'-Railton Road, Brixton. Ghettotone was the host Sound System every Wednesday night, and the reason that Dirty Desi and I were making our way there on this particular night. 'Yeh rude bwoy that lyric is wackad (wicked)' Desi suggested in appreciation of the latest lyric I had penned and recorded at home as part of the Deejay process and which was now blasting through the speakers of my car stereo.

Walking down the street late at night in ah England me can't feel safe
or free, cos the national front an the skinheads want to persecute an
tek me life from me. Them seh nigger, wog, coon, spade, if is one
him beg fi mercy when me flash me ratchet blade, seh them hate
Africans cau we inferior, an them ah European so them superior, all
ah chant seig heil an ah hail Hitler, all over them body them tattoo
swastika, if them did read bout the war it wouldah pay them better,
ah this country the nazi's want conquer an ah fi them relatives Hitler
did ah slaughter, never care that them have the same skin colour, any
how him buck them up them wouldah get murder, that's why me
know them ignorant an don't have nuh sense, just through we black
them ah come with violence, them nuh know render you heart an not
you garments, so when me ah deal with them me nuh have nuh
conscience, cos ah England me born an ah England me grow, ah
London me live an ah London me know, so whether dutty Babylon
or skinheads looking aggro, if them try test the lyrix them must get ah
blow. (Lezlee Lyrix, 1983)

'If is one him beg fi mercy when me flash me ratchet blade'. The words
barely have the opportunity to emerge from Ghettotone's speakers
when they are drowned out by cries of 'lick wood, lick wood'. It should
be noted that in Jamaica the cry was often 'lick Shot' as the police,
soldiers and gunman would fire a 'legal' or 'illegal' salute in the open air
(Jamaican dancehalls/lawns are generally outdoors) in honour of the
performer who was 'tearing down the lawn'. In Britain we would 'lick
wood' because gunplay was not an open part of our Reggae-dancehall
scene and, anyway, it would not be advisable to 'lick shot' inside the
types of building where our events were held. Again, we can see now
the Jamaican influence for these cries were mixed in with a cacophony
of approving sounds as the 'crowd ah people' stamped their feet whilst
using their hands, many of which were customarily filled with tightly
clasped beer cans or drink bottles, using their hands, England-style to
beat the nearest object to them, generally a wall, a door, a table or even
the Set's speaker boxes. All of this excitement added to the drama of
the moment as I tried for the third time to finish the 'skinhead lyric' in
an atmosphere that captures the essence of the Reggae-dancehall world,
a world where 'sounds' often speak more than mere words ever could.
The effect of this type of rapturous response was such that I struggled
to suppress the feeling of triumph that was welling up within me at
being so appreciated, in our space, by those whose approval meant

everything to me. For as the Deejay who is presently 'tearing down the lawn' with original lyrics on Ghettotone's Set, the separation between the 'crowd ah people'-the human voice and the technological wonder that is the Sound System is blurred during these moments, which makes the experience totally unique from watching others. I also knew, intrinsically, from experience that you have to remain composed in these situations otherwise you will not get to finish the lyric and the excitement that was being generated, coupled with the sharp rise in temperature, and enough ganja smoke to make the wholah London high, tend to affect your breathing. Being 'short ah breath' would tarnish your reputation as a 'professional' Deejay and so maintaining your composure, whilst sustaining the dramatic moment, is a crucial aspect of the live performance. Suddenly, as part of the ritual drama, my sparring partner Dirty Desi grabs the mic from my hand and cries 'Haul an pullup operator! Come ah gain deh Mr Lyrix'. Using my 'rag' (flannel) to wipe the sweat from my face I felt my heart outpacing the Studio One 'Armageddon' rhythm I was chatting on, and decided to seize the moment to settle myself and marvel at the amount of people who are crammed into this smoke-filled converted shop-front that is the 'Temple'.

This is our reality, our space, our media, our vehicle, our voice, which surfaces during these moments and takes on its own dynamic as it speaks the language of the Reggae-dancehall. It mirrors the thoughts, feelings and sentiments of those who truly overstand the validity of a form that not only allows the downpressed to win a cultural space, but also to utilise that space for upliftment, never forgetting that, although the lyrics must reflect the internal knowledges which describe an urban reality, the role of the Deejay is to entertain. Yet beyond this space its worth, value and potency remains 'hidden' within the realms of the wider public arena.

'Massive, just cool an listen the lyrics nuh', I suggest, 'cau you know me ah the lyrics originator pon this side of the Equator, weh dress slicker than the vicar an me chat non-stop like Alan Wicker (a famous chatty TV journalist of the time)'. This time I deliver the lyric in its entirety and receive the type of appreciation that only the Reggae-dancehall massive can forward, 'wicked piece, me lion', 'original style an fashion', 'the bwoy can chat, you see', 'touch me deh, rude bwoy', 'build ah spliff deh Lyrix', 'ah weh you want fi drink'. All of these accolades and offers rain down in tandem with the 'lick wood' concerto conducted by other members of the Reggae-dancehall massive, and in the background, by virtue of the Operator Rankin's skill with the echo chamber, the final words from the 'skinhead lyric' resonate through the air, 'if them try test the Lyrix them them must get ah blow, get ah blow, get ah blow, get ah blow', get ah blow...'

****

Chapter 4

'Me bornah England, me know me blak, me nah seh me British'!

Introduction

The fact that IC3, the police identity code for black, is the only collective term that relates to our situation here as residents ('Black British' is political and refers to Africans, Asians, West Indians, Americans and sometimes even Chinese) is a sad fact of life I could not ignore. (Newland, 2000:X)

In this chapter I will pick up on the themes discussed in the A~SIDE, presenting the type of empirical account that counters the problem status accorded to 'black youths', leading to their portrayal as a 'discrete social category'. I will demonstrate how the notion of 'adaptive response', in the guise of Deejay lyricism, was utilised by many 'black youth' to express their lived reality, on their own terms and in their own words. That is why I chose to open the B~SIDE with **re-memories**, which represents those reflections that describe what it was like to be a black person in Britain during the 1970s and 1980s. The point is that black youth, as "thoughtists" (Walters 2001), were more than capable of articulating their own downpression and often did so in a grounded intellectual fashion that is yet to be fully appreciated. I will therefore present a raft of Deejay accounts as forms of intelligent practical knowledge, which enabled many to negotiate a sane path through a hostile environment where 'walking down the street late at night in ah England me can't feel safe or free'. This means that Reggae-dancehall music, as a provider of a safe 'cultural space', will be shown in its most practical sense, wherein an alternative blak perspective was freely articulated in response to that which branded our 'lifestyles' as 'pathological' or 'deviant'. Moreover, this will provide the best example of how culturally and politically aware black youth were with regard to their real social position, as the recipients of racist exclusionary practices which were designed and sanctioned by the state to compound their inferior status. This awareness of the tribulations of 'real people' led to S. Jones' (1986) suggestion that we must recognise how much currency negative depictions of black youth, as inherently deviant and uneducated, have 'within the practical ideologies of state institutions'. For this, more than anything else, 'legitimises forms of repressive control' revealed in the various types of unjust treatment black youth would frequently encounter, whether innocent or guilty, at the hands of racist authority figures. More importantly, as Newland points out above, even in our contemporary social climate, 'the only collective term that' identifies us as peoples of Afrikan/Caribbean descent is the 'police identity code', IC3, which he uses as the title for a collection of Black British writing based upon the type of irony 'that is a sad fact of life I could not ignore' (Newland, 2000:X).

This type of ironic engagement with our everyday reality perfectly speaks to our condition as black people who were born in the UK and so, whether we like it or not, we are historically associated with this place as 'home'. The suggestion is that you can go on living in the womb of a rejecting 'mother', but certain aspects of your everyday reality remind you that you are scorned in the land of your birth. We shall now experience this in the critique from the street!

4.1 'Promote the youth, we haffi, promote the youth'!

Wake-up in the morning me haffi run couple laps, cau if me do it ah night-time I will get stopped by the cops. (Papa Levi, Saxon 1983)

Government pay Babylon just to harass, them love beat youth-man like Trevor Natch, an shoot people with them tear gas. (Trevor Natch, Diamonds 1984)

Promote the youth, we haffi promote the youth, fi mek them rise up we haffi teach them the truth, when them go-ah school them treat them like coot, dutty Babylon ah treat them like brute. (Champion, Jamdown Rockers 1983)

Several Deejay accounts graphically depict what it is to be a member of a community that is on the receiving end of racial discrimination and the practical steps taken to maintain both your liberty and sanity in a hostile environment. I opted to use Champion's lyric 'Promote the youth' as the title for this section, because it perfectly captures how black youth sought to deal with their own 'problems' during the late 1970s to mid 1980s. Their realisation that these 'problems' were, in many cases, not of their own making is relevant because it shows just how confronting adversity can be used as coping and transcendental mechanisms in a racist society, as is featured in the Deejay's performance. I suggest that this is so because the Deejay biographically documents an ongoing history in the present, through the medium of Reggae-dancehall music, which combines the performative with the informative in much the same way as the above **re-memories**. By doing so, they confront head on the more unsavoury aspects of what it is to be treated as a social problem by those who are supposedly in a position to be less judgmental. The inference is that the Reggae-dancehall is a space where these alternative cultural politics are freely aired and readily discussed by those who are otherwise excluded from this level of meaningful social dialogue within the recognised public arena.

The development, articulation and subsequent promotion of the trenchant 'hidden voice' of the largely disgruntled black youth acknowledged the reality that we were downpressed for various reasons. For instance, in the opening extract, Papa Levi describes how even a simple everyday occurrence, like jogging to keep fit, has to be thought through by the black youth who is aware of the ramifications of such an innocuous act. The reality being that when Levi penned these thoughts during the 1980s, the police force had a licence to 'stop and search' IC3's especially young black males. In fact we were all of the opinion that a black youth seen 'running' at night-time was regarded as a confession of guilt if you happened to be 'stopped by the cops'. That's why Trevor Natch suggests that the police are paid to 'harass' and always prepared to 'beat youth-man like Trevor Natch' or 'shoot people with them 'tear gas', because 'all over England it is happening, at the hands of police, blacks get ah beating' (Macka B, 1987), or worse. For as Macka B further suggests:

WHAT THE DEEJAY SAID

Spoken intro: Clinton McCurbin was murdered, his killers are still at large, I'm fed up with the fact that when police kill ah black they never seem to get charge.

Chorus: We've had enough, we've had enough of it, we've had enough of it, we've had enough of it, can't take it no more. We've had enough, we've had enough of it, we've had enough of it, we've had enough of it.

Deejaying: In ah Wolverhampton there was ah killing, police murder Clinton McCurbin, in ah shop called Next ah weh the murder begin, they seh ah stolen credit card he was using, before I carry on, do some thinking, if you had ah credit card which was stolen, an them seh mek me do some checking, you nah goh stand up like ah damn dingaling, so why him never move an do some running, maybe it was his or fi him idrin, you know the police will say anything, cau to them you is ah thief from you have black skin, but anyway, two dutty Babylonian rush in, jump pon the youth an ah sit-down pon him, draw back him head an bust the youth neck string, an ah kin fi them teeth like them kill ah chicken, he was only young, lord what ah sin, he should be walking round but he's in ah coffin, them don't treat we as human being, so we better get together an do something. (Macka B, 1987)

Rendering these observations in lyrical form demonstrates the manner in which Deejays express the opinions of black youth who are the recipients of police brutality, in ways that were not often considered by those who would seek to control/explain their actions. Thus the relationships between 'black youths' and those in positions of power especially the social theorists and other commentators (who write the distortions that pass as 'black reality') or those who govern/police according to this 'reality' are usually discussed from the perspective of the powerful. Throughout his lyric Macka B engages the babylon logic upon which this murder was justified and then uses black cultural logic to counter the official explanation as to how this black youth died. He does this by asking the listener to do 'some thinking' by answering a very simple question, 'if you had ah credit card which was stolen, an them seh mek me do some checking, you nah goh stand up like ah damn dingaling'? I would suggest that the answer would be to 'do some running', which in McCurbin's case did not take place and explains why many blacks were outraged by this killing at the time. Furthermore, as

Macka B states, in another verse of the said lyric, when naming several victims of police brutality, 'I could go on, the list is never ending'. The obvious conclusion is 'them don't treat we as human being, so we better get together an do something'. I make this point to illustrate the importance of facing up to the reality of your condition, something that Macka B clearly does when he challenges the 'legal' version of what is said to have occurred in McCurbin's case. It should be noted that, since this case, there have been several additional cases of police brutality/murder against Afrikan people and, to my knowledge, not one of them 'dutty babylon' has ever been convicted of a single offence. Hence, there is no need to wonder why many have no faith in an organisation that is a haven for rife racists, who literally 'get away with murder', and we are expected to believe the conclusions of internal babylon investigations into such incidents. The powers that be must think that we were 'born big' to have faith in such a system, not realising that if we were born this size, fully grown, 'we wouldah kill we mummah'-as my dear old mum always reminds me.

Lyrics such as Macka B's offered black people a similarity of experience, blurring the distinction between the teller of the tale and the listener, given that this was in many cases a collective biography experienced through the illocutionary force of the Deejay's lyricism. That is why it is crucial to recognise how effective this culture was at uplifting black youth during these difficult times, because the Deejays, who were encouraging you to 'wise-up and rise-up', were youths themselves. Equally the sense of realism presented in the lyric was experienced on a conscious level; by locating your-self in the Deejay's account during the performance another 'voice' spoke your personal thoughts. It seemed that the Deejay's account mirrored your reality as a 'black youth' deprived of a 'public' voice, which consequently enabled you to recognise the validity of the Reggae-dancehall as a place where you did have a voice. Within these spaces your perspective was given status and ultimately justified, as you bore witness to ordinary youths like Macka B and Champion encouraging you on the 'mic' to 'do something' and 'promote' yourself. Hence we gain a practical overstanding as to how 'within the alternative public spheres where black music was played and danced to, collective sensibilities could be shared and new ones forged' (Back, 1996:187). Thus according to Back's reasoning, the participants in the culture could share their concerns with an audience of their peers and could between them work out practical solutions that would assist their moving forward. This means that these songs elicit physical and psychological movement and change by making things happen, things that we can be seen to instigate and, more importantly, control the practical aspects of your every day experiences. For instance, when during the summer of 1983 many black youths in Brixton got so fed up with being stopped and searched by the police they began to 'leggo them pants'. Literally, they would drop their trousers as soon as they realised that the police were going to harass them, which caused the police to rethink their strategy, especially during the daylight hours in the middle of the always-busy Brixton High Street. This ploy was greatly assisted by Deejays like Dirty Desi who heard of these tales first hand, incorporated them into the live performance, thereby spreading the word that:

> The ghetto youth them nah tek nuh chance, when them sight the dutty Babylon bwoy ah advance, them undo the belt leggo them pants, threaten fi bust the brief and expose the lance. (Dirty Desi, Ghettotone 1983)

Understanding what this ongoing style of rendering and conveying social reality, in lyrical form, meant for the self-esteem of black youth demonstrates why it was necessary for us to maintain this 'cultural space'. Once inside this safe haven, these performed identities-made manifest through a particular usage of language-presented more realistic accounts of what it meant to be black during the 1970s and 1980s. In essence you were provided with a platform to air/discuss/debate the problems that you believed were most important in your young life from your own perspective. To this end, the fact that the Deejay spoke about how it felt to be under pressure at school and at home, or to be constantly harassed by the police on the streets, or by colleagues in the workplace-made you realise that many of these problems were not unique to you. In this way, you recognised yourself and your social predicament in this picture, whereas the way you were depicted in the mainstream media hardly represented a lived experience, that of a victim of white supremacist thought and action. This type of daily experience-as a racialised subject, which only compounded feelings of exclusion-in a society that informed you at every opportunity that black don't 'belong here'.

Paradoxically, given that there was, generally no visible distance in age or, more importantly, social consciousness between the performer and the audience, there was a heightened sense of belonging in this refigured blak community. I suggest here that black youth often pooled their knowledge of lived experiences to pragmatically determine the best way forward. Of equal importance, the fact that the audience can empathise with, and contribute through active participation to, the Deejay's performance results in transcendental acts of self-defence. That is why the personal commentaries on what it is to be targeted to fail in the wider community, are generally linked to the treatment received at the hands of racist police officers, many of whom still believe being black is synonymous with being stupid. In fact according to Papa Benji:

> If you can put a sentence together, their (police officers) mannerisms change. The way they were taught has blighted them that's why they don't see us as individuals. They recoil if you can talk well. That's why they try to treat us like idiots, cos it makes them feel better. They remind me of schoolteachers, nuff power and little commonsense. (Personal Communication 2000)

Benji argues it is necessary for many white racists who are in positions of power, to believe that black people are 'naturally' uneducable as 'it makes them feel better'. So his view that 'the way they are taught has blighted them...they don't see us as individuals', means that their prejudice is fuelled by a notion of 'natural' black inferiority, a consequence of their socialisation in a racist society. However, when the expected levels of inferiority are not forthcoming, 'they recoil if you can talk well'; for the racist authority figure this runs counter to their expectations, And Benji attributes this to having 'nuff power and little commonsense'. Commonsense in this context is, arguably, the good sense to realise that black people are 'individuals' and should be treated as such. This simple observation speaks of the challenge that black people face on a daily basis in a racist society; many have to constantly prove that they are nothing like the negative depictions that dominate popular culture and fuel a white racist imagination. Realistically this means that the attitudes and prejudices that are harboured by many 'ordinary' members of the white community, irrespective of class or political alliance, are as much a part of their make-up as any other minority/majority social group. As Benji suggested our interactions with the police force remind many of us of our experiences with school teachers, as both 'treat us like idiots' and are overt examples of institutionalised racism. The reality is that if as an adult, you receive the same type of treatment from those in positions of authority as you did when you were a child, then the problem permeates society at all levels.

To overcome both physically and psychologically those racialized constructs that compound your subordination by perpetuating 'natural' inferiority, you must be firstly aware of their existence. Having this awareness provides the locus for a collective identity that can be used to strengthen your resolve when faced with crisis situations that, in other circumstances, may appear to be insurmountable. Furthermore, due to the lack of recognised distance between the audience and the performer, in the sense that anyone who had something to say could use this platform to do so, it was our collective duty to promote ourselves in a more positive light. Therefore, the outernational nature of Deejay culture provided the necessary links with other Afrikans, who also expressed their dissatisfaction with our global predicament. This is where the term 'outernational' becomes wholly descriptive of a 'consciousness' that is not bound to geography; it essentially entails a notion of being everywhere at once. It is this type of outernational consciousness that led to many of the youths in Britain identifying themselves as peoples of Afrikan descent by embracing the notion blak. By doing so Afrikan traditions, folkways and mores, that still influence the manner in which many conceptualise self-noticeably through language and culture-are used as a resource in our ongoing struggles against Eurocentric dogma as 'brainwash education'. The suggestion is that an 'interactive consciousness' (Lewis 2001) equips those who recognise these aspects of their thoughts and behaviour, to challenge the types of misrepresentation that are critiqued throughout this work. That is why black music in this sense is an 'outernational song of ourselves', where cultural knowledge can 'cross barriers', because these outernational forms are our 'informal' and highly dependable 'routes of exchange', as Cooper (2000) reminds us. Thus where 'outernational consciousness' begins or ends cannot be determined, meaning that it transcends the notion of dispersal from one place that a 'Diaspora' consciousness is premised upon. Hence:

Traditions are revered in Africa because they were woven out of the substance of human experience: struggles with the land and elements, migrations, wars, conflicts and wrestlings with the mysteries of life and death. For African, traditions reflect human relations: relations between humans and animals, responses to the challenges of the unknown and the need for order. Through them, Africans relate their past to the present and explore their future. (Liverpool, 2001:16)

A concept like 'outernational' enables those of Afrikan descent, peoples who are now regarded as Afrikan/Caribbean/West Indian/black, to think themselves into being in a manner that defies simple explanations. This is because many black people realise that:

From you skin is black you is ah struggling man, all over the world not just England, we have many enemies including Babylon, cau we caan tun to them when we want protection, in ah parliament we have nuh representation, cau not many blacks ah tun politician, if them do them is the tool of the politician, cau in ah parliament you find the most corruption. (Leslie Lyrix, 1989)

The rationale behind this aspect of the culture demonstrates how recognising your condition through an exposure to the Deejay's lyric, becomes a mode of black survival emerging from our common identity. It then becomes logical that those with this type of political awareness realise, 'we haffi promote the youth, fi mek them rise up we haffi teach them the truth'. This means that there was an acceptance of a collective responsibility to uplift/teach in the Reggae-dancehalls where Deejays addressed the worst aspects of 'living in Babylon'. In this space black oppression was perceived and conceptualised as a global problem that affected all Afrikans psychologically, 'from you skin is black'. In turn 'conscious' Deejays realised that they had a certain responsibility to their community; this notion of the Deejay-as an educator-was 'hidden' from many who would endeavour to interpret the form, which is why Asher suggested:

When we were out there chatting all over the place trying to uplift the youts, the press an them people deh was not interested in what we had to say...Ringo told me it was the same over yard, cau them see the Deejay them as fool'. (Personal Communication, 1999)

These sentiments were borne out in the Jamaican context by Cooper's erroneous observation that 'the lyrics of the Deejays define the furthest extreme of the scribal/oral literary continuum in Jamaica' (1993:136). However, 'them people deh' in Asher's account are those invariably white, or white minded, authority figures that generally dismiss this type of 'black youth' cultural expression in the same fashion. This, in and of itself, is not a bad thing; it was this dismissive attitude that provided the youths with a tangible reference point, further emphasising the conceptual divide between their own and their downpressor's thinking. In other words whilst the Deejay sought to uplift in a language that is comprehensible to the youts, and so spoke for them, the downpressor 'was not interested in what we had to say'. Moreover, Asher's critique emphasises just how the Deejay's lyric was based on a lived experience, which often spoke to black youth by combining current affairs with some poignantly 'uplifting' cultural criticism. For instance, this was the case when Papa Levi critiqued the ideological clout of 'Live Aid' by stating:

> Bob Geldof song everybody start sing, through them dip in ah them pocket an give we ah shilling, Europe left my people starving. (Saxon, 1987)

The act of rejecting 'Live Aid' in Papa Levi's lyric demonstrates how this 'hidden voice' refuses to accept the existing frameworks for debating, what, for us, are personal and profoundly political issues. He, quite rightly in my opinion, makes it known that European acts of philanthropy ('give we a shilling') should be treated with utmost suspicion by Afrikans as in this case, they deny history. This utterance, that 'Europe left my people starving', would perhaps encouraged those exposed to these words to seek out more information on such matters. Even more significantly, once the Deejay has completed their performance, it is not unusual for members of the audience to reason with them about what they have suggested, enabling the Deejay to further explain their position. In fact, Levi told me that this lyric was inspired by Walter Rodney's famous work, 'How Europe Underdeveloped Africa', which I seldom hear mentioned in the white world when they are commenting on 'Africa as the white man's burden'. This includes the 'Live 8' debacle that occurred July 2005, where a bunch of white-led 'humanitarians' arguably used their celebrity status to further undermine the Motherland by arguably partaking in the biggest money-making distraction ever witnessed on live TV. Money-making for them, but not for the peoples of Afrika, whose situation has no doubt worsened, in much the same way as it did after 'Live Aid'.

The crux of the matter is that because our perspective on such matters was/is not known to the wider British public, it still retains its power to challenge the Eurocentric worldview that we have shoved down our Afrikan throats on a daily basis. These sounds of the black experience, illustrated here, challenge the popular misconceptions of the dependent, docile or doltish African. I remember, from my own experiences of the 1970s and 1980s, that it was almost 'natural' for many white people to expect blacks (especially the youth) to be like 'our Frank' (Bruno) step 'n' fetchit-ly stupid, or our Lenny (Henry)-self-abusing to be 'amusing'. If you did not fit into this stigmatised view, you were often regarded with suspicion, mentioned above in Benji's experiences of the police recoiling if you can string 'a sentence together'. This dangerous perception did nothing for the black youth in their social interactions with white authority figures, especially politicians, schoolteachers or members of the police force, who half expected you to be 'naturally' unintelligent. For this reason the sentiments behind Benji's declaration that 'the the way they were taught has blighted them' are particularly telling: this demonstrates why it was necessary to promote ourselves, using our own language, to counter the misconceptions that sought to tell us who we were or what we could be.

4.2 'wise up, rise up'

When considering racial exclusion and victimisation from the Deejay's perspective, it is not too difficult to appreciate why many black youth opted for a type of cultural expression which distanced them from the way in which they were depicted by the downpressor's. To be regarded as an agent of your own destruction presupposes that all is well and fair for all British citizens, irrespective of class, race, colour, gender or sexuality. Challenging these misconceptions in their lyricism enables the Deejays to expose the rationale behind their perspective on a failure to 'fit' into white society by broadening what is a narrow point of view.

Take for instance the following account by Papa Levi who, although London based, penned these thoughts on the 'riots' (for me, they are 'uprisings') in Handsworth, Birmingham, in 1984:

> Poor people are the pillars of society, but don't get no respect from those in authority, me nuh need the rich but the rich need me, if them want live life in ah luxury, ah poor man can work in ah factory, an at the end of the week collect him money, pay gas bill rent bill and electricity, after that his wallet is completely empty, but still him need food fi him whole family, ah nuh just in Afrika you find people hungry, it's a world-wide ting in each an every country, so heads of state I want you listen to me, spend more money on poor pickney. (Papa Levi, 1984)

Verbalising these common experiences of downpression in this fashion ensures that the Deejays become arbiters of change, both physical and psychological, by virtue of their uncompromising stance on the reality of living in a downpressive society. The 'rich' make sure that 'poor people' remain in their lowly position by ensuring that avenues of advancement are closed to 'the pillars of society'. Levi suggests 'me nuh need the rich, but the rich need me' if they are to maintain their luxurious existence. A situation that is not unique to the UK, or even one that affects black people alone, for it depends on sealing off openings in education other fields, that perhaps could lead to the social advancement of any society's disenfranchised elements. Therefore, it is not just the Afrikan or the other, ubiquitously portrayed as poor, peoples of the economically disadvantaged Third World who remain in poverty and 'hungry'; we face the same problem here as the 'heads of state' are not willing to spend their money to better the condition of the urban poor. Levi's lyric, then reflects the mood of the streets; real people do 'rise up' as a consequence of 'wising up' to their less than desirable social predicament. More so in the case of the more visible 'others' who are targeted solely due to their skin colour, which reads as a black badge of inferiority in the 'superior' white imagination, in a dominant culture where white standards of 'civilised' behaviour are the norm. This is the perspective that endorses the proverbial 'chip on the shoulder' as the only explanation for the 'recalcitrant black youth' who, although spawned from pathologically 'weak Caribbean communities', should still strive in our meritocratic society.

The real effects for the black person who encounters these racialised realities are rendered by the Deejays like Papa Levi who convert personal histories and experiences into lyrical form. The most potent form of lyricism, which elicits the greatest response from the audience, unifies the collective through the similarity of experience, and becomes an educational tool. Just by thinking through a racialized encounter the Deejay can create **re-memories**, in lyrical form, that conjure up an alternative reality that is a truer reflection of the black British experience. I am arguing that the tales that are told around the amplifier are a more accurate reflection of what it is like to be the victim/object/subject of racism from this perspective. However, as Levi's extract on the plight of the global poor suggested, this does not mean that victimisation is something that only affects the black downpressed, for as Benji (1999) suggested many whites fight us down because 'it makes them feel better':

> Bredrin, we were educated in a certain way to make us think a certain way, so it mek good sense to think that the white people who hate us are victims as well. In fact in 1982 I worked in the private sector as a draughtsman and this white boy, Barry Jones, said to me, "all you niggers should go to the Falklands first. Yeh they should out you lot first as you shouldn't fucking be here." I am not really into fighting but this rankled me as I thought if I was in the wrong place he would have done me something. The next thing I knew we ended up fighting on the floor. I got the sack for that and I honestly don't know what happened to him, but I know that when I started to Deejay these were the things I would chat about, what it's like to be hated in your own, ha ha, country. (Personal Communication, 1999)

Benji's insights are profound as he realises that we are all 'victims', to an extent, of the dominant ideology, but realising this fact and being in a position to effect real or meaningful change is a different matter. That is why he probably reacted the way he did to Barry Jones' jingoistic patriotism which advocated the extermination of 'all you niggers' and why he ended up in a fistfight with this person. To be faced with such hatred and hostility is bad enough, but when you think that this person was as much a 'victim' of Falkland-mania, (as were the Argentineans during this Thatcherite moment) another set of issues need to be considered. For instance, the fact that this guy brazenly made such a racist statement means that, irrespective of Benji's professional position, he could not see beyond Benji's colour. For the racist this is obviously enough to signify not only the fact that blacks do not belong, but also that 'we' (whites) should be able to do anything within 'our' power, i.e. 'outing you lot first', to expunge the unwanted black presence. This represents a more insidious side of these encounters; the racists who do, in certain situations, have that power to mete out their own 'justice' on the enemy within 'our' midst, more often than not do so, as suggested in the opening **re-memories**. Benji's comment that 'if I was in the wrong place he would have done me something' therefore speaks to a reality that is a consequence of being 'hated in your own, ha ha, country'.

In line with the above we can ask this question-what qualitatively changes in the social experiences of black people in a racist society when age or educational achievement/ability are not considered? These are factors overlooked by many of the theorists that I critiqued in the A~SIDE, whose narrow perceptions did little more than collapse the black presence in Britain into the main characters in an abstracted psychodrama that only compounded our supposed inferiority. This is a consequence of how black people have been misrepresented as members of a thinking community, that perhaps does not 'think' in the manner in which correct 'thought' is determined by the register of the dominant society. Yet, the lyricism I present here details how, and more importantly why, the 'hidden voice' makes sense of the changing urban environment from its own perspective. The simple fact is that racism defines blacks as outsiders whether or not they display signs of deviance or cultural difference, which means that dealing with the real consequences of these racialized definitions is a central concern for Deejays like Reds, who suggests:

> If me ah chat bout Babylon an how wicked them is me want ah man fi know weh me ah deal with is real, me goh through that nuff. I'm not saying we don't gwaan with certain tings but most of the people I know, who get 'bag-up' (arrested) by the police haven't done nutn so that's what I put in my lyrics to mek the youth them know wah really ah gwaan cos we are criminalized from birth in this society. (Personal Communication, 1999)

Sentiments such as these were widely expressed throughout the culture and, in many cases just as Reds' suggests, the Deejay is speaking of a first-hand experience of police harassment, showing them to be, for black people a major problem in our everyday lives. However, what is important to consider is the racially tense climate that the police were operating in and how this climate was influenced by the commonly held view, at street level, that black youth were a major social problem for the ordinary white citizen. Here we are witnesses to the disparity between black youth as a self-perception and black youth as a racialised construct, as detailed above in chapter 1 where these types of negative signification were discussed. For this reason it is unsurprising that Reds takes the view 'that we are criminalized from the day we born in this society; this is how it looks from the ground up to those members of society who are often targeted and get 'bag-up' (arrested) just for being black. The point is being that we were deemed to be the 'problem' by those who had the power to define and 'control' our actions, yet the fact that they were our biggest problem is not represented because there was no meaningful dialogue-that white society was aware of-between 'us' and 'them'. Consequently, if this is the 'reality' of the black presence, when viewed through the racialised white gaze, it is understandable that the justification for overt forms of racism were based on a need to curb the 'moral panic' caused by the black presence during this 'crisis' period. This meant, as will be evidenced in the next section, that the Deejays felt compelled to highlight these injustices through their lyricism in the Reggae-dancehalls.

4.3 'Entertainer, entertainer, we fi join hands together'

The potential of black youth to be anything other than deviant is, as far as the Deejay is concerned, seldom represented in mainstream discourse, irrespective of where you happen to live in Britain. The role of the Deejay's message was to present an argument that was universal in its appeal, in a language that traversed geographical boundaries, although often it highlighted specific local problems. This was achieved because the nature of the culture was itinerant (Deejays and Sets are totally mobile) and could speak across geographical borders in a 'voice' that was representative of a lived blak reality. In order to clarify this point, consider a further extract from Papa Levi's 'Riot in ah Birmingham' (1984) where he argues:

WHAT THE DEEJAY SAID

Well down in ah Handsworth the living it rough, to the poor man it
hard, to the poor man it tough, social security that's not enough, no
jobs around youts get dangerous, seh how long can the government
manhandle us, you nuh see the situation serious, problems we face
are various, police can stop-ah man just through suss, if you walk pon
street you haffi well cautious, police are always, suspicious, if you
drive big car them get envious, nuh believe poor people can be
ambitious, we come last and them come fuss, but the system is
getting very monotonous, future fi the youth don't look marvellous,
even if you born as a true genius, from you live in ah the ghetto you
nuh have nuh status, if you complexion dark that mek it even wuss,
this lyric dedicated to all the conscious (Papa Levi 1984).

Levi reasons that, for many, being black is synonymous with being
'poor', both financially and culturally, because the manner in which
blackness is negatively represented in a racist society means that black
people are seldom 'judged' on individual merit. This implies that, as a
black youth, your common experiences of racism and social exclusion
are not geographically determined. A consequence of this reality, Levi
suggests, is that the dominant view perpetuates the 'problem' status of
'black youth' and explains why many in positions of power, in this
instance the police, act accordingly and are 'always suspicious'.
Consider this:

> This group has made it quite clear that it does not intend to succumb
> to any attempt to integrate it into the mainstream of the
> society...they reject efforts to solve their problems as inapposite.
> Accounts of their dishonesty and arrogance are not uncommon and
> they themselves do nothing to suggest that the accounts are
> inaccurate. (Cashmore and Troyna, 1982:28)

In light of suggestions like these is it any wonder that black youth
realised that the chances you have to achieve your potential and be
judged on individual merit are slim in a 'system' that has become
'monotonous'. As a consequence, for the black youth the 'future don't
look marvellous, even if you born as ah true genius' because who is
going to encourage you to develop your 'gift' in a system that promotes
black inferiority? Here we clearly see the articulation of a position that
challenges the negative view of black youth, presented in the sociology

of race, which did little to assuage the treatment black people received from the government, or their agents the police officers who 'manhandle us'. The crucial point here is that Levi's argument, even as the standpoint of one individual, refutes the misleading view that black youth 'do nothing to suggest that the accounts of their dishonesty and arrogance are inaccurate'. In actual fact Jah Bones' idea of the 'fortified cultural strongholds' within which these negative, and overly deterministic, racialized constructions were challenged, remained 'hidden' from this bigoted gaze. Afrikans do have potential, but by treating us collectively with such overt contempt it is not surprising that our 'genius' is overlooked: 'if you drive big car them get envious, nuh believe poor people can be ambitious'. Even in these moments when you are 'included', in that you are fortunate enough to have earned the trappings of 'success', you remain in a tenuous position due to the way blackness is configured and socially projected as a negative sign. I made this point in Chapter 1, arguing that negative black stereotypes have much currency within popular culture and that the mainstream media are largely responsible because they 'continue to rely on racist stereotypes, emphasizing negative aspects of behaviour, and suggesting deficiencies in morality and intelligence that stigmatize an entire population' (Gandy, 1998:157).

The ramifications of this type of stigmatisation are experienced by all sections of the black community irrespective of the type of cultural politics that they embrace. Once you are branded/labelled by those in a position to maintain these overly negative constructs, you face an uphill battle in your endeavours to challenge these gross misrepresentations. Furthermore, the constant trauma one faces in this kind of social battlefield, as detailed in the above *re-memories*, is not considered in theories that cite a 'generational breach' as a consequence of the failure of black youths to access their 'parent (West Indian) cultures'. This view suggests that the societal and cultural 'failures' of black youth were the result of an agonistic relationship with their (generally older) kin, which naturally explained their 'cultural and political disposition', but did not consider that the:

> Political obsession with race was a dense residue of institutional racism which pervaded the United Kingdom. It was a ticking time bomb for a generation of black kids born and/or educated in the UK. They were supposed to do better than their mums and dads, and

were about to put themselves on the white collar job market having been advised at school that they should view themselves as British and at home that once they had an education doors would swing smoothly open. (Bradley, 2001: 255)

Bradley's commentary details how black youth were encouraged to view themselves as British by the education system. This was because our education was supposed to 'open' these doors to equal opportunity in the job market, irrespective of what colour your skin or 'collar colour' happened to be. However, parental encouragement is also tainted by realism, stemming from the fact that we do not live in a society where black people are viewed as equal to their white counterparts. Black women, especially during this moment in time, were "invisible" and, in Sister Audrey's experience, many black parents told their children that:

"We (blacks) must realise that we have to work twice as hard as white people to achieve sometimes only half of what they have because it's their country." Well, I'm sorry but I was never into that mentality and if I work twice as hard then I want twice as much. (Personal Communication, 1999)

Sister Audrey's view is important for us to consider because to many of our parents generation, we were as English as our white counterparts. This outlook was based upon a different type of racial experience with white folk; many were not born and raised in a society dominated by white people. Therefore, the specific problems the 'black British' faced were alien to many of our parents, whose social experiences were grounded in an Afrikan or Caribbean experience, the likes of which would not be faced in a white man's country. On occasions when their generation were informed that they were not welcome here, they had memories of a home beyond these shores that strengthened them. This was something that could only be imagined by British born blacks who had not travelled beyond these shores. Further to this, Sister Audrey (1999) recounts that her parents would instruct their British born children to answer taunts of:

"Go back home" with "This is my country, I was born here and have as much right as you to be here", which, no disrespect to their generation, showed me that they never understood what we were really up against. I really wish it could have been that easy for us when we were youts. It would have saved us a lot of grief.

Failure to consider this 'grief' is the reason why many West Indian parents did not appreciate how difficult it was for their children to fit into a society that did not cater for their socio/cultural/racial or educational needs. The reality was that black people were considered to be here in England to carry out specified, generally menial, tasks after which they would 'go back home'. When they failed to do so, both they and their offspring became a major problem for many ordinary whites, who did not wish to have immigrants as permanent neighbours. The issues were exacerbated when the offspring of these unwanted immigrants were placed in the hands of educators who often regarded them as less capable than their white counterparts. Whether this was believed or acted upon by all educators is not important here, what I do hold to be important is that this racist viewpoint infiltrated the popular imagination, because commonsense dictates that:

> If the children of us immigrants were to get equal educational opportunities then in one generation there would be no large labour pool from underdeveloped countries, prepared to do the menial and unwanted jobs in the economic system…for our children armed with a good education, would demand the jobs—and the social status that goes with such jobs—befitting their educational qualifications. This would be a very bad blow for Britain's 'social order' with its notions about the right place of the black man in relation to the white man in this country. (Coard, 1991:40)

Coard's position is that those who are in a position to maintain the 'social order' continue to do so even in situations when their education, training or official position should ensure a level of fairness when dealing with black people. Levi's suggestion that the 'future fi the youth don't look marvellous, even if you born as a true genius', is particularly poignant because it is premised on not only being aware of this predicament, but also on acting upon it. It takes collective action to combat a problem that negates the fundamental civil rights of the black community by reducing them to an oppressed 'other'. Therefore, it is the Deejay's duty to highlight this aspect of the culture by promoting a sense of unity in the struggle for our liberation against all forms of oppression, for this is principally the role and purpose of this 'hidden voice'. Hence:

> Entertainer, entertainer, we fi join hands together, an teach the younger generation something that's proper, positive not negative that will help them future, so that generation will be wiser when them older, education at school could be much better, cau fi the youth blakness society nuh cater, an you know we caan depend pon maggie tatcher, or any other blasted prime-minister, you fi listen Daddy Reds round the mic centre, cau we haffi teach the youth them more culture. (Reds, Ghettotone 1983)

Reds' pragmatism shows when this 'hidden voice' is at its most potent: in identifying a problem, acting in accordance with said problem and deciding upon a course of action that aims to improve the livity of the black community in general. This, is not just in a contemporary context, but also offers an alternative to the 'young generation' by mapping out what needs to be done to secure a better future, as articulated above. For Deejays like Reds, it is not enough to point out that which 'nuff nuh know' in isolation, given that this will not empower the collective because it goes against the notion of the 'entertainer' as the provider of practical knowledge based on lived experiences. Further weight is added to Reds' point of view when he states that 'entertainer entertainer, we fi join hands together an teach the younger generation something that's proper', because this aspect of Reds' account regards the conscious/original Deejay as the creator of 'proper lyrics', which will be fully discussed in Chapter 6. However, it is the idea of those Deejays who are regarded as teachers coming together that is of interest here because it demonstrates a level of conscious engagement that advocates collective action as an 'adaptive response' to a racialized reality. In fact for the Deejay to openly acknowledge their role as 'teacher' means that within the culture there is the ability to not only identify, but also to solve our problems by using our own traditional methods, which are founded upon collective action.

This represents the essential part of Deejay culture that posits the 'each one, teach one' mentality, which is a recurring theme in the Reggae-dancehall and offers a practical solution to our shared problem. Why? Clearly because the children (the youths) really are the future, and so protecting their physical as well as psychological wellbeing is paramount when in the endeavour to make this society more liveable for them in years to come. One way in which this can be achieved is acting in a 'positive not negative' manner, and acknowledging the fact that 'education at school could be much better, cau fi the youth blakness society nuh cater'. If we know this to be true, then it is up to us to ensure that the youth learn to regard blackness as a positive and not a negative sign. For example, to look to the 'prime-minister' for assistance is misguided, as the political parties have historically sanctioned racist exclusionary practices. That is why our internal register, which determines who we ourselves consider to be intelligent/conscious/educated, remains unknown to these racial/ cultural outsiders.

The critical point is that we are taught/socialised into believing that to be white is right/normal/civilised and to be black is wrong/ other/savage. Therefore, the only justification a white person requires to exercise this normalised superiority, over the perceived other, is a white skin, the chief determinant in this racialized notion of belonging. As Levi mentions, 'through the complexion of them skin colour', many whites are in a position to regard us as 'ignorant and inferior' and act accordingly. It is important to consider that there was not much in our (blacks and whites) general socialisation that curtailed this distorted view during that era. An awareness of this fact meant that it was imperative to expose the iniquities of the system fronted by Thatcher's, right wing Tory party. According to Dirty Desi:

> Cau flash it oppah, roots an culture, maggie tatcher, even labour, either either, blakman suffer, under pressure call we nigger, cannot prosper no job offer, become hustler, couldah mugger, or bag snatcher, sometime burglar, even daughter ah tun stripper, couldah beggar, even wussah, police capture, lock in panda, sometime rover, cannot wonder, judge don't jester, mek we prisoner, even lifer, under jailer, baldhead Rasta, wah we prefer, Etee-opia or tun chanter, fi high power, lord but if you happy an you love it say forward. (Dirty Desi, Ghettotone 1983)

Dirty Desi makes the point that our oppression is perpetual as it is governmentally determined that we (black people) 'suffer', regardless of who happens to be in power, 'maggie tatcher, even labour'. That is the main reason why we 'cannot prosper', for how can one prosper without any 'job offer'? Desi puts forward that this partially explains why many of us do in fact 'become hustler, mugger, burglar, even daughter (woman) ah tun stripper'. This particular take on certain acts of desperation suggests that they are not merely a pathologically determined black problem, he demonstrates that sometimes people under pressure will do what they deem necessary to survive. Moreover, Desi's account refutes the notion that there was a blanket rejection by 'black youths' of any type of meaningful integration into the mainstream society, due to an unwillingness to adhere to socially acceptable forms of behaviour. It is for this reason that he said we 'cannot wonder'; in thinking through our predicament to ascertain just why we are so victimised during the physical act of 'wandering', when looking for employment as a black person would most likely result in 'no job offer'. For black youth 'wandering the streets', like 'running at night-time', is the type of behaviour that often culminates in our incarceration. Desi:

> When I wrote these types of lyrics I was studying and spent a lot of my time thinking through my situation, because I remember my girlfriend's brother was unemployed and was always getting stopped by the police even though he spent most of his time looking for a job. One time they even locked him up on a mistaken thing and it made me realise how vulnerable I was. That's why I thought my only choice was to chat about these things and make people aware, cos I had no intention to go to Ethiopia, God know. (Personal Communication, 2001)

The last part of Desi's account is particularly interesting for he makes it clearly known that his intention was to stand-up and fight his corner in the UK; for him the notion of looking for better in Ethiopia was unrealistic. He argued, 'baldhead Rasta, wah we prefer, Etee-opia or tun chanter, fi high power', thereby presenting another option for those who would 'prefer' to 'tun chanter fi high power' and voice these concerns on Sound Systems. The idea of representing the 'high power' is, in the first instance, recognising the role of the Sound System as providing the amplified platform for a voice that acts as a medium for change. Secondly, it is also a manner in which we can carry out the 'works', as inspired by our belief in the divine as the 'higher power' because, as Desi stated, 'God know'. That is why 'Etee-opia', was a metaphor to make black people aware of their Afrikan roots, because as a globally oppressed other we need to unify in the struggle against our common enemies. However, this did not mean that you had to physically relocate to this geographical region in your endeavours to overcome the Babylon system. Simply recognising this fact as part of the everyday struggle meant that the downpressed must collectively 'join hands together' and learn to use whatever means they had at their disposal to effect real change in racist British society. This was the case when the British Deejay Lana G suggested that we can even use 'politricks' (politics) to ease our situation and during a performance suggested to her audience:

> **Spoken intro:** Rahbit, hear me now star, Jesus Christ, Jesus hear me now. Anybody know what's happening June the 9th (1983)? June the 9th man come on come on, what's happening June the 9th? Election alright alright Election Champion hear me now eh hear me now star.

> **Deejaying:** Election, is ah damn election, rahbit, election is a damn election, them ah goh figure out who ah goh run the land, seh don't vote margaret she's a wicked woman, let's all get together an think as one. Vote Labour, Labour, that way we'll be safer, safer, if we all vote Labour. Four years ago we vote Conservative, answer one question about what did they give, 3 million unemployment an nowhere fi live, I beg you tell me is that progressive. Vote Labour, Labour, that way we'll be safer, safer, if we all vote Labour. If you want keep yuh job vote Labour, if you want ah few bob vote Labour, Labour we ah goh vote for, we ah goh vank (vanquish) Margaret Thatcher, rahbit. (Lana G, Sir Lloyd, 1983)

Lana G's comments on why black youth should vote against Thatcher, and her Tory government, crucially underline the notion that we will be 'safer' under a labour government'; 'safer' because we will be more likely to 'keep our jobs' and 'safer' from the policies that gave rise to the likes of the SPG. For the above, Lana G receives a rapturous ovation because the youth, present in the Reggae-dancehall identifies with her political stance, given that, 'tatcher's' Tory government were deemed to be the worst enemy of the black community. Consider the role of incitement and catharsis represented in the call, 'if you want keep you job vote Labour' and the obvious response from an audience of her peers, which allow the audience to purge themselves of the traumatic experiences of being black in Babylon. By expressing her views of the political system and how it can ensnare us politically, Lana G provides black youth with collective/alternative choices with regard to thought and action. The idea to present the notion of choice was strategic, as this 'hidden' dimension of urban blak consciousness realised that 'either either, blakman suffer' regardless of the ruling political party. However Lana G illustrates the pros and cons of which party to vote for in her lyric, with regard to practical everyday issues such as the real chances of employment and public safety for the black community whether young/old, male/female in the recognised public arena. Her conclusion was telling and echoed the conscious political sentiment on the street-that voting for the Labour party couldn't worsen our condition, so 'we ah goh vank (vanquish) Margaret Thatcher, rahbit'.

Conclusion

In this chapter I have presented various Deejay accounts that challenge the misleading idea that black youths were the 'recalcitrant' agents of their own destruction. Levi's reasoning about the reality of those black youths who do have potential, but yet never being presented with an opportunity to display their gift in a system that regards them as inferior, is important for us to grasp. What is crucial and telling about arguments like that of Levi is that his own intelligent rendering of this socio-cultural, racialised reality was not even considered by the 'experts' on the black experience, due to the spaces within which it was articulated. The reason for this occurrence is clear in the sense that the 'hidden voice' retains much of its 'truth'-telling quality by remaining in the Reggae-dancehalls. This in turn means that black youth turned these alternative public arenas into spaces where they could simultaneously promote their brand of blak cultural politics, whilst challenging the system. The potency of this voice was based upon offering a similarity of experience, which blurred the distinction between the teller of the tale and the listener. This was achieved through the word-sound-power of the Deejay's lyricism, which uplifted black youth during this snapshot in history, encouraging them to 'wise-up and rise-up'. Equally the sense of realism presented in the lyrics allowed the audience to locate themselves in the Deejay's account during the performance, when another 'voice' spoke your 'personal' thoughts on the most fundamental of civil rights, which is personal safety.

The suggestion is that these experiences would uplift, thereby bolstering your self-esteem as a black youth, enabling you to cope more readily in your racialized encounters with white authority figures. This is what I meant when I suggested that the pragmatic nature of the culture cannot be undervalued, as there was no other place for black youth to experience this type of cathartic/uplifting experience. I am arguing that the Deejay's account mirrored your reality as a 'black youth' deprived of a 'public voice', therefore, within these spaces your perspective was given status: you were encouraged to recognise where the problem truly lay. Utilising this safe cultural space enabled the youth to reject the existing frameworks that were used to explain their 'antisocial behaviour' and it furnished them with new ways to appreciate their own intellectuality. The lyricism of the Deejays would elicit physical and psychological change by making things happen, things that the collective can be seen to instigate and control. It was viewed as your duty to point out to the youth that part of the reason why we 'fail' is because the education we receive does not 'cater' for our blackness. That is why we have to 'promote' ourselves through a positive 'voice' that presents more realistic cultural politics that seek to include a more meaningful black presence. Otherwise, as Levi suggested, the monotony of the system will ensure that the 'future fi the youth don't look marvellous', a reason to learn how to maximise our potential and, through this, uplift ourselves. By recognising and acting on our own genius, in a society where many of our problems are not of our own making, the Deejay's perspective reflects a form of 'consciousness', which is determined from within the culture itself.

Chapter 5

'Conscious' Deejays know weh fi chat!

Introduction

Conscious: mentally recognising, to some degree and extent, one's own inner feeling and thought, or their objective reference. (Webster's Dictionary 1997)

Conscious: awake and aware of one's surroundings and identity. (Oxford Dictionary 1998)

The producer decides if he wants to sell conscious music or gun music. Right now violence is selling, so they want violence, but that will change. After a storm, there's got to be a calm. People have a time when they really tired of some shit, really tired. Fed up. They don't want to hear that any more. So, in my book, if it's not conscious, it's not going far. (U Roy, cited in Foehr, 2000:189)

In this chapter I will focus on the 'consciousness' that determines how this 'critique from the street' becomes a viable source of Africentric knowledge, irrespective of whether or not the 'producer', who decides its worth or marketability, has. I will outline how being regarded as 'conscious' is one of the foremost accolades that any Reggae-dancehall performer can receive, as demonstrated above by U Roy, one of the pioneers of the form. In doing so I will also demonstrate how self-generated concepts, like 'blak' and 'outernational', more accurately describe what is transpires within the culture interms of complex patterns of thought and behaviour. That is why the above dictionary definitions when taken together, encapsulate many aspects of what it means to be 'conscious' from the perspective of Reggae-dancehall Deejay's. The reason for making this claim is that certain types of lyrics are not deemed to be 'conscious', primarily those that deal with 'slackness', 'gun talk' or 'burialism' yet, confusingly, often the Deejay that delivers these types of lyrics may well be regarded as a 'conscious' Deejay. Part of the reason for this paradoxical occurrence within Reggae-dancehall culture is linked to being 'aware of your surroundings' and being able to pitch your lyrics at different types of audience.

As this evaluation progresses, we will overstand how the idea of pitching your lyrics provides an insight into what the Deejays themselves, and the audiences they seek to entertain, believe constitutes a good 'conscious' lyric. We shall also become familiar with the mechanisms that allow Deejays/Sound Systems to lyrically/musically 'destroy' their opposition, as an acceptable part of these cultural practices. These same mechanisms enable Deejays to 'claim' to be 'original', when in fact what they are actually doing is often incorporating, challenging/versioning, or building on another Deejay's ideas. Therefore, we need to consider how the notion of being conscious/original is an aspect of the tradition of the form, that is ultimately drawn upon to judge the lyricism/performance of the Reggae-dancehall Deejays. Of equal importance, is this notion of 'consciousness' which, whilst crucial to the manner in which Deejaying is appreciated from the inside, has never to my knowledge been the subject of serious scrutiny.

5.1 'It's conscious time'

Look into yourself my friend and try to get wise. You gotta be a conscious man (Jolly Brothers, 1978).

Well I'm Macka B. and I'm an M.C. I talk the truth and I talk reality, conscious lyrics are my speciality, and I do it to the best of my ability, lyrics to shock you like electricity, lyrics of peace, love and humanity, lyrics of freedom, pride and equality, lyrics of what is going on in ah society, hear my style, check the vibes, check the music, check the groove, talking facts, talking live like a reader of the news, tell a joke, make you laugh, it's a talent god has given me that I cannot abuse, what I do is what I say, and what I say is what I choose, lyrics from my dreadlocks down to my shoes, I might not change the world with my views but I might just light a fuse. Conscious conscious, come everybody get conscious. (Mack B, 1990)

148

In Chapter 1, I spoke of the 'hidden voice' from the streets that disrupts the facade of a 'settled' black British community, which uses particular self-generated concepts to present a challenge to racism and its concomitant exclusionary practices. An example of this perspective is provided by Macka B, who uses his lyricism to question 'what is going on in ah society'. His view of the social is woven from the fabric of a lived reality, rendered in a form palatable enough for 'real people' to recognise their own images in this particular tapestry. Macka B's lyric provides an access point to the reasoning behind this take on social realism, when he suggests 'talking live like a reader of the news...I might not change the world with my views but I might just light a fuse'. The suggestion is that the real changes the Deejay can effect will more than likely occur at the local level, and this is enough to convince Macka B to proceed in his endeavours to 'light the fuse'.

To 'change the world with your views' may not be possible, but at least you are 'conscious' of these limitations and more importantly, are aware of where your influence is most required and desired. The 'lighting of the fuse' through imparting the type of knowledge that will explode into thought and action is the specified aim of the 'conscious' Deejay. This is a significant point to make when rationalising why these youths decided to 'chat the mic'-many Deejays performed more often than not without financial remuneration-and appreciating this factor is totally relevant to this discussion. Therefore the Reggae-dancehall becomes the site for broadcasting alternative news, where the motivation for the 'newscaster' (Deejay) to present the results of their journalistic endeavours is premised on a recognised need for the black community to be uplifted. In fact, this is where the 'conscious' Reggae performer comes to the fore according to Sister Audrey, who states:

When you have travelled all over the world spreading the message with Prof them (Mad Professor and the Ariwa Posse), you soon realise that our condition is dread so it can't be about material things. We need spiritual and cultural upliftment, reminding us of who we are and what we can achieve because the people we see in a position to do so do not represent the black community. They are not reminding people of the Afrikan struggle. (Personal Communication, 1999)

Sister Audrey's view is representative of the notion of an 'interactive consciousness' that transcends the personal, not just in terms of material gain for the individual's benefit, but also in its purpose of 'reminding people of the Afrikan struggle'. The suggestion is that this take on radical black cultural politics is premised on the expectation that at 'least one will rise up from each generation and tell the rest how it goh' (Sister Audrey, 1999). Thus, within the 'conscious' worldview, the immediacy of the problems that afflict the Afrikan in the present are re-linked, Sankofa-like, with aspects of a known history of oppression. When the Deejay decides to chat 'roots an culture', a more positive black self can be projected through their lyricism during these moments of heightened 'consciousness'; 'we need spiritual and cultural upliftment, reminding us of who we are and what we can achieve'. Other types of lyricism are excluded during these moments within the Reggae-dancehall, because these performances are meant to uplift as well as entertain. The point that I make is summed up in the above extract from the Jolly Brothers when they argue that there is a need to, 'look into yourself my friend and try to get wise'. As they say in Jamaica, it is only as a result of this type of conscious self/soul searching that those 'who know better' will be in a position to 'do better'. Furthermore, although 'consciousness' is a fundamental aspect of this cultural critique, what is crucial to overstand is that being regarded as a 'conscious' performer would depend upon the 'choices' you make and how your 'works' are received within the black community.

The rationale behind this statement is captured in Macka B's 'what I do is what I say, and what I say is what I choose', meaning that the choices are determined by the reasoning of the Deejay who present, practical knowledge based upon practical consciousness. The knowledge that is contained in the 'verbal exchanges' I spoke of in Chapter 2, often imparted by virtue of frequent interactions with Jamaican people, and-in this case- an exposure to Yard-tapes. Overlooking the significance of this factor in the acculturation and socialisation of many British Deejays is the main reason why the culture is often misunderstood. Moreover, because the Deejay is intrinsically linked to the Sound System, a Jamaican phenomenon that Gutzmore argues 'is the medium of the Reggae message' (1993:217), an amplified platform is provided to discuss various issues from a blak perspective in urban Britain:

> The definitive conventions of sound system culture laid great emphasis on its communicative functions. News and underground information was transmitted and alternative analytical statements aired, recording the community's views of historical and political events in ritual processes which also served to establish the limits of the community itself. (Gilroy, 1987:183)

Those who are immersed in the culture have an awareness of what constitutes a 'conscious/original' lyric and, obviously, that which does not because the yardstick by which the performers are measured is outernational. That is why the most significant feature of the Yard/Session-tape was that the listener was provided with various types of reasoning in their unexpurgated form, much akin to Macka B's suggestion that he is a conscious caster of news that 'might just light ah fuse', creating an environment that the culture thrives on. Once this aspect of the form is known we will begin to appreciate why, for instance, entire Sound Systems will also be regarded as 'conscious' if they are renowned for concentrating on upliftment. One of the first Sets that I 'followed' as a blak youth in the 1970s, Jah Shaka, is still regarded as Britain's premier 'Roots an Culture Sound'; this name is synonymous with upliftment to this very day. Hence those who have an internal knowledge of the form are in a position, generally through a process of reasoning, to judge a Sound System's aesthetic value. This will range from the Selector's ability to 'play good tunes', to the actual quality of their musical output or a Deejay's lyricism.

Although the act of creating a lyric is often a very individualistic enterprise (justified within Deejay culture as the ubiquitous 'written by me'), the consciousness that manifests in these accounts relies upon the communal experience for their 'truth'-telling qualities. These Deejays not only 'know weh fi chat', but also *when* to 'chat it' in order to elicit the most favourable response from the 'crowd'. Part and parcel of being 'conscious' is the ability to 'look into yourself' and use this knowledge to identify how your personal experiences are shared in the everyday experiences of the wider black community.

I went to dances as a youth to hear about me. What it was like to be me in this place. Of course I didn't have to chat the lyrics myself and didn't want to Deejay, but I went because what they said was how I felt and I could reason with them and tell them (the Deejays) yeh, that's just how I feel about white people or the police. It didn't matter what they said as I could always relate to it. It was always relevant because we were treated the same. (Derek, Personal Communication 2001)

Therefore, being 'conscious' as a Deejay means that you have the awareness to 'build lyrics' that are attuned to the cultural politics of your peers and the wider black community, which form part of the culture's internal registers. For this reason the Deejays I feature in this study argue that the one main difference between them as conscious/intelligent/original and the pirates/imitators, is that they 'chat what them see an what them know and not another man's tings cau we too intelligent fi that' (Asher Senator, 1999). Asher explains why many British Deejays decided to chat strictly original lyrics and not be branded a 'pirate', or 'lyrics thief', who basically mimics another Deejay's performance. It is also the reason why it was crucial for me to flag up this point in chapter 3; it is necessary to acknowledge the critical role pioneer Deejays such as General Echo, played in the creation of this outernational culture where 'argument' as 'knowledge' reigns supreme.

British Deejays were influenced by these shifts in Jamaican Deejay culture, and during the late 1970s to early 1980s, instead of 'pirating' the lyrics of the Jamaican Deejays who were the main sources of inspiration, many began to come 'original'. What then happened was that the lyricism of the British Deejays could now be distinguished from their Jamaican counterparts because they spoke for the first time about 'life on-yah, cau we did born-yah'. However, when assessing the notions of both 'originality' and 'piracy' in the context of Deejay lyricism, it becomes apparent that true piracy is unacknowledged imitation, as all Deejays draw inspiration from other performers. Therefore, in order to ascertain what represents 'conscious' intellectuality and 'originality', within the Deejay culture of the Reggae-dancehall world, we need to consider the Deejay's own sense of how this self-expression is judged. This is because there is a noticeable difference in the lyricism of the 'conscious' Deejays featured in this study and those who, whilst not being 'unconscious', do not 'have the ability to build lyrics on the same scale of meaning and relevance as the lyrical man them' (Dirty Desi, Personal Communication 1999).

5.2 Time to come 'original'

Within Deejay culture, 'Pirating' is regarded as out and out copying/imitation with little acknowledgement to the lyric's 'originator', much as is suggested in the case of 'King Yellow' in Chapter 3. Although it should be noted that whilst 'King Yellow' was not renowned as an 'originator', he played a highly significant role in the promotion of a more 'professional' approach to the art of Deejaying in an outernational context. Furthermore, his popularisation through the recorded release of certain Reggae-dancehall favourites, for instance 'Soldier Tek Over' (General Echo) and 'Operation Radication' (Sassa Frass/Burru Banton), which were correctly cited by Gilroy (1987) for their influence and appeal in the wider British public arena. However, Gilroy has erroneously attributed certain 'popular trademark devices', which were adapted by two British Deejays 'Laurel and Hardy', to Yellowman such as:

> His chant of 'left right left right' from 'Soldier Take Over' which had conveyed the onward march of Seaga's military to the dance-halls of Jamaica became 'Evening all, what have we here' the sound of British police preparing to make an arrest'. A fragment of Yellowman's dialogue with the feared Eradication squad from 'Operation Radication': Him look pon me shirt, him see seh it a red. Him seh me ave a good mind fe lick off you head' was similarly transposed so that it as a conversation between a youth from south London's black ghetto and his local bobby: Him look pon me neck, him sight Rasta scarf. Him seh "Do you know about the fire down at New Cross". (1987:193/4)

Note that I have included the names of the Deejays, in parentheses, who 'originated' these lyrics, to display how an 'insider' perspective alters the manner in which the culture has been understood up to this point. 'Operation Radication', was featured on the Yard-tape circuit for at least two years before Yellowman recorded it; the creation of this lyric is attributed to two performers, Lord Sassa Frass and Burru

Banton. The reason for doing so is the fact that I first heard Sassa Frass chat about the 'Raiding Party' on a 'Black Star Sound System' (1980) Yard-tape that ironically also featured Yellowman as well. It was on a Yard-tape featuring 'Gemini Disco' (1981) I first heard Burru Banton's 'Radication Squad' and the notion of being a 'lyrics Banton' is synonymous with being 'original'. The point here is that both performers were involved in ongoing 'verbal exchanges' about who 'first chat' this lyric; I want to underline here that this is not an unusual occurrence as many Deejays make similar claims.

On 'Creation' Sound System in 1983, as part of a 'burial' lyric, Papa San stated that 'me used to have a lyric named Radication, but through it get stale me give Burru Banton, Toyan get jealous an seh him want one'. Whether or not this is true cannot be stated here I have never heard Papa San chat that style. Yet knowing that he is regarded by many as the most prolific and original lyricist the Reggae-dancehall has ever known, I would not be surprised if he did 'first chat' this lyric. Papa San was taking on all comers and tearing down the 'lawn' at that time, even as a youth of approximately 12 years old. However, it was Burru's own ability to 'chat non-stop' that he himself suggests, resulted in 'them changing me name to the lyrics Banton'. This is why, to my knowledge, he was the first Deejay to carry this title. Consequently, he wrote a lyric entitled 'non-stop' from which the ubiquitous 'eh uh eh eh uh eh eh eh Boom wah this, wah that, ah Burru banton ah chat' was taken and used as one of the most popular Deejay introductions of all time. I must also state here that many performers such as Asher Senator, Dirty Desi, Papa Benji, Mikey Reds along with myself, believe that the Jamaican Deejay 'Nicodemus' was the first true 'lyrics Banton'.

Nicodemus was already chatting 'non-stop', 'ah full up di riddim' with 'style an fashion' when Burru came along. Nicodemus was actually known as the 'champion Deejay' during this moment and was uniquely renowned for continuing his performance and delivering his original lyrics, irrespective of what was happening around him. For instance if the 'needle stick' causing the record to 'jump', whilst in the midst of his lyrical flow, he would realign his delivery to the beat of the rhythm by rapidly chanting something like, 'play-by-the-champ-cau-we-nuh-ramp-in-the-camp' and carry on with perfect timing. Similarly, if the crowd reacted favourably and the 'operator' restarted the record, he would more often than not just carry on delivering his lyric whilst the tune was forwarded which served to generate even more excitement. The reason why Nicodemus or Nico D, Demus, Senator D or Grandfather Demus all names by which he was commonly known, became the 'Champion Deejay' in 1980, was due to a Deejay clash he was lined up to have with Brigadier Jerry. It was rumoured that General Echo would have been included, had he lived, because until his brutal murder he was the most popular Deejay on the island, bar none. It was for this reason that, in the end, to establish who was the number 1 Deejay in Jamaica, the clash was held between Nicodemus and Brigadier Jerry. Both Deejays signed an agreement to be at the venue in Ocho Rios where they would clash on Jack Ruby Hi Fi's Set. Ballot boxes were readied to decide the victor, but Brigadier Jerry failed to show and Nicodemus, who did turn up, won by default. A telling moment in the dance was when, several hours later in the evening, the following transpired:

Jack Ruby: Jack Ruby presents the ballot box. One mark, Demus, the other one mark; gimme di forward one yah. One mark, Briggy…the agreement was signed around di table. Nicodemus, did you agree to be here, without any fear?…I can't see Briggy up til now. Demus, tan up mek dem si yuh boss…ah wah time yuh deh yah from?

Nicodemus: From 2'oclock Rasta, Jah know, yeh. Seh ah nuh any gal can come model with me, ah nuh any gal can come model wid me, them haffi pass up them GCE, them haffi pass up them GCE, cau Nicodemus in ah higher category, me baddah dan Brigadier Jerry, me sweeter dan ah neesberry…where is Brigadier Jerry, me hear seh him gaan buy up some cherry, me hear she him gaan buy neesberry, while Nico deh ah Ochi eating fry fish an bammy, me seh we can't find Brigadier Jerry, but watchah man but yuh nuh hear, yuh nuh hear weh me hear, di reason mek Briggy don't come here, ah true him know di money nah goh share, cau Nicodemus gaan clear. (Jack Ruby, 1980)

Nicodemus boosts up his status as the Reggae-dancehall 'teacher' by excluding 'any gal' who is not educated from 'model with me', whilst notifying Brigadier Jerry's fans that he, too, is included in this sense, as Demus is in a 'higher category'. The lyric also explains why 'Briggy' did a no show in Demus' eyes, because 'ah through him know di money nah goh share', so naturally 'Nicodemus gaan clear'. In Britain when we heard this particular Yard-tape it was unlike any we had experienced before concerning two heavyweights of the Deejay world. It did not much matter that Briggy didn't turn up, a factor that was explained as an aspect of his Rastafari principles, which was good enough for many of us Yard-tape aficionados in the UK. It also goes some way to explain why this 'clash' is one of the most famous and sought after Yard-tapes, which still creates much passionate debate over two and half decades later. However the above from Nicodemus, the original lyrics Banton, demonstrates the value of Deejaying as that critical aspect of Sound System culture, which gave birth to the British Deejays who lyrically 'pass up them GCE'.

A Deejay considered to be a 'lyrics Banton' is recognised within the culture as being able to 'ride' the rhythm properly and chat 'non-stop' in an 'original' fashion. That is why so many performers still affix this title to their Deejay name, hence Buju Banton, Mega Banton, Lusty Banton and the British Deejay Starkey Banton (to name but a few), as recognition of the fact that they have these attributes. Hence the word 'Banton' is another example of how a 'self-generated concept' is representative of the internal registers by which the culture is known to its adherents. It is important to place certain influences in their proper historical context; there is no dispute among those from within the culture that Yellowman merged the two styles, 'Raiding Party' and 'Radication Squad' and 'created' his popular hit 'Operation Radication'.

To further explain this significant point I will now focus on General Echo's 'Soldier Tek Over', to reveal how the knowledge contained within Yard-tapes provides an alternative history of the genesis of the form in the British context. In the lyric, Echo conveys a sense of the terror caused by the massive, hostile, military presence on the streets of Kingston, Jamaica and an air of dread is evidenced when he suggests:

Spoken intro: Murder, from the top of the main at the itrol tower. You want see me sitdown pon me veranda one night you nuh an me hear me gal come een an seh. 'Them ah come, them ah come, them ah come, them ah come'. Guess ah who she ah talk? Soldier iyah, soldier, ah soldier she ah talk, hear how them march! Left right left right, left right left right.

Singing: But lady lady lady, why do you holler, nobody see weh you draws (knickers) cover, 'go in ah it, go in ah it, go in ah it'. Lady lady lady, why do you holler, nobody see weh you draws ah cover, 'goh in ah it Echo'.

Deejaying: Ah weh me seh ah soldier tek over, choh mek ah till you seh ah soldier tek over, choh lord ah god me haffi run fah cover, choh mek ah till you seh ah soldier tek over, choh lord ah god them ah goh curfew me area, choh lord ah god me haffi hide under the cover, choh mek ah till you me haffi run fah cover, choh lord ah god them just ah put on the pressure, choh let me till you, look out look out some ah drive up in ah jeep, look out look out some ah drive up in ah jeep, ah beg you stay around the corner an peep, ah beg you stay around the corner an peep, choh lord ah god ah seh, soldier tek over, choh mek ah till you said ah soldier tek over, choh lord ah god me haffi run fah cover, choh lord ah god them just ah put on the pressure, choh mek ah tell you them ah curfew me area. But hear me star. Me nah lef me ID ee ee, me nah lef me ID, Why? Cau me nuh want soldier beat me, ah till you me nuh want soldier beat me, choh lordah god me ID haffi certify me, me ID haffi certify, choh mek ah till you seh ah soldier tek over, choh lordah god ah said ah soldier tek over, bamwiddly-widdly, ah worry- demahworrydem ahworrydem ahworrydem ahworrydem, Echobadah dandem, Echobadahdandem, Echobadahdandem, me said ah soldier tek over, how them march, left right an go round, left right left, 'go in ah it Echo'. (Stereophonic, 1980)

Echo's lyric captures the feeling of tension in Kingston, Jamaica during this moment of intense 'pressure' from the soldiers who had 'tek over' and whose hostile presence had terrified his 'gal' and made him and the rest of the community 'run fah cover'. What makes the performance even more effective, is the fact that he switches his mode of delivery to accentuate each aspect of his overall argument. It is for this reason that he begins by speaking to the audience as he introduces the theme and then goes on to sing his 'version' of the introduction to the 'Johnny Dollar' rhythm, which is one of the most popular Studio One tunes ever recorded. Echo cleverly matches his 'left right, left right' chant to the marching drum beat that introduces the dub version of 'Johnny Dollar' and anyone who has experienced this 'riddim', pumped through a Hi Power Set, knows the kind of vibe that it generates in the Reggae-dancehall. Echo then presents his account of the lives of 'real people' who do not often have the opportunity to express their opinions so openly, when chanting 'look out look out them ah drive up in ah jeep, ah beg you fi stay around the corner an peep'. Warning the community that under 'curfew' conditions they had best walk with their 'ID' or be prepared like him to 'hide under the cover' or even 'run fah cover'. Was clearly because 'me nuh want soldier beat me', or worse.

I must stress that it is imperative that we realise this: at the time of Echo's murder, during the highly volatile political climate of Jamaica's 1980 General Election, it was rumoured on the Yard-tape circuit that the 'Soldier Take Over' lyric had contributed to his death. One Jamaican performer, who I will not name for obvious reasons, informed me that it was partly due to the said lyric that 'the bwoy Jim Brown dust him'. In fact in the moments before Echo chatted the above lyric, the exuberance of Donovan, the Deejay that introduced him to the audience, resulted in the following exchange:

Donovan: An me seh bubble we ah bubble an we nah seek nuh trouble. You (the selector) ah hear me Rasta, you better find you fashion style before me cuss bad wud in ah the place. Choh you see although whole heap ah Officer in here, you ah hear me Rasta, ooh...

Echo: Cool runnings, Donovan, cool runnings.

Donovan: Lord have his mercy upon them yah man weh sweet like ah papa Echo, Jesus Christ...

Echo: Forward again, forward again. An me like hear dah music yah start you see, ting called the Soldier Tek Over, great sounds called the Soldier Tek Over.

One can almost experience the tension of this moment when Echo interjects by taking the mic from Donovan, then cleverly defuses the situation by instructing the 'Operator' to restart the record to the prompting of 'Forward again, forward again'. By doing so he allowed those in attendance—especially the police officers and soldiers who were ever-present—to recompose themselves, because law enforcers were and are still heavily armed in Jamaican Reggae-dancehalls. This led the Deejays to take a cautious approach in dealing with these Officers,

158

as will be evidenced in the next two extracts where Sassa Frass and then Burru Banton detail their encounters with the Radication:

> Seh just the other day me coming from ah party eh, ah so me buck-up pon a raiding party, some fudgie want to search me, choh lord ah god some fudgie want to search me, ah weh him do, him tek off me tam him start to play in ah me head, him seh him ave a good mind fi goh lick off me sledge, him look pon me ganzie (A form of knitted sweater) him sight the Emperor, hey youth man you look like ah murderer, him look round me waist him see me gold an green, him seh me ah fire bare sub machine, him look pon me pants an him sight it in the socks, crank-up him gun the bwoy shot me one box, hey officer weh mek you fight dreadlocks, seems to me you nah nuh love in ah you heart, you grudge me fi me diamond socks an me Clarks, said ah please Mr Officer, choh right yah now me want you name an you number, do it Jah, me dah goh caah you to commissioner, woy, him decimate me character. Him caah me go ah station him get statement, go ah court house him don't ave nuh argument, hey massah judge him grudge me fi me garment, the clothes weh him have on belongs to government, the house weh him live him seh him nah pay nuh rent, seh leave Sassa Frass an mek him be confident, Jah Love in ah the president yard, said ah Jah Love in ah the president yard. (Jah Love, 1980)

Sassa captures and details, in much the same fashion as Echo's lyric, the feel of what it was to experience this belligerent presence on the streets of Kingston during this moment and the air of menace that permeated their neighbourhoods. Similarly, Burru Banton's 'Radication Squad' offers a tale of this form of 'legalised' brutality, which does not enjoy the semi-satisfactory ending as described in Sassa's lyric. Importantly, whilst waiting for the B~SIDE to be played, there was a brief and ominous silence, as Burru began his performance, that speaks to the seriousness of this moment:

> **Spoken intro:** Special request fi the promoter ah the dance who seems to for get seh ah whole heap ah Radication. Well hear come I play the musical disc called the radication Squad...(momentary silence)...Sorry fi that interruption through certain vibration, me lion, special request to the promoter ah the dance, special request to all Radication officer. The ting called Radication Radication.

Deejaying: Lord, woy, hear me now, Radication Radication, hail Jahman, Radication Radication, well watch yah man eh, as me trod along, seh as me trod along, seh as me trod along, I hear ah voice of ah man, seh this time man it was the Radication, some come in ah jeep some come in ah van, the woman in ah buckers (a style of shoes) an the man them in ah tam (hats or berets), but when them come out you hear the door just ah slam, slam bam, slam, that's the Radication, slam bam, slam, that's the Radication, seh soldier up ah camp an police in ah station, put them together call them Radication. Boom, room for rent supply within Almond Barracks run out an Radication run in, Radication Radication, hail jahman, Radication Radication, well watch yah star. Them come yah in ah tens an in ah thousand, them fire 16 (M16's) them nuh fire M1, them com pon the land fi confront bad man, me step it pon ah minivan ah go ah Barbican, fi guh check fi ah girl name Sharon, jahman me seh me run up in the Radication, well them deh man ah tell me fi hands up me hand eh, them deh man deh drunk them put me in the car trunk, them handle me bad, me claim how them mad, them seh them come from Radication Squad, me coming from ah dance from over Patrick City, but man me run-up in ah raiding party, two home guard them want come search me, hail jahman ah mussi grudge them grudge me, lord, woy. (Gemini Disco, 1981)

In 1983 I met the late great Jamaican Deejay Johnny Ringo, who was a regular on 'Gemini Disco' and one of the performers featured in the session when Burru's performance took place. Ringo, along with his sparring partner, Welton Irie, had travelled to England with the rest of the 'Gemini Disco' crew to feature in a series of Reggae-dancehall sessions. One such session took place at the 'Peoples Club', Paddington, London, where his Set played alongside Brixton's 'Frontline International'; I was one of the Deejays performing on 'Frontline' that night. After the session we were reasoning about various issues and it was then that I asked Ringo what happened during Burru's performance. He informed me that, just as Burru was about to 'chat', one of the Radication officers came over to the Set, told the selector not to start the record and 'warn Burru fi mind him mouth'; in other words to watch what he was about to say. The point is that these extracts demonstrate how the stories of everyday livity are conveyed, via Yard-tapes, to an outernational audience that emphasises the reach of the 'live event' in a manner that is yet to be fully appreciated. These performances were the template upon which our lyrics/styles were often based because they were easily adapted or incorporated into our 'black British' worldview, especially where our relationships with the police were concerned. One example I can present to demonstrate this influence on 'what the Deejay said' is one of my 'original' lyrics, as featured on a Sir Lloyd 'Live LP'.

> **Spoken intro:** Special dedication to the...Bwoy me hot but me know how fi chat. Champion, tek in this me know you love them style yah. Original, originated by me, the king champion hear them style yah, eh.

> **Deejaying:** Cau me seh SPG them just ah rush me, SPG them want fi crush me, SPG them want fi hold me, SPG them want control me. Seh just the other day jahman me gaan ah West End, me gaan ah Regent Street fi goh meet me girlfriend, me see ah van load ah beast favour hog more than men, them mek a little circle then them come back again, them pull up with a skid, bare tyre did ah bun, but I man stand firm, why should I run? I don't have nuh fear fi noh evil one, me under Jah Jah protection, hail Jahman me under Jah Jah protection, ah weh them do. One tek out him truncheon, swing it in the air, he said hey nigger what you doing up here, me never seh ah word Jahman me keep me silence, cau anything me do them ah goh bring me violence, them search through me pockets want fi see the contents, is a good ting me never have ah draw of ishense (weed), an while them ah search me them ah give me hard time, ah tell me seh me must know bout street crime, when him see seh me clean, him haffi let me loose, ah then the bwoy start with the verbal abuse, him seh the whole-ah we ah thief, him hate all blacks, me seh shut you fucking mouth I pay you wages with me tax, I pay fi you uniform you boots an you socks, you don't fit fi come ah dance an carry speaker box, seh bwoy like you couldn't stop me from tracks (going about my business), puppah Lezlee at the microphone attack, cau as ah so me chat boom dance haffi pack. (Sir Lloyd, 1983)

This extract is demonstrative of the manner in which the Jamaican Deejays gave their British counterparts so much thematic material to work with that the true extent of their influences cannot be overstated. It is clear how I maintained the level of critique, with regard to the unjust conduct of those whose duty it is to 'protect and serve', in much the same way as the Jamaican Deejays, whilst transforming the gun toting Radication Officer into the baton wielding British Bobby. That is why it is an aim of this work to present a more informed and inclusive history of this form because experiencing the Reggae-dancehall in this fashion gave us an insight into everyday Jamaican livity. This actuality refutes the ludicrous idea that Yard-tapes were 'limited circulation cassettes' that had a minimal effect on 'dancehall's global/local intersections' (Stolzoff, 2000); this statemtnt overlooks the outernational resonance of Jamaican culture in the alternative 'world music market'. The most notable aspect being the alternative take on social and political relations contained in Yard-tapes which were used to 'originally' recreate this aspect of Jamaican life in our British context.

By presenting this viewpoint I am in a position to convey the true significance of the Jamaican cultural influence, with regarding the outer form, and inner direction, that British Deejaying was to take in the context of Britain's changing urban environment. The Jamaican Deejay 'Charlie Chaplin' suggests 'every Deejay have a message fi give, whether them chat slackness or culture' (Creation Sound System, 1983). The idea of the Deejay 'message' is of critical importance to this evaluation because many who premised their theorisations of the culture's influence in Britain, by taking a lead from Gilroy's perspective, did not include the messages contained in Yard-tapes. For instance, Gilroy maps the influence of Yellowman's 'popular trademark devices' beginning with Laurel and Hardy's 'Your Nicked' (1982) tune, as previously discussed, suggesting that when Laurel and Hardy stated 'Him look pon me neck, him sight Rasta scarf. Him seh Do you know about the fire down at New Cross':

> The originality and appeal of the tune lay not simply in these exchanges, but in the toasters' ability to switch between the different speech idioms which characterised the policeman (south London respectable working class) and his black prisoners (black London patois, the language which marked the boundaries of the Rasta community even when other signs and symbols were not used). These ideas were developed further by another DJ also signed to the Fashion Label: Culture Smiley. So named because of his refusal to chat 'slackness' in his rhymes, but renamed Smiley Culture by his management. (1987:194)

In the context of British Deejay culture, Smiley Culture/Culture Smiley was known to use both names and did so the first time we performed together on Ghettotone in 1983, which is also when I first met Asher Senator, and before Smiley had a manager. It was his 'refusal to chat 'slackness', coupled with his 'originality' (to be evaluated in chapter 6) that led to him featuring in this particular session, which was a birthday celebration for Maxi Priest. However, what is most significant about this event is that it featured a host of British performers who were known as 'The Crucial Posse'; a concept created by Maxi Priest to unify the black musicians in Britain and also as a means to 'get paid' as professional entertainers. I will be detailing this idea of what it means to be 'professional' in chapter 7; it is a highly complex and contentious aspect of the culture. Although 'Laurel and Hardy' could be regarded as 'professional Deejays' they were dismissed as 'comedians' (much like their namesakes) and were not recognised as Sound System Deejays in the Reggae-dancehall, or more importantly as 'originators'. Their 'ability to switch between the different speech idioms' of London and Jamaica was, as I suggested in chapter 2, a 'natural' part of the 'verbal exchanges' many of us experienced in our daily interactions. In fact it was commonplace in the Reggae-dancehalls to hear various regional accents mixed in with Patwa, which was the dominant language of the Deejay performance. For instance, you would hear Macka B and Pato Banton speaking with a 'Brummie' (Birmingham/Wolverhampton) accent during their performances, (they were born and raised in the Midlands) and Smiley Culture's 'Bajan' accent was clearly heard in many of his performances.

It is not unusual for the British Deejays to feature this type of regional/local/international expression in all aspects of their performances. As such, the inclusion of cockney speech idioms including 'rhyming slang' in the performances of London based Deejays were commonplace and cannot be attributed to any one performer. Attributing this kind of 'originality' to these particular 'Deejays' is misleading and denies the usage of Patwa as a language in its own right, which transcends any notion of a simple 'code-switching' device as I stated above. This does not mean that Patwa is not 'consciously' deployed as an anti-hegemonic tool for, as Gilroy states, it was an important part of 'the basic strategy of linguistic exclusion with which the community had protected itself from the encroachment of unwanted white listeners' (1987:194). I put forward that, because this usage of language reflects the polyglot nature of the form, it is so familiar to many members of the black community, irrespective of where they hail from and that it is not in the least bit surprising that British Deejays would perform in this fashion as conscious and 'original' lyricists.

5.3 Questioning 'consciousness': the 'roadman' mentality

Be conscious, in every little thing you do, be conscious in every little thing you say. (Leroy Smart, 1979)

Me did ah talk to one sister weh tell me seh she want ah conscious man, weh want goh back ah Afrika an live. Me tell her seh ah conscious man can live anyweh in ah the world. She look confuse, but me know seh any of the man them weh live pon the road we overstand weh me ah seh, cau from you conscious you know fi flex mongst friend or foe. That's why me use to Deejay fi the roadman-them, cau them really know wah gwaan. (Champion, Personal Communication, 2001)

In his extract Champion makes known that the 'sister' he was reasoning with failed to 'overstand' how his notion of 'consciousness' differed from her own and, crucially, states that those who are familiar with his worldview 'the roadman them' would 'overstand'. The sister's view of a 'conscious man' is aligned to that of the so-called 'back to Afrika' movements; it is argued that they believe that the only place the Afrikan can truly strive is in Afrika itself. On the other hand for Champion 'consciousness' is based upon survival and transcendence, which is why he uses the term 'roadman' to describe a level of awareness that allows you to 'live' wherever you choose to in the world. This is the very same point made by Dirty Desi in his lyric 'baldhead Rasta, wah we prefer, Etee-opia or tun chanter, fi high power'. It is this overstanding that encouraged Champion who 'use to Deejay fi the roadman-them, cau them know wah gwaan', to recognise that the sentiments reflected in his accounts were identifiable to those who shared the same worldview.

The notion of being able to live 'pon the road' is important to this argument, as the suggestion is that there is a more practical set of life-rules, grounded in lived experience, of which black people are made aware if they are to survive in a hostile environment. The suggestion being that although much of the inspiration was coming from the Jamaican Deejays, we had to use our own street knowledge and wisdom to tell our particular stories in our own voices. Hence Macka B (1999), who incidentally stated that he, too, began his career chatting both 'slackness' and 'culture' lyrics, reasoned that in 'the early 1970s there was a spate of Reggae tunes giving us inspiration and guidance, telling black people to be conscious in our acts and deeds'. He suggested that the continuous exposure to the lyricism of the Jamaican Deejays had a profound affect on his thinking because:

> The messages in these tunes influenced the way I viewed the world and at this time I really became interested in what the music was saying. I used to play the violin and sing in the school choir, but when I heard Prince Jazzbo, U Roy and I Roy I thought that they were speaking of my condition as a black youth in a white world. (Personal Communication, 1999)

Here we have an indication of how important it was for Macka B to have role models, like these Jamaican entertainers, who provided exposure to practical information as well as introductions to examples of the Deejay style. I think that this is captured magnificently in his transformation from a one time violin-playing schoolboy, who sang in the 'school choir', to one of the most militant Reggae-dancehall Deejays the world has ever produced. The suggestion is that playing the violin and singing in the school choir are reflections of acceptable forms of 'cultural expression', from a highbrow European perspective, which did not enable Macka B to express his disapproval at living in a racist society. Once he left the school environment and suffered redundancy three years later, he suggests that the experience led him to 'focus even more on music and the messages, and that's when I started to write lyrics and practice Deejaying at home'.

Champion echoed a similar tale of the impact and relevance of Reggae music's message; the early 1970s was the period that introduced a significant shift in the social perception of Reggae Sound Systems and the types of performers who were affiliated to them. It was during this time that the British Deejays, who would spontaneously adlib during the silences between musical changes, began to provide more topical social commentary on the B~SIDE. For instance, there were early 'British' pioneers like Capone and Mickey Bennet on Jah Shaka, Castro Brown, Gunsmoke and Densil on Sir Coxsone Outernational and Pebbles on Sufferer Hi Fi. Many of these pioneer Deejays were born in Jamaica and partly raised in Britain explains the reason for their inclusion here as British Deejays. Pebbles, according to Bradley, suggests that he was 'the first British-born Deejay to hold the mic on a major sound system' (2000:379). It is important to consider that these social commentaries were influenced by the lyricism of the Jamaican Deejays who dominated the British Reggae music scene, which was heavily reliant on imported Jamaican music in the format of recorded releases, and to a lesser extent, the emergent Yard-tape phenomenon. However by the late 1970s, the shift in the perception of the Deejay was profound in terms of what was now expected of them within British Reggae-dancehall culture. Ironically, it was because many British Deejays pirated verbatim the live performance of their Jamaican counterparts, that the lyrics received much wider exposure. That is why this is one of the most important periods of the burgeoning British Deejay scene which coincided with a massive influx of Jamaican performers, who often brought the latest Reggae-dancehall cassettes with them. Due to the popularity of the Yard-style during the summer of 1980, one of my brothers (Rankin/Dr Vibes) and I went to the 'One O' club in Catford, south-east London, because the Jamaican Deejay:

> Ranking Joe with sound operator Jah Screw brought the Ray Symbolic Sound System to the U.K. for the first ever U.K. tour by a Jamaican sound. (Saturday Night Jamdown Style, 1980)

However, although we were captivated by his performance, it was not too dissimilar from that which we were exposed to in the UK because much of what he chatted we were familiar with through our exposure to Yard/Session-tapes or pirated performances. This was the case with the Deejays on Frontline International, Welton Youth and Colonel Flux, who it must be noted played a crucial role in disseminating the Yard-style in the British Reggae-dancehalls. Frontline's Set was popular because it recreated the Yard-vibes and according to Rubin Ranks:

> Man an man did ah try a ting an me did love the way Briggy did ah gwaan, so ah nuh nutn if me did ah talk fi him style cau me never

claim it. Sometime ah one fi just tek up the mic an try ah ting fi them self (Personal Communication 1997).

Rubin argues that his piracy was a way of showing appreciation/respect (the 'imitation is the best form of flattery' scenario), to his role model. At the time Briggy was the number one 'roots an culture' Deejay and renowned for his originality as suggested above. However, what is significant is that Rubin's rationalisation of his own piracy, based on the suggestion that he never 'claimed' to originate the lyrics performed, differs from the pirates who pretended to be the originators. Therefore, his notion of just 'trying a ting' suggests that he was modelling and perfecting his own Deejay style along the lines of his major influence. Rubin's rite of passage was also taken by many featured in this study, including myself, who agree that this was how they 'learned' to Deejay. At the same time, his 'live an direct' version of the original lyric, featured in these Session-tapes, furthered the message by exposing more of the black community in Britain to the Reggae-dancehall vibe. This type of exposure unquestionably encouraged many of the British born youths to, in Rubin's words, 'tek up the mic' an try ah ting fi them self'. Many British Deejays did so to directly counter those pirates who were deemed to be unimaginative and unrealistic, because they often spoke of what was happening on the streets of Kingston Jamaica verbatim, and this did not make sense in the British urban context. On this very issue Reds states:

> I got tired of hearing Deejays going on like Yardies and chatting about M16's and all that stuff. I never knew nutn about them ting deh and I couldn't identify with that stuff, so when I used to go Saxon an hear Levi an Peterkin chatting about London, it made me start practising my own styles, cos all I did was wrote what I knew an not all that gunman, Fantasy Island shit. (Personal Communication, 2000)

Reds could not easily identify with the gun lyrics that dominated Deejaying during the run-up to the murderous Jamaican General Election (1980), which claimed the lives of many. He also makes known how important it was for him as a blak youth to hear a tale of London livity, with which he could identify and so not be subjected to that 'Fantasy Island shit'. This is a crucial factor in the acquisition, recognition, and subsequent usage of your 'own voice' as it allows you to actively participate in the culture as both observer/audience, or the observed/performer, on your own terms. However, and far more importantly, it was the positive messages that were coming to these shores from the Jamaican Deejays, via recorded releases, Yard-tapes or pirated performances, that further encouraged many black youths to embrace this genre of performance, for as Champion states:

> My mum was strict and wouldn't let me go out late an that, cau weh we did live on Croxteth (A housing estate in Wandsworth, south-east London) it was a bit wild in the night-time with the youth them an the police, so me used to listen to man like Jazzbo when him did ah tell the youth them fi 'Step forward' cau 'the Babylon a brute' or when Jah (Big) Youth ah tell we bout Garvey. Cau even though it was Jamdown them did ah talk bout, me see the same tings a gwaan round yasso, so later on when me start put pen to paper me realise that nutn nuh change fi the youth them on-yah, an me chat that because me know bout that. (Personal Communication, 2001)

Champion raises an interesting point about the universality of the Reggae message for the conscious blak youth, because, even though Jamaican Deejays like Prince Jazzbo were commenting upon the types of downpression they would face, mainly in Kingston, the youths here could identify themselves as being caught up in the same struggle. This meant that the British Deejays were now being presented with an alternative framework within which they could articulate their socio/cultural problems, by directly contrasting their struggles with those of the Jamaican Deejays, as stated in the SPG lyric above. Of equal importance, Champion informs us that exposure to these types of message was instrumental in orienting his own lyrics to the suffering of black people in Britain. According to Champion, 'we did always try to bring the Yard-style culture-vibes to London people', which is why their Set was called 'Jamdown Rockers'. A point embellished by Macka B (1999) who reasons that his mission as a Deejay is:

> Me doing my little bit to help my people cau every time you hear a word it conjures up an image, therefore my mission is to fashion my words in a way that reflects the plight of the Afrikan and doesn't reinforce the negativity that is associated with the Motherland. If you look at the world and look for the poorest people, invariably they will

be black, so my lyrics are like a stepping stone to help us get back to where we once were and Reggae music is the vehicle to carry the message. (Personal Communication, 1999)

We plainly see that for Reds, Champion and Macka B, Deejaying on Reggae-dancehall music is the most practical way to provide an alternative voice, that deals with the outernational plight of the Afrikan oppressed. Moreover, by suggesting that 'Reggae music is the vehicle to carry the message', Macka B demonstrates the relationship between the performer and the audience and the types of reasoning that are disseminated within the culture. The suggestion is that people will tune-in to his lyrics to be uplifted/enlightened because within the culture he is regarded as the type of Deejay who has something relevant to say about the types of problems black people encounter in a racist society. His 'message' is 'consciously' constructed in a manner that is both easily digested and informative, and the provider of the type of 'stepping stone' that black people require to 'get back to where we once were'. Macka B makes known how the associative power of words and their ability to 'conjure up images', whether they be 'positive' or 'negative', must be comprehended and utilised by the conscious Deejay because they are potent forms of 'ideological weaponry'. This is why he demonstrates how crucial the notion of overstanding 'wordplay' is within these types of counterculture that challenges the 'negativity associated with the Motherland'. By explaining that he 'fashions' his 'words in a way that reflects the plight of the Afrikan', he obviously made a 'conscious' decision based on what he deems to be his 'mission' and purpose, which is to deliver a message that will uplift black people.

5.4 Burying 'consciousness'; 'I'm not here for liberties'!

****

Re-memories

'Weh Frontline deh?' I asked as I arrived around midnight at 'The Crypt', in Deptford High Street, for our return 'clash' with Frontline International and Revolutionary Hi Power. This was a couple of weeks after our greatest triumph as a fledgling Set 'weh just born weh day'. It

169

was the night when 'the Yard man them', Al Campbell and Lui Lepke, chatted on our Set and led to, as previously suggested, my becoming known as Lezlee Lyrix; I had 'nuff argument'. The streets of Lewisham had been alive with anticipation for this return bout because many could not believe that the great Al Campbell and Lui Lepke had chatted on a small Set like Ghettotone. This was unprecedented because at this time Al Campbell (a singer) and Lui Lepke (a Deejay) were two of Jamaica's most famous Reggae artists, in England to perform on stage shows, and would have been expected to appear on a top Set like Frontline International. For this reason even a few of our sworn 'enemies' from the Saxon Posse were there as well as many other Soundman from the London area. In our corner we had a full complement from the 'Rockers Posse' who were a 'youth Sound' from 'ghetto' (Milton Court Road Estate, Deptford, south-east London) that were avid Ghettotonians who would help us 'string-up' our Set and their Deejay, Daddy Dego, would often 'spar' (perform) with us. On that particular night we sounded extra 'clean' and our prized possession, the one 'Quad box' we owned (which, it was rumoured, Caesar a co-owner of Ghettotone, had built from some wood that had once boarded up his shop front) made me feel especially proud as the bass 'tumped' out of it. Quad boxes are the four-phase speaker boxes that were built for maximum effect (bass wise) and not portability; any Sound System folk will inform you that carrying them from the van and into the venue, which sometimes involved several flights of stairs, was no easy task. They usually had four 18 inch high powered speakers of 200 or 400 watts, which were a sight to behold let alone to experience their earth shaking qualities. That night we were also in the possession of a few 'dubs' that the selector Rankin was itching to play to demonstrate that we, too, could acquire these 'exclusives', the soon to be released tunes that in those days were truly 'specials' and only played by one or two Sets.

The time was approaching 1 AM and there was still no sign of Frontline, 'them must be fraid' Desi said as we listened to Revolutionary Sound System warming up the crowd; taking their turn to entertain the expectant masses who were grumbling their discontent at what appeared to be a no show by Brixton's biggest Set. 'Them deh yah' Tee from the Rockers Posse shouted, beckoning us to follow him outside to the car park where Frontline's Sound-van had pulled up.

'What the fuck is that; you see that, Lez?' Rankin shouted, but all I could do was stand there gob-smacked and totally overwhelmed by the size of the 'removal truck', from which Frontline's posse were unloading their equipment. In all of my years of going to sessions, man and boy, I had never seen a Sound-van as big as that in my life. Java Sound System from West London had a small coach, which they would use to transport their Set and their posse, but this was unbelievable. However, as if this initial shock wasn't enough, imagine how we felt when we witnessed **Seven** 'Quad boxes' being wheeled in on a type of customised 'sack barrow' and strategically placed amongst the columns that gave the Crypt (formerly an underground tomb) its eerie character and made it the perfect place for what was to follow. In fact whilst they were stringing up their Set, our awe-struck crew were walking around the venue inspecting these magnificent speakers', whilst secretly fearing the inevitable outcome of their imminent introduction to this arena, which now had an air of dread/dead anticipation permeating its tomb like structure.

'MIC CHECK ONE TWO, MIC CHECK ONE TWO', the words boomed out of Frontline's mass of speaker boxes, as they began the preliminary testing of the Set's equipment to ensure that all was correct and functioning properly. However, this was done whilst we were playing our Set and their 'mic stage' was so loud it was dominating our endeavours to entertain the 'crowd ah people' who had 'corked' the venue and were eagerly waiting for Frontline to 'sign-on', when it was their turn to do so. 'Just cool, man, we have two more tune fi play an then you come in, scene' Desi argued; 'MIC CHECK ONE TWO, MIC CHECK ONE TWO AH FRONTLINE TIME FI PLAY' was the only response from Frontline who had set up their 'itrol' tower directly opposite our own. At this point Caesar was fretting and wanted us to 'sign-off', but out of our naiveté we continued and Desi was calling him a 'weak-heart' and a 'friars'. Rankin stated that it was because he was used to being signed off as 'Caesar' the 'Lovers Rock' Sound, but we were supposedly made of sterner stuff, when suddenly; 'AH LOT OF PEOPLE GOING TO SUFFER TONIGHT…CAUSE THE BATTLE IS GETTING HOTTER, IN THIS IRATION, IT'S ARMAGEDDON'. The telling words from Willie Williams' hit 'Armageddon Rock', accompanied by the thumping Studio 1 bass-line, sent a shiver down my spine. I can still feel the shame we felt standing there shaking our heads in disbelief as the moment they signed on properly, Frontline completely 'drown us out'. To make things worse, we only realised we were still playing when 'Natty', Frontline's Selector/Operator, pulled up the tune to play something else and when he did so we were utterly consumed again.

The owner of the Set, 'Trevor Frontline' (who is the coolest Soundman I have ever met, nothing seems to phase him and I have never heard him raise his voice in anger), later informed me in that gentle but firm tone of his, 'everybody needs a lesson in manners sometimes and that's what it was. Sound business ah nuh overnight ting so ah one must know them place'. That is why he hired the removal van and brought his full range of speaker boxes into the fray 'to bury us' without apology because that is the nature of the business. Ironically, it was my performance against his Deejays in our first meeting that led to me chatting Frontline on several occasions and after the demise of Ghettotone in November 1983, Trevor asked me to become their main Deejay, which for me was an honour as few Sets could match them for sound quality and entertainment value, a lesson that we so painfully learned that night. 'Yes, we were clean and, in our own lightweight division, quite heavy', Dr Vibes stated, 'but':

> We sounded like a drum-pan compared to them and when they played 'Mighty Diamonds' 'Unruly Pickney' on dub, me ah tell you the truth it is the one and only time I have ever felt well and truly buried. I mean it was futile for us to even try to play and when they did let us in they warned us that if 'we gwaan with any slackness, them ah goh sign we off again'. Surrounded by all of them Quads and pummelled by Natty's selecting. It was the most humiliating experience a big man could goh through, being handled like ah baby in front ah so much people that you know. (Personal Communication, 2001)

****

In the previous section, Macka B suggested that he 'fashions' his 'words in a way that reflects the plight of the Afrikan', which I suggested was a 'conscious' decision based on modes of thought and action that are recognisable from within. In a not too dissimilar fashion Papa Levi (1997) suggests that:

Consciousness is me doing what Selassie I know is right for my people, cau who know better do better, me did haffi leggo the slackness and chant strictly culture. (Personal Communication 1997)

Levi raises an interesting perspective on what it means to be 'conscious' as he provides an insight into why he believed he had to 'leggo the slackness and chant strictly culture', for it demonstrates how he realised that his role as a Deejay was crucial to the struggle. He knew that he had to make a 'conscious' decision to do what he knew to be 'right for his people', which meant focusing his talent on the 'cultural/conscious' aspect of his performance. His decision was welcomed in the Reggae-dancehall where Papa Levi was viewed as a paradoxical character who, because of his embracing of Rastafari and his 'natty dread', would often cause consternation amongst heartical Rastafari due to the nature of his 'slack' lyrics. Never more so than during the moments when he was 'burying' another Deejay for he was known as one of the best burial Deejays, in much the same way as Champion (2001), who suggests:

Me hear seh the best-selling cassette from them time deh (the 1980s) is the one weh me an Tippa (Irie) clash. Me just goh deh fi seh weh me haffi seh fi win, an end up ah tell Tippa bout him mummah (his mother). Him never talk to me fi years, but I'm not here for liberties an them caan tell me nutn. (Personal Communication, 2001)

The inference in Champion's statement is clear, and within 'our' culture, the hurling of aspersions against somebody's mother is the ultimate sign of disrespectful behaviour and arguably the worst type of 'slackness', which is why many Deejays fall out with each other during these types of exchange. Champion also acknowledges the fact that the Session-tapes from the heyday of the British Deejays are being redistributed as a new generation display a significant interest in what was being said during this moment in history. Champion demonstrates how complicated it is to dichotomise 'slackness and 'culture' in the context of the Deejay performance because, although he is widely regarded as a 'conscious/culture' Deejay, he openly admits that he would say anything to an opponent to win a clash. The main reason for this attitude is summed up in his 'me seh weh me haffi seh fi win'; therefore there are no boundaries because 'I'm not here for liberties', which justifies him telling 'Tippa about him mummah'. He argues that this is another aspect of the 'roadman mentality', as on many occasions in ordinary life you may have to get 'slack and tell simmody bout them self when them try tek liberties with you' (Champion 2001). This attitude sums up the **re-memories** I used to open this section, which provided an insight into what it was to experience 'burialism' first hand and how central it is to the form as a totality. It should also be pointed out that many performers were 'burial' specialists and would often, like Dirty Desi, 'start the 'fuckry' because:

> I loved to bury a friars and would chuck-it, hoping that they would retaliate so I could do my ting. Like the time when Asher start trace me an me just give him what him deserve. Cau me haffi mek them know that you can be intelligent an still dust-out ah a bwoy, an mek the crowd rail-up fi that. (Personal Communication, 2001)

Thus in the context of the Reggae-dancehall 'burialism' of all types was expected and accepted, in some way shape or form, by Deejay and audience alike. For example, as a youth I attended countless 'Buck-Down' competitions between our local Set, Jah Shaka, and a host of other popular Sets, including Sufferer, Fatman, Sir Coxone Outernational, Count Shelly, King Tubbys, Neville The Enchanter, Soferano B, Prince Trojan, Quaker City from Birmingham and many others. These dances were proper burial sessions just like the one in the above **re-memories**, everything was exaggerated as the Soundman them were 'extra', showing off their new dubs/specials and equipment to the extreme. This stylish and ritualised behaviour was what made these dances so exciting and for those who were on the receiving end of a musical or lyrical drubbing, it was a shameful and embarrassing experience. According to Liverpool (2001), this ritualised practice is a constant feature of Afrikan expressive cultures and is the basis of the 'Kaiso' (Calypso) performance which, like American rapping and Deejaying, is dependant on this combative element because:

> The Hausa word "Kaico" from which came "Kaiso"…means "you will get no sympathy; you deserve no pity; it serves you right."…calypso reflected the verbal war atmosphere that took place when two singers clashed. It was also an expression of approval from the crowd. They would "throw back" the line ending, when they

approved a good Kaiso, a well worded line or rhyme...Sometimes they used two sets of musicians and two choruses-which suggests that the war was probably fought among the bystanders as well. (2001:372)

Liverpool could arguably be describing any Reggae-dancehall clash scenario or the ritualised aspects are linked to Afrikan traditions and thus exemplify the role of that which is known as 'the changing same' (L. Jones, 1995). The point is that if you appreciate the ritualised aspects of this type of behaviour then it transcends any notion of 'slackness/burialism' as sheer vulgarity, because it is placed in the context of the performance as a totality. Given that Liverpool is 'Chalk Dust', one of the greatest Calypsonians ever to 'tek up the mic', he brings that insider perspective that makes links of which 'outsiders' would not be aware. His Africentric perspective broadens the analysis in ways that are seldom acknowledged, much less understood, by "foreign enthusiasts"; those who the wordsmiths are often intent on burying in the first place. There is no point whatsoever in pretending that these outernational forms are all inclusive, as in many cases they are not. Quite often they are our most potent, alternative media outlet. In fact their strength lies is in the manner in which they shape-shift to resist the gaze of outsiders, who will perhaps never appreciate the aesthetic quality of what we do, as Afrikans, in Babylon shitstem. For this reason many commentators fail to appreciate that the dichotomy between 'slackness' and 'culture' is often a false one, misrepresentative of what actually happens within these alternative public arenas.

To clarify this point I will elaborate on the 'art' of 'burialism' by re-presenting the occasion to which Dirty Desi referred, his 'burial' of Asher Senator, is one of the best 'cultural' Deejays around. It occurred during a Deejay clash-dance October 21st 1983, which featured Lezlee Lyrix on Ghettotone versus Papa Levi on Saxon in the Lewisham Boys Club, south-east London. The scene was set when Asher Senator, who was performing on Saxon that night, 'chatted' a style called the 'Alphabetical Burial', which my sparring partner, Dirty Desi believed was 'slackness' and signified a challenge; for he was well prepared. In the actual lyric Asher did not mention Desi's name directly, but the inference was there (in Desi's view at least), as he was performing on our Set when Asher chatted the lyric. It is crucial to remember, as Liverpool suggested above, that during these 'verbal wars' the overriding mentality is one of 'you deserve no pity; it serves you right'. The said idea used by Trevor Frontline to explain why he disciplined our Set because 'ah one must know them place'. Therefore as soon as Asher finished his performance and Saxon signed off, Desi seized the moment to present his own drama on plastic:

> **Spoken intro:** Heh heh heh heh ha ha. Rasta you see that, ah man call me name. Wait deh, wait deh, wait deh, wait deh, the man them seh aggro. AGGRO! yes Rasta. Call my name first I ah goh call yours last heh heh rahbitit. Man call Barry Brown happens to be the talk of the town. Bumbuhclaat, if you happy an you love it say forward, lift it...People I goh tell you ah secret, I goh tell you ah secret. You know why them call me Dirty Desi? Heh heh, me have the duttiest mouth (dirtiest mouth). When I bury I do it properly. I don't goh round in circle scene. Straight to the point, heh heh ha ha. (Ghettotone, 1983)

The above was uttered whilst the vocal, Barry Brown's 'culture tune' 'Thank You Mama' on the 'Heavenless' riddim, was playing with Desi supplying the odd bits of humour, enhanced by Operator Quick's skilful mix-down, another crucial ritualised aspect of the Deejay performance. In this instance it readies the crowd for what is sure to be a derogatory lyric, for the audience has been forewarned by Desi that he has 'the duttiest mouth'. Additionally Desi acknowledges the fact that Asher did not 'cuss' him directly when he suggested that, 'I don't goh round in circle scene. Straight to the point', but chooses to turn this to his advantage. Once the vocal had run its course and Desi had set the scene, he chatted the following lyric after cleverly hyping up the crowd ah people with a series of 'special requests' to the local posses who he knew would be against Asher. This was because Asher came from Brixton, an area in south-west London that has historically been accorded the enmity of many from the Lewisham area, especially in the clash-dance scenario. To this end:

> **Spoken intro:** Special request to the sister called Black Beauty, special request to the Cirus posse, special request to D'unes posse, special request to the Rockers posse big bowyah, you see me now me get to the point, I don't need to goh round in circles I can chat one ting an out oonuh out cold, hah hah hah, but hear me now, but watch ah man cau.

Deejaying: In ah it, come mek we jump up in ah it, bim. In ah it, come mek we jump up in ah it. Asher get face-ti, him must get hit, him run up him mouth an him have too much lip, put me hand dong me throat, me bring-up vomit, kick weh him foot mek him drop-in ah it, draw up me cold me full him-up ah spit, like a lion tamer me lash him with me whip, me tek him out side-ah, me fling him in the skip, send him back to the sewer with the rest of the shit. Rasta, cau if you happy an you love it say forward.

Spoken intro: Yes, well that was that an that is ah fact. I don't need to keep on burying, Rasta, heh heh, you see me now, me out ah that cau me too intelligent scene, watch me now, me ah entertainer watchah, best.

Deejaying: Ah wededem ah goh do fi shut me mouth, ah wededem ah goh do fi shut me mouth, seh I nuh ignorant but if me vex me might ah shout ha ha ha ha ha ha ha. 'Forward, forward, murder, gwaan bury'.

Spoken intro: Wait deh wait deh wait deh, hey me have ah style you nuh, me have ah wicked style hear how it goh now, hear now.

Deejaying: Dirty Desi ah the MC murderah ha ha, Dirty Desi ah the MC murderah, Dirty Desi ah the MC murderah bim, cau Dirty Desi ah the MC murderah, seh Asher trace me, me haffi answer, first me think carefully an then me start fi shower, I might get rude or out ah order, whatever it tek fi do the job proper, I tell you already I'm the headmaster, cau if you happy an you love it say forward.

Spoken intro: Ha ha ha you see me now, me can bury all night, but it's not in sight, dynamite, special request to the man call Oliver, how ah man can come in ah the ghetto come chuckit star ha ha ha. Special request to all ghettoites, Mr Dirty at the mic, hear we go again star, style an fashion, ration. Bim.

Deejaying: Cau Dirty Desi ah the MC murderah bim, cau Dirty Desi ah the MC murderah, seh Asher trace me, me haffi answer, first me think carefully an then me start fi shower, I might get rude or out ah order, whatever it tek fi do the job proper, I tell you already I'm the headmaster, me nah chat nuh slackness if me tun ah Rasta, you caan

chat slackness an praise the Emperor, before you come ah dance tek
a bath or shower, you ah smell up the dance with you body odour.

Deejaying: Yeh well right now, Dirty ah get out ah that, an in ah
supn better, special request to the man call Blackie, aanyah, rahbit.
(Ghettotone, 1983)

Desi presents, in the most dramatic style, the art of burialism in full
effect; he demolishes his opponent with no quarter asked or given,
fulfilling his promise that 'when I bury I do it properly'. But it is what
happens after he has delivered the first lyric that captures the essence of
my argument about the difficulty in separating the 'slackness' and the
'cultural' performer, if we are discussing 'consciousness'. This is where
Desi states that 'I don't need to keep on burying, Rasta, ha ha, you see
me now me out ah that cau me too intelligent scene, watch me now, me
ah entertainer watchah, best'. For by stating 'me ah entertainer' he
demonstrates that he makes 'conscious choices' during his performance
and his role as an 'intelligent' Deejay is to entertain. Hence 'first me
think carefully an then me start fi shower, I might get rude or out ah
order', which includes the amount of emphasis one places on key
words, sounds, or phrases during the performance as act; thereby
making it known that he will do 'whatever it tek fi do the job proper'.
Desi has that awareness of what type of lyricism/performance is
expected from the Deejay and delivers 'whatever it takes' to defeat an
opponent and conquer the crowd. If Desi was Rastafari he would know
what was expected of him on a 'conscious' level, due to his familiarity
with the internal registers that determine how a performer will be
ultimately rated. This was the rationale behind his comment 'me nah
chat nuh slackness if me tun ah Rasta, you caan chat slackness an praise
the Emperor', which again speaks to the levels of conscious thought
and action that are crucial to the Deejay's choice of lyricism.

The above highlights how problematic it is to determine whether a
Deejay is 'slack' or 'cultural', for many chat styles containing various
key elements that could comfortably locate them in either 'camp'.
Furthermore, although Desi was renowned as a 'slackness' Deejay he
was also regarded as one of the most 'intelligent' because of the
poignant nature of his 'conscious' lyrics already seen in the 'SPG' and
'Flash it Oppah' extracts cited above. Moreover, the Deejay will be
'conscious' of where they can chat certain types of lyrics because if Desi

chatted burial lyrics in a 'roots an culture' dance he would expect to be booed off. The main reason for this is because many in the crowd recognise the powerful nature of the spoken word, which when put together as Macka B previously suggested, 'conjures up an image'. In this instance it demonstrates just how potent these forms of lyricism can be, for once the words left 'the duttiest mouth' and combined with the rhythm track of a 'conscious' tune ('Thank You Mama'), their internal dynamism culminated in Asher Senator's burial.

There is, however a more sinister side to 'burialism', which has caused major conflicts and almost cost Papa Benji his life in 1984, thanks to a promoter setting up a clash/burial dance between Benji and Papa Levi, without Benji's consent. The consequences of dealing with these types of unscrupulous characters, in the Reggae-dancehall world, will be discussed in Chapter 7 when I consider professionalism in Deejay culture. The 'reason' for the threat to Benji's life was because he did not agree to this type of clash and stated that:

> I wasn't into that slagging each other off an all that, an me know seh Levi cuss people mother an them ting deh. I'm a big man and if it was lyrics for lyrics that would be different. I told the promoter that and he still put my name on the flyers. On the night of the dance I didn't bother to turn up. Two twos (a little later) I was attacked by the promoter who chopped me in my back with an axe. I thought what the fuck is wrong with them, them want kill ah man over them fuckry. (Personal Communication, 1999)

The serious impact of this type of mindless assault is self evident and Levi, too, was shocked by this occurrence. It was one of the factors that influenced his decision to switch his emphasis from the 'slackness' of 'burialism' to something more conscious and uplifting. Furthermore, Levi's decision to chat 'strictly culture' emphasises the profundity of Champion's 'roadman' mentality, as a necessary factor in the lyricism of the conscious Deejay. As Leroy Smart opined in the second of this section's epigraphs, we must endeavour to 'be conscious in every little thing we do, be conscious in every little thing we say'. This, more so when we consider that the spoken words has a habit of taking on its own dynamic, quite often with the most dramatic and damaging consequences as we shall witness below.

Conclusion

Throughout this chapter I have endeavoured to provide an insight into what it means to be 'conscious' from the Reggae-dancehall Deejay's perspective. We have discovered, being truly 'conscious' is quite an ambiguous and therefore highly problematic idea. The main reason for my arrival at this conclusion is that 'consciousness' is, on the one hand, the Deejay's presentation of a heightened level of awareness that can be communicated during certain moments, which are geared towards upliftment. On the other hand, this notion of 'consciousness' can be subsumed during moments when the expectance of the audience shifts to another aspect of the culture, as in the case of 'slackness' as the art of burialism. Therefore, this paradoxical occurrence demonstrates the intricacy of the politics involved in the Deejay performance, meaning that 'slackness' and 'culture' as generic constructs, are context dependent and aligned with specific moments. Therefore, as was evidenced in Macka B's account, 'consciousness' as it was transmitted from Jamaica to these shores through the medium of Reggae music during the 1970s, stressed the need to be 'conscious in our acts and deeds'. This means that the act of being 'conscious' cannot be ascribed to the performer as a total 'cultural' (in the uplifting sense) or political being. This in turn suggests that being 'conscious' is in the 'doing' and often occurs in that moment during the performance when the Deejay seeks to uplift; just as it was in the profundity of Echo's 'Soldier Tek Over' lyric, an example of 'slackness' personified in 'conscious/culture' mode.

The reading of the performance as 'act' must be appreciated in the context of the 'message' that is delivered during a particular instance, establishing the political context for the 'conscious' performance to be accepted within the culture. Paradoxically, if the scene is set for burialism, you would not hear uplifting 'roots an culture' style as this is not what is expected, or required, during this particular Reggae-dancehall scenario. It is often the case that a Set can bury another with 'roots n culture' tunes because many do not rely on slackness lyrics, cussing, tracing or slagging off their rivals to get a favourable response from the crowd. Now it is perhaps easier to appreciate my suggestion that to dichotomise 'slackness' and 'culture' in any simplistic fashion is untenable, it too conveniently reduces the performer or Set to either one camp or the other by underplaying the significance of the performance as a totality. Champion's notion of the 'roadman' helps us to overstand why certain skills and ability are necessary parts of the Deejay performance, everybody has choices in their everyday lives and, therefore, why should things be different within the context of the Reggae-dancehall? What then becomes crucial is for the Deejay to recognise the moments when their particular skills will be most appreciated and they must have within their repertoire 'all kind-ah style'. For this reason I now wish to evaluate in the next chapter the notion of what it means to be 'original' from the 'conscious' Deejay's perspective, as the lyrical content of their performance determines how they are 'rated' in the Reggae-dancehall community as portrayers of social realism as 'roots an culture'.

Chapter 6

'Originality, learn to study'!

Introduction

> The DJs have produced a significant body of creative language in varieties of Jamaican Creole, not just at home but also in the Diaspora. (Cooper, 2004:299)

> I play or write me...Music is the language of the emotions. If someone has been escaping reality, I don't expect him to dig my music. (Charles Mingus, cited in Small, 1987:339)

> Originality, learn to study, bwoy, Originality, learn to study. Me draw me inspiration from the almighty, cau God mek the world also he made me, so me nuh love chat the o either the e, if me ah goh chat them me ah goh chat deeply, me talk bout invention and discovery, me talk bout the famous in history. (Papa Benji, Diamonds: 1984)

In the previous chapter the notion of originality from the conscious/intelligent Deejay's perspective was, according to Asher Senator, 'chatting what them see an know and not another man tings'. This, we shall discover, is complexly linked to the manner in which this 'verbal art' is determined because, for many, the ability to Deejay is a 'natural' gift from the divine. Benji explains that a crucial part of being 'original' is the ability to 'draw me inspiration from the almighty, cau God mek the world also he made me'; this means that this presence must be constantly acknowledged as part of the re-creation process. For these reasons I will make known, throughout this chapter, the mechanisms in place within the culture that enable the Deejay to claim that what you hear is original/intelligent/conscious. I will detail the cognitive processes behind these claims by considering Deejays as grounded intellectuals, because intellect is defined within their own frames of reference. Explaining that 'originality', like 'consciousness', is determined by how I/we 'play or write' me/us, in the context of a worldview that does not seek to 'escape reality'. Thus recognition of your intellect as a Deejay is—in this case—both locally and globally determined, because your lyricism represents a British urban reality that links to the wider struggles of the Afrikan Diaspora. Moreover, I will argue that the lyrics are sources of knowledge and historical documents, and must be appreciated in the context of how representative they are of a voice that is grounded in the experiences of specific communities, powerfully articulated in outernational 'varieties of Jamaican Creole'.

6.1 Breaking the 'silence': Jah know seh ah London we deh!

I remember when I first started chatting an nuff people tell me seh me couldn't last because I was chatting so different, I was chatting about being a blak youth in London. Later on me fine out seh nuff of who was saying that was just pirating the Yard-style and once everybody get the tape, yuh done know seh is them who couldn't last. (Champion, Personal Communication, 2001)

Just the other night at a MC jamboree, ah youth deh pon the stage ah call himself dirty, ah chat Desi style bout 83, but Desi just cool him never get angry, cos him know what mek a perfect pirate MC, ah Ghettotone tape an ah good memory. If you want more proof that pirates exist, them rearrange me lyrics like best in ah this, ah chat them in ah combi an ah gwaan like them criss, Desi said Lezlee mek them feel yuh fist, cau when them chat them against you they're taking the piss. But me nah go ah jail fi assault and battery, ah bwoy ah imitate then it must be flattery. (Lezlee Lyrix, Ghettotone: 1983)

Selassie I know seh me foot mek fi walk an me mouth mek fi talk, me seh me born as a natural Deejay. (The Lone Ranger, Soul to Soul Sound System: 1980)

In the extracts the overriding sentiment concerns what it means to be recognised as a 'natural' or 'original' Deejay, because to be a 'pirate' or imitator meant that you were more or less a joke in the eyes of many Reggae-dancehall fans. However, recognising 'originality' is not always that straightforward when the form is largely associated with Jamaican performers, a perspective that fundamentally argues that Reggae music can only be produced in Jamaica by Jamaicans. This viewpoint stunted the growth of the British Reggae industry, and is exemplified in the case of 'Lovers Rock', which was seen as inauthentic or 'formula' (inferior) genre for a long time (Henry 2002, Bradley 2000, Gilroy 1987, Clarke 1980). For this reason Champion suggests that when other Deejays were being 'rated' for 'their' lyrics, what they were actually doing was mimicking the Jamaican Deejays. He suggests that his detractors were uncritically accepting the pirates re-presentation of Jamaican lyricism as 'authentic', whilst largely ignoring the content of his rhymes, which related directly to the black experience in London. Champion's position leads us to consider how the process of writing and performing lyrics, in the British context, became accepted as a valid representation of social reality. I am suggesting that lyrics are sources of knowledge and, once disseminated (e.g. via the system of taped exchanges), allow the listener to access other perspectives that increase their cultural knowledge. The same point was made in the previous chapter, based on Rubin's suggestion that he never actually 'claimed' ownership of the Jamaican lyricism he was presenting 'live an direct' to the British 'crowd ah people'. This means that there was no expectance on his part to be rated for the lyrical content of his performances, because he freely admitted that he was copying the likes of Brigadier Jerry. It must be noted that many listeners did tend to 'rate' the pirates too highly and this is why, according to Papa San:

> Dancehall pirate ah them deh me fraid ah, thief San lyrics gwaan like originator, so when me ah talk it them ah call me imitator, when him talk it them ah seh that him greater. (Papa San, Saxon, 1986)

Hence, even though piracy was acknowledged throughout the culture, this did not mean that the attempts of many British Deejays to present an original account of the black experience in Britain were not met with various types of resistance. It was this type of resistance to which Champion alluded as he argued 'when I first started chatting an nuff people tell me seh me couldn't last because I was chatting so different'. To demonstrate what was so 'different' about the way he used to chat, and why it was possibly resisted, Champion provides the following insight:

When I first took the mic, summer 81, I was round my bredrin's yard and I knew I couldn't sing so me just do ah ting. I had some rhymes that I made up pon spot, you know more humorous dan anything else, but the man them did love it cause I was chatting about what happens out ah-road. To me it was more like when you ah reason an mek two joke, so to me it wasn't a big deal and through me never really hear the Yard-tape too tough them time deh my flavour was different. Little later in October 81 I had a clash with ah Deejay on 'Dub Natty' (a local Sound System) an me dust him, cau by this time I had started to build proper lyrics even though me never have nuh name. After me rough him up, which was no big deal cau the bwoy did ah pirate; every-ting was Jamdown this an Jamdown that, so me seh me ah goh show you wah gwaan in ah London. The man them (the audience) did quiet at first an then them start galang bad when me run him out (his opponent ran out of lyrics). Then them start call me the Champion an you done know how the rest ah it goh, the name just stick. (Personal Communication, 2001)

Champion raises many significant points on how British Deejays gained acceptance on their own terms in a culture that was associated with, and dominated by, Jamaican originators or their pirate counterparts. Therefore, it is quite useful to consider that Champion's explanation of his 'difference' (regarding his style and delivery), as well as the actual content of his lyrics, was based on the fact that his exposure to Yard-tapes was limited. This meant that he created his lyrics both spontaneously, 'I had some rhymes that I made up pon spot, you know more humorous dan anything else', and more deliberately as witnessed during the clash by which time he states 'I had started to build proper lyrics even though me never have nuh name'. However what is also interesting is the 'silence' Champion suggests he was greeted with during the early stages of the clash, 'di man them did quiet at first'. Two pivotal moments to place there; firstly his breaking up of this 'silence' by stating to the 'crowd ah people' that his intention was to 'show you wah gwaan in ah London', and, secondly whilst doing so 'running' the pirate 'out' of lyrics. This 'silence' sums up the collective experience of many British Deejays, who were initially greeted with this reaction, because what was being expressed differed from the pirated performances that dominated the early Reggae-dancehall scene. Much of this kind of resistance was based upon not only the differences in lyrical content, but also the stark contrast, in many instances, between the 'British style' and the 'Yard-style'.

Within the culture the concept of 'style' encompasses all aspects of Deejaying, including, language, delivery, vocal dexterity, rapport, lyrical content, and the Deejay's accent, which is often the most distinguishing factor when comparing the two 'styles'. Therefore, the 'silence' triggered by an exposure to a novel form of lyricism that differed from the Yard-style, was resisted because it sounded 'different' and also featured the type of narrative that spoke of a uniquely blak experience. For if you are to truly express your innermost feelings, then, surely you firstly need to acquire your own voice, which speaks of your social/ cultural/political reality and presents an alternative worldview. Additionally, because the scene was dominated by Jamaican Deejays, during this seminal moment, many commentators were unaware of this emergent British voice, which explains why it remained 'hidden' from their gaze. The fact that your voice was initially greeted with silence was an obstacle that had to be overcome by the Deejays who were adamant that they had something of equal value to contribute, within the Reggae-dancehall arena. For instance, Asher Senator (1999) spoke of the same 'silent' experience in 1981 when he, along with his 'sparring partner' Smiley Culture, performed on a local Set called Bucanon in the Wandsworth area:

> Me and Culture were in the dance and nuff Deejays were just chatting Yard-style when we took the mic an started chatting our own ting. First is like them never know weh fi do, you wouldah thought that we came from another planet when all we was chatting was south (London) stuff. Anyway after we 'juggled' and did a couple of Combi's people came round the Set and started to beat down the place. It's funny but Jah know that was the first time I felt, yeh man you can do this ting. (Personal Communication, 1999)

Interestingly, Asher suggests that it was the positive reaction of the crowd that convinced him that he had something of value to offer by chatting 'different' from the pirates and imitators. Thus, like Champion, he was not deterred by the initial 'silence'; the skill and ability to deliver their own brand of lyricism, led to them establishing themselves as conscious originators who were not expected to chat the Yard-style. The point I am making is that an appreciation of how the lyrics were

186

actually produced and the rationale behind their creation, sheds light on the Deejay presence in Britain as something more than just blatant piracy. This needs to be fully understood; we partook in the tradition of a form that was dominated by Jamaican performers who became the yardstick by which our contributions were measured. This situation changed when many British Deejays decided to recreate their own experiences in a more representative voice, drawing on the known social world in a language that described life as a black youth in Britain. Champion stresses the need for this type of appreciation, in any endeavour to know 'our' reality, when suggesting that his first experience of Deejaying 'was more like when you ah reason an mek two joke', which in his own words was 'no big deal'. It is this almost nonchalant attitude towards Deejaying that is critical to the naturalness of the culture because:

> In this respect an improvised performance is not unlike a conversation—which is also...an improvised art. Both musical performances and conversations are occasions for exploration, affirmation and celebration of identity and of relationships, and both depend on the existence of a commonly agreed language. (Small, 1987:339)

Champion took a 'natural' aspect of the 'commonly agreed language' of self-conceptualisation, based upon everyday livity, which includes reasoning and cracking jokes, and then transferred these sensibilities to his Deejay performance. Benji is of the same opinion that the lyrics are almost 'naturally' inspired:

> I talk what I see and mek it funny. Really, I think I'm an educated man who puts lyrics together in a certain context, I don't want to chat eenie meenie minie mo, or flash it in ah A, flash it in ah B and all that bollocks. I didn't want to chat like that, I wanted to use the gift to uplift and chat good constructive lyrics and that's why I wrote Originality, learn to study, bwoy. Because nuff bwoy need ah lesson in writing sensible lyrics based on what you know and experience and a few of them who are chatting now need to listen to what we were sayings years ago. You know what Lez, we were miles ahead then, lyrically, and probably still are now. (Personal Communication, 2000)

,

The reasoning behind 'good constructive lyrics', coupled with the role of the divine in the creation process cannot be undervalued as every Reggae-dancehall performer I have ever reasoned with cites this omnipresence in some way, shape or form, as the provider of the 'gift' to 'chat-mic' in the first place. That means that the art of Deejaying operates on various levels and always has done which is why Benji can compare what he used to chat with what is being chatted now. I agree with him when he states that we were 'years ahead'; as many do still only 'chat bollocks'. Deejaying on a conscious level means there has to be a coming together of the natural ability to chat and the social awareness that is required to be an originator. For instance, Macka B (2000) argues that his ability to Deejay is 'natural' because for him:

> It's a God given ting the talent to be able to talk and rhyme and people find it entertaining. And as a Rastaman I an I cannot abuse that talent. I see so many problems in the world and sometimes you just feel helpless. But give thanks that we have the media where we can make it be heard by the people you nuh. That is the way I have to go forward. The preaching of righteousness is a must and Reggae music to me is a vehicle for that preaching. (Personal Communication, 2000)

The British Deejays would, like their Jamaican counterparts, suggest that their ability comes from the divine, quite often singing popularised church songs in the Reggae-dancehalls. This is not too surprising when we consider the major role that white Christianity played in the suppression of our Afrikan worldviews, languages, cosmologies etc., as part of the African's socialisation and indoctrination into Europe's New World. Consequently, this in turn sanctioned and justified our role as the African inferior/godless/heathen/other, to the European superior/godlike/Christian/self, during the chattel slave era and beyond. This is an affliction that explains why many Jamaican and British performers would claim, in much the same fashion as the Lone Ranger did above, that 'me born as a natural Deejay' because:

> More time me get ah gift from the almighty one, fi trod through the land as a true Christian, me tour Miami, USA an Japan, me tour China, Canada an England, with me bag over me shoulder me clutch it in me hand, me walk with the rod of correction...(Papa San, 1983)

The assumption is that to Deejay is effortless for those who are 'naturals', the divinely 'inspired', because you transfer your 'interior knowledges', social realism and witticism from the 'road' to the Reggae-dancehall arena. This is achieved as you 'trod through the land' using the 'gift from the almighty one', which is in this case the metaphoric 'rod of correction' that enables the Deejay to preach a 'social gospel', grounded in a lived experience. It is interesting to note that this lyric was chatted by Papa San 14 years before he fully embraced Christianity, further compounding why the slackness/culture dichotomy does not make sense in any analysis of the culture. In the past Papa San would chat the worst and most explicit forms of slackness, but he never distanced himself from the divine. Another factor that lends credibility to this claim for the recognition of the divine, in whatever shape or form, as the provider of this 'gift', is that unlike 'orthodox' types of musicianship, there is no 'formal' learning involved in Deejaying. According to Papa San's view the dancehall becomes the 'Deejay school', which is why many up and coming Deejays are called 'prento', which literally means apprentice. Furthermore that this is the key stage in the Deejay's development is given currency by the fact that within the wider black community, people who have the 'gift of the gab', highly proficient orators, are said to have 'lyrics'. Therefore the cultural sensibilities that allow the community to recognise a person who has 'lyrics' are similarly used to determine the merit of the Deejay that is performing in the dancehall. However, whereas in ordinary interactions with other community members your reputation as a person who has 'lyrics' is often restricted to the local, when you present yourself as a 'Deejay' within the arena of the Reggae-dancehall you often become outernationally known. If you were engaged in a conversation with a member of your local community, being born in Britain would allow you to utilise certain patterns of acceptable speech to enable a meaningful conversation to occur. The same happens whilst Deejaying as using known words, sounds and gestures (the 'illocutionary' act), ensures that a meaningful exchange takes place between audience and performer. Thus the language we used in Britain, Patwa, was more than just Jamaican language it was 'the language of the black experience' in Britain and contained a myriad of words and phrases from this pool of blak cultural knowledge.

I am arguing that this logic is employed when constructing lyrics, for as a British Deejay you realise that you do not rely on one pattern of recognised speech for mass communication. In fact, the very nature of the culture as an outernational entity, which links various Afrikan 'oral traditions' with Europe's 'New World' polyglot cultures, excludes this notion in the first place. Therefore our utilisation of other types of speech/language, especially the Island talk from the Caribbean and British regional dialects like 'cockney' or 'Brummie', are our ultimate marker of difference from the Jamaican style of Deejaying or American East Coast, rap. This is the reason why, especially in the context of urban London, there was a proliferation of Cockney phraseology in both the Deejay's written accounts, as well as during those moments of spontaneity. Recognising this key component part of British Deejay lyricism is crucial to this discussion, because many theorists have regarded this feature as a kind of novelty when, in fact, and as will be argued below, it is for many of us a 'natural' part of everyday 'black' speech.

6.2 Re-writing reality: 'that's real, that's us'

Ah just de truth what, ah just culture me chat. Me born in ah England under the Union Jack. (Trevor Natch 1985).

Papa Levi: Bwoy Lezlee, you sound like ah hinglish bwoy when you chat. (Saxon, 1983)

Lezlee Lyrix: You ah call me hinglish bwoy. Me nah try fi chat like nuh Yardy, I was born in London, you idiot. (Ghettotone, 1983)

The second extract was taken from the aforementioned clash that I had with Papa Levi in 1983 and curiously Levi attempts to ridicule me by suggesting that I sound too English (hinglish), which is interesting because, like myself, he was born and raised in south-east London. The point here is that this snippet of a much larger exchange demonstrates what was at stake when the British Deejays made their claim for recognition of a style that was uniquely their own. They were under pressure to sound more 'like ah Yardy' from even some of their own British-born Deejay peers. As a consequence of this pressure many

Deejays were even more determined to accentuate (literally) the differences between them and their Jamaican counterparts, stylistically and lyrically, by stressing that which made them so noticeably different. For example many Deejays, in much the same way as Trevor Natch in the opening extract, were openly expressing that Britain was the land of their birth, 'me born in ah England under the Union Jack'. Similarly whilst reasoning with Reds (1999) about what it takes to build 'proper lyrics' he stresses:

> I always made sure that my lyrics reflected London themes, so that anyone who lived in London would instantly appreciate what I was dropping was original, whether it was what I said or just the way I said it. Like in one lyric I talked about driving me jam-jar fi goh check me spar, down the frog an toad before the dance overload. (Personal Communication, 1999)

When I asked Reds why he felt it was necessary to merge the cockney rhyming slang, 'jam-jar' (car), 'frog an toad' (road), with Jamaican terms like 'spar' (sparring partner/friend) he simply stated:

> Because that's real, that's us, we don't just chat one way we chat all kindah style all the time, so that's how I write, the way I talk about how we live in London. Most of the youth them here have never been Yard and in fact nuff of them parents don't even come from yard like Smiley (Culture) comes from Barbados. So it used to make me laugh when people thought we couldn't write lyrics cos they were looking at it from the wrong angle. Would you expect a Yardy to sound or write like Peterkin? So why should I sound, or even try to sound like one of them, it's ridiculous. (Personal Communication, 1999)

Reds raises many crucial points, none more so than when he inquires whether you would expect a Jamaican Deejay to 'sound or write like' one of his British counterparts, Peterkin, whose 'fast style' (rapid rapping) was to take Jamaica by storm in 1983. This sums up the dilemma that was faced by many British Deejays of this era, because many still viewed the 'authentic' performance as the Yard-style. That is why it is interesting when Reds argues that 'people were looking at it from the wrong angle', which is the suggestion I made in my above exchange with Papa Levi. Furthermore, those who were viewing our

191

performances through this particular lens failed to consider the levels of dialogue that took place between Jamaica and Britain as a consequence of the system of taped exchanges. The most obvious example was the speed with which Peterkin's 'fast style' was copied, firstly in Britain in 1982 and then across the 'black Atlantic' in 1983 where it was being performed in Jamaica as well as in the USA. For instance various New York based Sound Systems, including the most popular at the time—'Third World'—featured performers like Colonel Desi, Shelly Thunder, Santa Rankin, Shinehead, Papa Biggy and a host of others chatting the 'fast style' on their Session-tapes.

Yet although Peterkin's style was mimicked by several Deejays outernationally, when the Jamaican Deejays began to chat their own style of 'rapid rapping' it was, in many instances, recognisably different in delivery and style to that which we were exposed to. Moreover as the 'fast style' criss-crossed these musical highways, Papa San (whose delivery was even quicker than Peterkin's original pattern), was hailed as the best Jamaican exponent of the form. This was the point that Reds made about the differences between how we 'write and sound' as British Deejays when compared to our Jamaican counterparts. It must be stated that Peterkin's opening line was a well-known Jamaican bubbling style, which is why many like Bradley (2000) suggest that the 'fast style' was originated in Jamaica. Personally I have heard many rumours to this end, yet have never heard a single Yard-tape featuring a Deejay chatting quite the same way as Peterkin did. When he first chatted 'Me neat me sweet' in 1982, as it was known then, he was adamant that it was his invention and challenged anyone to produce a Yard-tape with any Deejay chatting like that. In my opinion the nearest to this style of rapid delivery prior to the 'fast style' that could even be considered, however remotely, is featured on a Stereophonic (1980) cassette with General Echo doing a rapid style called 'me baddah dan them' and Donovan doing something similar on the same Set.

Another even more remote possible influence, is featured on a Black Star (1980) cassette with Brigadier Jerry chatting 'the ten tongue style', which was in essence him chatting partially in what Jamaican's call 'Gypsy'. This is where you divide words by ingeniously introducing a key letter or a number of key letters sequentially to make syllables where there were none before, so for instance 'me' becomes 'me-pee', 'milli-pee', or milli-gee. I was told by my elder Jamaican-born siblings (who incidentally taught us 'Brits' how to speak this way) that 'Gypsy' was created by the chattel slaves in Jamaica to enable them to communicate in the slave master's presence, thereby excluding the master from what was being said. In fact many of the black youths I grew up with were familiar with this form of expression and we would often speak to each other in this way in front of white authority figures. Most notably in the presence of the police and schoolteachers, because, when uttered with rapidity, to the untrained ear it sounds like mindless babble, which is why they called it 'the ten tongue' style in Jamaica. Many Deejays followed Brigadier Jerry's lead outernationally and the Jamaican Deejay Welton Irie had a number one hit with 'Army life' in both Jamaica and the UK in 1982, where he used this style on the choruses of this particular tune.

However, let us consider the following extracts as I attempt to clarify Red's most salient point about the differences between the Yard and British fast-styles; where I place a comma in the extract is where the Deejay pauses for breath, which exemplifies the marked difference in their performances:

Ah through me neat me sweet, me know fi dweet, me wash ah me hands me wash ah feet, me brush ah me teet me comb ah me hair, eat me bulla widdah me pear, the good clothes ah weh me wear, me pants an shirt seh them nuh tear, me gaan clear everywhere, do you hear. (Peterkin Ghettotone, 1983)

Listen Papa San ah bubble up pon ah version, them ah wiggle them ah dance them ah crawl them ah laugh them ah crawl them ah eat them ah peep them ah jump them ah wine them ah wiggle them ah jook them ah peep them ah knock them ah stall an ah laugh them ah stall an ah fall them ah laugh an stall an ah bawl, the general ah warn them an teach them general ah warn them teach them gwaan, general ah trouble them teach them gwaan, easy. (Papa San, 1983)

There is a noticeable difference in timing that comes from Peterkin sustaining the flow of his lyric by regularly pausing, although at a much quicker pace than when Deejaying 'normally', whilst Papa San's style was more dynamic as it was snappier due to the fact that his lines, although much shorter, were delivered in an incessantly rapid burst with no pauses during the performance. In fact in the same session Papa San suggests that 'me have long brett (breath) me mussi drink

193

donkey water (a form of tonic)'. This was because he was renowned for sustaining the dynamism of his live performances by mind bogglingly Deejaying for extremely long periods, before pausing for breath, in the same way that he does in the above extract. For many British Deejays, myself included, Jamaican Deejays seemed to be far more relaxed on the rhythm track on the whole than we were. Their mode of lyricism, based on their usage of Jamaican language coupled with a remarkable sense of timing, meant that they blended with the rhythm in a style that was uniquely their own, as we also performed in our own way. For this reason Reds' notion of 'looking at it from the wrong angle' when assessing 'proper lyrics', provides a valid interpretive perspective on this genre of black British cultural production; that of a creative art that needs to be appreciated from within its own frames of reference. Furthermore it counters, as I suggested above in Chapter 3, the dominant view that these types of cultural form are primarily oral, largely spontaneous and in the context of the lyricism of the British Deejay, heavily indebted to American Rap music. I have argued above the British contribution to outernational Deejay culture needs to be fully appreciated, an appreciation that is not forthcoming in the following commentary, which rather peculiarly argues that:

> With the influence of **hip hop** and street culture came the 'fast-talking originators' such as **Smiley Culture** and **Tippa Irie**…Fast-talking had much in common with Jamaican **dancehall**, which relied less upon musicianship and more on studio trickery and the prominence of the MC. (Wood, 2002:262/3)

To suggest that this type of 'hip hop' influence on the creation of the 'fast style' has no basis whatsoever and is as preposterous as the further suggestion that 'studio trickery' is responsible for this style of Deejaying which, like 'Jamaican **dancehall**' seemingly lacks 'musicianship'. This point was tackled previously when I suggested that much of what occurs within the culture, defies orthodox ideas of what a 'musician' is. If this is not the case then how can one explain the examples from the 'fast-talking originators' just discussed, in the Jamaican and the British contexts, who performed 'live an direct' in the Reggae-dancehall on Sets and not in the recording studio? This is a crucial point when considering who is actually commenting on the form and where their knowledge comes from. It is usually the case that many of these commentators were not there and so speak from a position that borders on ignorance. However, this can be placed in its proper context by one whose involvement in all aspects of a culture, that was/is a coping and transcendental mechanism for the Afrikan downpressed, can provide accounts of a distinctly British Deejay style. In fact Dirty Desi, along with Papa Levi and many others, would often imitate American party style rap (accent included) as another aspect of their role as entertainers. This would generally occur when musical shifts in the Reggae-dancehall crossed to that side of the Atlantic and was more about adding humour to the proceedings rather than as a means of expressing serious social commentary. Thus you would often hear Deejays introduce and bubble along to Soul/Funky music with the ubiquitous, 'I'm the Deejay cat from around the block and I'm guaranteed to make you rock, like Superman, I don't give a damn and like Donald Duck, I don't give a fuck'. Furthermore, you would also find this type of imitation on many of the Yard-tapes that came to these shores during this moment, as Welton Irie and Johnny Ringo would perform these 'Yankee' (as the Jamaicans called them) styles on Gemini Disco and other top Jamaican Sound Systems. What made the British Deejays become known as originators was not dependent on forms like American rap, because over here, lyrically and stylistically, it never wielded that type of influence. According to one of Britain's most successful American style rappers, Einstein, who began his mic career as a Reggae Deejay called Cocksman:

It was around 1984/5 the youths started to really copy American rappers and out of this came Derek B, Mello, MC Duke and London Posse. That's when I switched my style from ragga to rap style and changed my name as I liked the vibes of the hip-hop scene. (Personal Communication, 1998)

Einstein's perspective mirrors my own recollection of these events and the fact that I have met, reasoned, and performed with many of the top British rappers and have yet to hear anything to the contrary. Add to this the fact that by 1984/5 British Deejaying was fully established, and it serves as proof enough about the extent of the supposed African-American influence. I am arguing that what the British Deejays were doing was not that spectacular from our perspective when considering the actual form the lyrics took. You were in effect writing in the

WHAT THE DEEJAY SAID

language in which you 'think', then performing these 'thoughts' in the Reggae-dancehall on the riddim track, live an direct. Consequently, it was our performances that ensured we would be regarded as originators in our own right, primarily because our style and delivery was spectacularly different from the Yard-style. Therefore by appreciating how originality is determined from within the culture as a form of grounded intellectuality, we gain an insight into why the 'hidden voice' was so potent and popular amongst black youth in Britain. This claim makes for a more realistic discussion about the way we used 'black talk' as it is not restricted to over-intellectualised notions of so-called 'black language' use, cultural hybridity, syncretism, or 'code switching', none of which can explain why we chose to Deejay in this way in the first place.

Many write and perform in a style that is nearer to 'hinglish', for once you were regarded as 'original', people would expect to hear 'proper lyrics'. Therefore uppermost in the mind of these Deejays was the lyrical content and rhythmic delivery. I would further argue that 'black language' use, in the British context, is more about themes and content than how Jamaican you sound, which is why there is no set lexical/grammatical formula employed during the writing/creation process from the Deejay's standpoint. For this reason many of the lyrical extracts within this study contain what appear to be inconsistencies with regard to the spelling of certain words, when in fact they are the subject of the myriad forms Patwa takes when written. For instance, many of the lyrics featured here were written by the Deejays themselves, especially in the case of Papa Benji who sent many of his compositions to me via email, which means I have transcribed them in the exact fashion that they were written and have noticed these inconsistencies. This too, is the case with Macka B who generally has a transcript of the lyrics on his albums, in which these inconsistencies are also seen. Hence words are spelt according to how you understand their sound and feel along the lines of how you express yourself lyrically to an audience of your peers, which obviously includes other Deejays. The point I am making is best demonstrated in the following extract by a Deejay called Daddy Dego who chatted as near to 'hinglish' as any other Deejay I have heard or performed with. Yet because of how originality was determined in the British context, Daddy Dego was regarded as one of the best Deejays in London during the 1980s. It must also be noted that the theme of the lyric is directly related to a personal experience of racism, which echoes the sentiments I expressed in the first **re-memories** featured in chapter 4, as Dego states:

> Calypso Calypso dread, me seh Calypso Calypso boom, me seh Calypso Calypso right, me seh fi listen to Dego, seh me on my way me gone a Plumstead, me walk down the road man me sight two skinhead, ah smoke one spliff both of them look red, seh when me tek a stock me haffi bow me head, if me never bow me head Jah know me wouldah dead, them swing after me with one long piece of lead, them try out me but me out them instead, next ting I man know them in ah hospital bed, the doctor tell me them appear underfed, dread, you can gwaan like you heavy boom, you can gwaan like you ah natch, hear me Desi, but if you chuck it pon Daddy Ghettotone then you get brainwash, Rasta till you, me she Calypso Calypso. (Ghettotone 1983)

Dego begins his performance with 'Calypso Calypso', which is his acknowledgement of the version of the 'Answer' rhythm that started with a steel band drum roll. In fact, chatting in a recognisably Calypsonian style (using a stylised Eastern Caribbean accent) was popular and many Jamaican Deejays were travelling to the Eastern Caribbean to perform during the early 1980s. Many of the popular Jamaican Deejays such as Peter Metro, Josie Wales, Charlie Chaplin, Nicodemus and Johnny Ringo, were featured on various Yard-tapes chatting the 'Calypso Calypso' style and I myself had one such style as well. This is another factor of which "foreign enthusiasts" and other commentators were unaware and thus Calypso's profound influence on many Reggae rhythm tracks, lyrical content and Deejay performances, has seldom been acknowledged. Testimony to this profound influence is Dego's usage of the 'Calypso Calypso' to present a tale about an experience he had in what was then, and still is now, one of the most overtly racist parts of south-east London. This highlights a significant part of our local history because as a teenager one of the few places we could hear Reggae music, in the early 1970s, was in a Church hall that was in the centre of Plumstead. As a consequence of its location every Wednesday night we were forced to 'run the gauntlet' under attack from 'skinheads', 'greasers' and the like, as we endeavoured to return home safely. That is why Dego's choice of this area in his account was so relevant because Plumstead was/is synonymous with racist attacks and racial abuse. Consequently the spate of racist attacks and murders that have occurred in places like Plumstead and its neighbouring areas—Thamesmead and Eltham—have come as no surprise to those who are familiar with this history of racist Britain. That is why Dego's lyric is critical to this account of the black British experience. It spoke of a lived reality from a blak perspective, known to all who were aware of the danger these 'white man areas' represented to the black community. More significantly the fact that in his story he comes out on top, 'them try out me, but me out them instead', adds to the drama of his performance as a necessary aspect of that cathartic moment that allows the audience to purge themselves of the harshness of this (racist) reality. Symbolically 'ducking' the 'long piece of lead', as conjured up in Dego's manipulation of words and sounds, perfectly captures the effects of the originator's rhymes in that mind space that allows you to momentarily share the reality. Partaking in the antiphonic exchange between the Deejay and the audience, during this type of performance, meant that all concerned shared in this triumph over a most recognisable enemy, the skinhead.

> Of course we felt good when a Deejay chatted about dusting our enemies especially the fronters. Those were the things we would reason about and sometimes that's where the Deejays' got their inspiration from. I remember chatting to my bredrin who used to chat mic about nuff tings and the next thing I'd hear it on the Set. I remember it used to make me feel good cos in some ways that was me out there, my thoughts an ting. But you know what, thinking about it, if we didn't have that where would we express ourselves? I don't remember the media dealing with the issues from our perspective, an remember them time deh we never had Freedom (Pirate) Stations like now so of course we would support the youts who chatted how we felt. To me it was a natural thing to do. Give inspiration and be inspired to do something positive for yourself. (Derek, Personal Communication 1999)

Derek states, it is the content, theme and delivery of the Deejay's account that are of critical importance because when the crowd ah people are exposed to a 'proper lyric', it is as if they become one with the Deejay who gives voice to their innermost concerns. This is why the notion of antiphony alone cannot truly do justice to what occurs during a Deejay performance; it is more than just a mere call and response from a leading party to an audience and is perfectly captured in Derek's reasoning. For any separation between the performer and the audience is an artificial one, which is evidenced in the notion of to 'give inspiration and be inspired' in a positive fashion. In fact in Dego's case there is a sharing of a tale of an ongoing situation, which addresses the realities of racism that many of those in attendance have either experienced first hand or personally know someone who has. Presenting this type of account, based upon everyday experiences, is what made certain Deejays stand apart as originators; what they were documenting was the ongoing black British experience in a language that was familiar to those who shared this worldview. Moreover, these experiences were seldom articulated as graphically or realistically in the mainstream media because many social commentators had negative preconceptions about black youth in Britain. This in turn meant that they would neither be aware of the vocabulary nor the space within which these grounded intellectuals articulated their oppression in accordance with the vibes and strength they drew from their community. That is why Cashmore and Troyna (1982) displayed the extent of their ignorance when stating that 'we choose to see insecurely rooted black youths'...from 'inner-city areas' as 'educated on words which they find irrelevant – and do not know how to spell anyway'. They obviously overlooked the cultural mechanisms that are intrinsic to the body of a language that, when used strategically, enables you to resist your downpressor in cognitive ways they could not begin to imagine. Therefore, it is obvious that what it means to be 'educated' (and thus be in a position to make statements that are 'relevant' in 'words' that mirror a distinct and counter-perspective), is dismissed because 'the western rationalist approach to reality can function on a comprehensible or logical dimension only by means of invented antithesis: it is caught in its own line of sight' (Finkenstaedt, 1994:322)

Whatever rationale, 'logical dimension', led them to 'choose to see black youth' in such an unfavourable light, meant that these theorists failed to comprehend how language provides a culturally fortified space that reaffirms a more positive sense of self, through the power to name and define your own reality. According to Small, black cultural sensibilities as outernationally expressed within the language of performance, create a 'psychological living space' (1987: 35), within which, as Jesse Jackson constantly reminds us, a person of Afrikan descent can recognise that 'I am somebody'. Comprehending the notion of what it means to be 'simmody' is, in Jamaican language, one of the ways to convey your utmost respect to another human being. To say that 'you favour simmody pickney' best demonstrates the profundity of what is at stake in this analysis of the practical usage of language, for the Jamaican is not just suggesting that you look exceptionally well, the suggestion is also that you belong to, and come from, a proud set of parents/folk/people. By merely suggesting that you look like (favour) somebody's child is self-empowering as it reaffirms your 'somebodiness' from within your own cultural frame of reference. The word triggers a concept that gives meaning, value and autonomy, to the black community in general. That is why the Deejay draws inspiration from the knowledge in the black community and by so doing resists the kind of 'invented antithesis' that relegates blacks to a set of pejorative terms that purposely undermine our very existence. This type of resistance is based upon a conscious choice in the discursive spaces that are the Reggae-dancehalls, where language is used as part of an ongoing process of knowledge exchange and equips black people with the tools to cope with our 'structural placement' in a white racist society. Thus when performing in an uplifting fashion the Deejay's account actually draws upon and increases, during that moment, the 'some' (amount) of a 'bodies' (the black community's) cultural knowledge, because the struggle for the reaffirmation of a more positive racial/cultural/social/political self is ongoing.

The Deejay can actually shift aspects of their performance to accommodate the vibes they are receiving from the audience, so someone may shout out something which then becomes seamlessly incorporated into the live performance as witnessed in Desi's burial of Asher (in the previous chapter). Similarly, Dego informed me that the last few lines of the lyric were improvised in reaction to the response of the audience, a factor that is evident when we consider that the narrative shifts from Daddy Dego as an individual, to Daddy Ghettotone as representative of the collective. To this end in closing the performance he states, 'you (in this instance the skinheads) can gwaan like you heavy (act hard), you can gwaan like you a natch, Desi (this is acknowledging the presence of his sparring partner), but if you chuck-it pon Daddy Ghettotone (symbolising the black presence) you will get brain wash, Rasta know'. Deconstructing the lyric in this fashion, we can observe how cleverly Dego manipulates both white and black cultural sensibilities, by virtue of his intelligent usage of language as a 'hinglish' lyrics originator. A usage exemplified in his description of the behaviour of the two skinheads who 'started' on him in the first place, as them 'ah smoke one spliff' (a clever inversion of a supposed black habit) and 'chucked badness', when it was generally suggested that only 'black youth' had this 'penchant for violence'. Hence, the fact that Dego vanquishes one of our most recognisable enemies, 'the skinheads', elicits the greatest response from the crowd who had already 'kicked-up' before he got the chance to ask them whether they shared his reality, 'if you know it ah the truth ball forward'. In this way he reaffirmed that sense of being that is experienced within the Reggae-dancehall when you truly know that you 'belong'. For the fact that beyond this autonomous 'cultural space' lies your enemy (the skinhead et al) is offset by the safety you feel amongst your 'own' and is therefore of no consequence during these ephemeral moments, because in here, right now, you truly are 'simmody pickney'.

Exchanges such as those between the Deejay and the audience, illustrate why the Deejay who was born in Britain would opt to use this linguistic form as a truer representation of an autonomous blak self. The point is I have often experienced a performance where the Deejay's ability to locate me within the narrative, through their particular skills as wordsmiths, actually had me considering whether the thoughts were theirs or my own. This is the point I was making about reaffirming the 'somebodiness' of black people because the experience is something that is easily comprehended and aesthetically pleasing to those who share the Deejay's worldview. Furthermore it is the theme/content and style of delivery that are crucial to whether or not that which is being presented will be accepted as a valid source of original knowledge. In other words, the Deejay needs to be aware of what is going on in the black community so that when they present certain reasonings they can touch a raw nerve and elicit the greatest response. During a session which featured Diamonds and Saxon (1985), the Diamonds Deejay Cinderella uttered the following as part of her performance:

> Listen, I'm ah supe, Jahman I'm no prostitute, cos I'm ah supe
> Jahman I'm no prostitute, ah pure Diamonds leaflet that I distribute,
> cau pon Diamonds set I make all my loot, so when me come in ah

the dance you better bow an salute, cau from me born until now me still remain cute, cos I'm an MC, I'm ah lady, I'm no prostitute, hitch it, hitch it, pull it up. Just cool Miss Irie and the Saxon posse, cau ah Diamonds rule every raasclaat time. (Diamonds 1985)

Cinderella demonstrates how to elicit a favourable response from the crowd ah people, by merging both 'slack' and 'cultural' elements into her reality performance, by firstly outlining why she is not a 'prostitute', meaning that she is not a 'slack' person and is in fact a 'lady' and then conducting herself in a most un-'lady'-like fashion when she starts to cuss bad-wud. However, this literal take would be a far too simplistic reading of her performance because Cinderella's opting to swear at this point was a way of boosting Diamonds' Set, as well as her own credibility in the realms of entertainment. Hence it was an opportune moment to remind those in attendance that 'ah Diamonds rule every raasclaat time'. This is why 'chatting reality', whether it is deemed to be 'slackness' or 'culture', invariably 'moves the crowd', even if that movement is mental as opposed to physical. The performance brings to life a whole aesthetic world that is known within the culture. For this main reason I will now focus on the types of reasoning that allow the originator to be separated from other Deejays during the live performance.

6.3   Rhyming with reason! 'Proper lyrics'

While nuff of them ah right an rahbit, we write an arrange. (Trevor Natch, 1984)

I wrote 'Originality' because I thought people were just rhyming for no reason, in the e's and the o's and the shans and all that, I thought let me just read-up certain things and if you're gonna be original be conscious, it's like everyone was saying how they could write, that they're original but they wasn't chatting anything of any consequence. So I said let me do something that was really original, factual, put some facts in it to make people think a bit. (Papa Benji, personal Communication, 2000)

According to Benji's account he was fed up with listening to the Deejays that seemed to rhyme for no reason, yet would constantly state that they were 'conscious/intelligent' and 'original'; for him what they were 'chatting' had no substance. He composed 'Originality, learn fi study, bwoy' to separate himself from the purveyors of the 'ees the o's and the shans', which means that the final word of each line would end with the same sound. For instance, the lines will always end in 'man, van, can, ran', or 'snow, hoe, show, etc etc.', the very Deejays that Trevor Natch dismisses as those who can only 'right an rahbit', whilst 'we (true originators) write and arrange'. In other words he believed that they could only make 'sounds' without any substance, for this is just how 'right an rahbit' were used by Deejays, especially during the late 1970s to mid 1980s. Quite often these types of 'sounds' were central to the Deejay performance as was the grain and tone of the Deejay's voice (Henry 2003: 447/9) as they were employed to signal the beginning or ending of a performance. For many Reggae-dancehall tunes begin with other forms of instrumentation, but the Deejay performance usually coincides with the introduction of the bass drum. Thus when the Deejay is waiting for the rhythm proper to start, you often experience them mixing and blending sounds with words (scatting) as an intro, which is why I suggested in chapter 5 that Burru Banton's 'Boom wah this, wah that' was taken and used as one of the most popular Deejay introductions of all time. Therefore, Trevor's categorising of certain Deejays as only being able to 'right an rahbit' was a mark of total disrespect for their ability to rhyme with reason, in fact he relegated them to the realms of 'sounds' alone. Noticeably Trevor takes the highly popular 'right' out of 'right an rahbit' and transforms it into a marker of difference by employing the homophonic 'write' as a symbol of his originality. For those who 'right an rahbit' are unable, according to Trevor's rationale, to 'write an arrange', which means they lack the natural skill or ability that are necessary to the original Deejay. This reflects the logic behind Dirty Desi's previous comment on how these types of Deejay were perceived within the culture, for their main difference was an inability to 'to build lyrics on the same scale of meaning and relevance as the lyrical man them'. Within the culture it is generally understood that these Deejays would chat that which lacked a definite structure and thus the content of each line did not necessarily fit together with the previous one, for example:

Spoken intro: Tell them star, hear them style yah, originate by me only hear them style yah, alphabet style.

Deejaying: Seh a, seh b, seh c, seh d, seh anything me chat it ah goh end with e…chat it in ah a sometime in ah b, me chat it in ah c all kindah stylee…to you eh, me said ah this one dedicated to you, brah man box me gal an little gal you don't screw, me favourite drink that the one the Malibu, them have one quiz it name give us a clue, said anything me chat it ah goh end with o, you put the g together an that spell go, seh go seh Nico pon the go seh go, seh go seh go Nico pon the go, the killing of the man me seh the killing of the woman, the killing of the man, the killing of the woman all nation hav to bow, right yah now cos am ah yow I man ah yow, tell them ah, me flash it one…(Nico D, Ghettotone 1983)

This type of rhyming in the Deejay world is known as out and out 'bubbling' where the performer chats to create a vibe, generally as a prelude to a more lyrical performance by an 'intelligent' Deejay. Alternatively, it can also occur during the Studio One/Lovers Rock session where the beats are generally mellower and 'woman an man' can dance together in a less frenetic atmosphere than they would encounter during a Deejay session. As we can see the emphasis in this type of lyric is on 'bubbling' and the lines only make sense in isolation, for there is no noticeable link between each line and they could in fact be 'chatted' in any order. The performance of Nico D (who took this name from Nicodemus) fits comfortably into Benji's category of the Deejays who stated 'they could write, that they're original but they wasn't chatting anything of any consequence', as they were into 'e's and the o's and the shans and all that'. The main reason for this occurrence is that much of the lyrical content is spontaneous and known within the Reggae-dancehall as 'head-top-lyrics', or that which the Jamaican Deejay Ninja Man calls 'lyrics pon spot'. The lyrical content is often quite erratic in its construction and execution, which is why many times the 'bubbler' Deejay will 'fraffle' (stumble over their words) when chatting this type of style. However, it must be noted that many of the most popular Deejays (with regard to recorded releases) are, ironically, these 'head top' bubblers, as they rely on catchy forms of gimmickry and repetition, which people can just 'move' to without overly considering what is being suggested. Hence Capleton's (1999) warning that 'ah nuh boom boom boom an just dance, listen to the powerful words we ah chant', which makes known that sometimes we need to put more thought into what we listen to as Reggae-dancehall fans.

Many of the more accomplished Deejays, myself included, would chat 'head-top' lyrics depending on the vibes or if two or more Deejays decide to chat a 'combi' that was unrehearsed. Champion reasoned that many times he would chat 'head-top' styles and once he had listened to the recording of the session, if the lyric in question had potential, he would turn it into a proper style. Many Deejays have offered similar stories about perfecting their lyrics in this way but, as suggested, the 'bubbler' rarely composes anything of real substance as they generally just 'vibes-it'. This is clearly seen in Nico D's performance; the effectiveness of his contribution is in the 'bubbling' nature of his delivery, not the lyrical content. Therefore, this type of Deejay would not be expected to convey profound lyrical insights into the social world; this was not their main purpose and, according to Dirty Desi, 'on occasions when them mek them mouth miss', challenging a more lyrical Deejay, the crowd would expect them to get buried by a performer who would still rhyme with reason.

To gain a clearer insight into the originators' perspective, let us compare Nico D's lyrical extract with the following taken from an Asher Senator performance during the same Reggae-dancehall session and it is poignant that within the lyric he sounds out this type of Deejay. The main reason for this occurrence is that the intelligent/conscious/original Deejay makes it known, generally as frequently as possible, that what you are hearing is their 'style an pattern/fashion' and not pirated, which is why Asher declares:

So go Jah know now me gaan pon the O, me pass through rain an me pass through snow, but where fat lies I seh the ants will follow, an where the weather cold there is Eskimo, an Asher don't fire gun an me nuh fire crossbow, the only ting me fire is the lyrics in ah row, just once, not twice, fi me lyrics precise, cau nuff MC me ah show you sound nice, but what them a chat me wouldn't chat it to ah mice, me put mouse in ah trap, face-ti MC in ah vice, an tighten up the vice till them ball out Christ, but the Lord his name don't say it in vain, cau some MC like them don't hah nuh shame, going around chatting lyrics from ah next man brain, ah school them did deh them, them must get the cane, but me lyrics them mix fi me lyrics them nuh plain, me have more lyrics dan the count of rice grain, it's true, it's a fact, me lyrics caan stop, an right now Rasta you know seh them on an on like ah train pon ah track. (Ghettotone, 1983)

The most obvious difference between the two extracts centres on the issue of skilfully fitting words and sounds together to convey some type of message or coherent story, the very point Benji was addressing above, because the lyricism of the intelligent/conscious/ original Deejay transcends any idea of rhyming without reason. Unlike Nico D's extract, Asher's rhyme can only really make sense when recited in the order that it was designed to be delivered in, as demonstrated above. The emphasis is on continuity with regards to storyline and rhyming skills, as well as the manner in which the performer delivers the lyric in time to the rhythm track, which is then 'mix-down' by the Operator to add further emphasis to significant words or phrases. For all Deejays rhyme in some shape or form and generally bend words and sounds to maintain the continuity in tandem with the Operator's 'mix-down', a crucial aspect of the overall Deejay performance. In fact in many instances a good Operator is the difference between an effective and an ineffective Deejay performance, because a bad Operator who cannot 'mix-down' will 'mash-up' the vibes, which is why Deejays will always suggest 'oppah, mix me down but nuh bother mix me up'.

In light of the above all of the Deejays I have reasoned with suggested that they could openly display their skills as wordsmiths in the moments when they actually performed the products of their minds in public, which is ultimately the reason for spending their time privately constructing these accounts. This is why Asher states in the extract that he chats his lyrics, 'once, not twice, fi me lyrics precise', he makes clear that what you are experiencing is thoroughly thought through, with little or no margin for error. Furthermore, many less lyrical Deejays tend to repeat lines or whole verses as a means of 'filling up the track', whereas the 'originators' pride themselves in never having to repeat what has gone before; 'me nuh love chat one ting two time' (General Echo, 1983). This is unless of course they get a 'forward', which means they have the option of restarting the lyric from the beginning or changing the style/pattern completely, chatting something different on the same rhythm track. Also it is noticeable that Asher stresses, 'the only ting me fire is the lyrics in a row', an obvious distancing from the British Deejays who would unrealistically chat about firing guns like Magnums and M16's. Another crucial point for consideration is how Deejays play on terms that are recognisable within the culture and cleverly mould certain sentiments, lyrically, throughout the performance to get the principal point across. For example, when Asher states 'what them ah chat me wouldn't chat it to ah mice, me put mouse in ah trap, face-ti MC in ah vice' he uses the recognisable mark of disrespect within Jamaican culture which regards such a person as a 'mice' or 'mouse'. So Asher is forcibly stating that 'what them ah chat', their lyrics, he 'wouldn't' lower himself to 'chat' to those within the community who are accorded minimum amounts of respect if any at all, the 'mice'.

Asher's sentiments are indicative of the levels of seriousness encountered when discussing notions of originality/consciousness with many performers as they seek to distance themselves from their less lyrical counterparts. A point that Asher stresses when he states that such Deejays are pirates, because they 'don't have nuh shame, going around chatting lyrics from a next man brain' and should endeavour to come original. However, this attitude creates its own problems and in fact led to a series of conflicts between Benji and the two owners of Diamonds Set, whose perspective on entertainment differed from his own. This was because Benji (2000) was in his own words 'a fanatic' who was 'obsessed with Deejaying and writing fresh lyrics', as it allowed him to 'express' how he 'felt about things without compromise' and led to the following confession:

> We had a sound meeting and Big John and Percy (Diamonds) told me that um, the crowd weren't responding to my lyrics, because you chat too deep, and can't you, you know talk about girl lyrics an all that; make it a bit milder. I was like, fuck you man I talk what I see and mek it funny cos I ain't no gimmicks Deejay and to be quite honest that was the demise of our relationship. (Personal Communication, 2000)

Benji describes in his account how his idea of what it meant to Deejay on Diamonds conflicted with that of the Sound System owners, who were more interested in light-hearted gimmicky types of lyricism than profound social commentary. The major point of contention was the content of Benji's lyrics, which they thought were 'too deep' and making it difficult for the crowd to be entertained. Benji's idea of what constitutes a 'good lyric', which the 'crowd ah people' would appreciate, was not that which the Sound owners wished him to chat. Benji's reasoning is based on the fact that he considers himself to be 'intelligent' and therefore he 'constructively' talks about 'what he sees'; unlike the type of Deejay who, more or less, sing nursery rhymes as they disjointedly rhyme without reason. If we think back to the discussions in the previous chapters about the role of 'reasoning' in black culture, then we begin to realise why Benji places such emphasis on the fact that he is an 'intelligent' Deejay and is thus part of a community that is capable of profound social commentary. Of equal importance, as a consequence of this exchange with the owners of Diamonds, Benji wrote the following lyric entitled 'In Demand' in which he states:

Spoken intro: I Daddy Benji round the Mic MC, special request to each an everyone bout yah. Well Diamond, just happiness, right, Hey. Ah musical shackattack I do play on the track. 'Settle cau me an Benji in ah this, scene'. Yes Lezlee, the man call Trevor Natch, the man call Lezlee Lyrix.

Chorus: Becau, in demand Diamond in demand, yeh, in demand Diamond in demand gwaan, in demand Diamond in demand, lord in demand Diamond in demand.

Deejaying: Seh when me chat the mic me nah goh fool the public, me nuh care if you bright or you brain couldah tick, cau just like Mr Spock Benji have nuff logic, some-ah seh Benji too technical an them want me chat shit, but me nah belittle myself an chat idiotic, so hear them set ah lyrics weh me put pon plastic.

Chorus: Becau, in demand Diamond in demand, yeh, in demand Diamond in demand gwaan, in demand Diamond in demand, lord in demand Diamond in demand.

Deejaying: Me nuh like nuh criticiser or damn hypocrite, becau them caan chat the mic but them love turn critic, if you give them the mic to chat see how quick them reach the toilet, so all prento Deejay better button them lip, me don't respect nuh guy who only chat in private, cau when it comes to the dance nuff ah them start panic.

Chorus: Becau, in demand Diamond in demand, yeh, in demand Diamond in demand gwaan, in demand Diamond in demand, lord in demand Diamond in demand.

Deejaying: Me rule under Taurus not Capricorn, right now me nah chat deep right now me ah warm, when me chat pon the microphone Jah Jah know me perform, cau Diamond in ah Willows Club a kick up ah storm, before we arrive jahman the place did calm, man an woman come to the dance an them ah fold them arm, some get so bored Jahdahman them start yawn, when Diamonds start play man an woman start swarm, cau the Diamonds MCs fire lyrics like corn, an right about now becau we in demand, it name.

Chorus: Becau, in demand Diamond in demand, yeh, in demand Diamond in demand gwaan, in demand Diamond in demand, lord in demand Diamond in demand.

Deejaying: Me nuh chat no fantasy and no soft porn, cau if me chat slack I seh me might get scorn. Me seh pull it operator. (Diamonds, 1985)

It is noticeable how thoroughly Benji deals with his detractors throughout the entire lyric, by making the audience aware of the accusations that have been levelled against him from the outset by arguing, 'when me chat the mic me nah goh fool the public, me nuh care if you bright or you brain couldah thick, cau just like Mr Spock Benji have nuff logic'. Benji reasons that it is pointless for him to try and 'fool the public', intelligent or not, because as an intelligent man it is logical for him 'like Mr Spock' to use his 'gift to uplift'. That is why he forcibly states 'some-ah seh Benji too technical an them want me chat shit, but me nah belittle myself an chat idiotic, so hear them set-ah lyrics weh me put pon plastic'. The irony present in this aspect of the lyric sums up how a 'voice' which is 'hidden' has such power of critique in real life situations, because the nature of the culture allowed Benji to use the amplified platform provided by his critics, the owners of Diamond's Set, to chant them down. Not only does he effectively make his case but also to begin his performance by stating 'Well Diamond (Percy), just happiness', is a sure way of 'wrong-footing' your intended victim(s) as part of the burial ethic outlined above.

Benji, whilst offering his perspective on the role and purpose of the original Deejay, pointed out that he did not have to get too technical to deal with his critics, 'right now me nah chat deep right now me ah warm', which is the clearest way to state that you best know how not to 'fool the public'. He stresses that 'me nuh like nuh criticiser or damn hypocrite, becau them caan chat the mic but them love turn critic, if you give them the mic to chat see how quick them reach the toilet, so all prento Deejay better button them lip'. This aspect of the culture is often a serious point of discussion and occasionally leads to verbal or even physical conflict; many who reckon they can perform either as a Deejay or singer, often tend to do so during practice sessions or when the dance is empty which is either before or after a session. The fundamental point is that Benji did not believe that his critics acknowledged that it requires a level of skill, dedication, education and divine inspiration for original Deejays to continuously deliver at this level. Hence 'when me chat pon the microphone Jah Jah know me perform', which is his way of further distancing himself from those who fancy their chances on the mic, but do not have what it takes to back up their claims as performers of any note.

Anyone who is familiar with the culture knows that this type of backbiting is common amongst Sound System folk (in much the same way as this form of conflict permeates other realms of everyday life) because the Deejays, Operators and Selectors are in the limelight and those who are not in the limelight often cause the most disharmony in the group. However, when these 'criticisers' own the Set, it can create some serious conflict situations, which if nothing else detracts from the good works that can be achieved by maintaining a more harmonious working relationship in a group enterprise such as this. Therefore Benji states 'me don't respect nuh guy who only chat in private, cau when it comes to the dance nuff ah them start panic'. However, what is of even more significance is the fact that Benji uses the word 'guy' to totally disrespect his critics and other wannabee Deejays, because in Jamaican word culture, calling someone a 'guy' was the same as calling them a 'battyman'. Thus as in the case of Asher's usage of 'mouse', or Rastafari's notion of 'men', the Deejay draws on these 'self-generated concepts' to deal with what are largely internal conflicts in a 'commonly agreed language'.

The critical point is that this is how the culture operates most effectively as an alternative public arena where issues can be addressed in a conscious /intellectual fashion within a space that is 'hidden' from the wider public gaze. Moreover, because Benji recreates the scenario of the meeting and moulds the events into his narrative, his critics knew exactly how he felt about their comments. He effectively uses his participation as a Deejay, crucial to the Set's popularity, to remind them that 'when Diamonds start play man an woman start swarm, cau the Diamonds MCs fire lyrics like corn, an right about now becau we in demand'. The lyric aptly demonstrates that the ability to take a given situation and rhythmically render it, in such a skilful fashion, cannot be overstated. In fact, to bolster this argument, consider the following extract which effectively had myself, Desi B, Papa Benji and other members of Diamonds' Set openly discussing with Trevor Natch his reasoning on what it meant to be an originator born in Britain:

> Lord ah just de truth what, ah just culture me chat, ah just de truth what, ah just culture me chat, ah just de truth what, ah just culture me chat. Me born in ah England under the Union Jack, from me's a bwoy me start to wear me thinking cap, I can see out ah me eyes because it don't have cataract, from long time I see Iran fighting with Iraq, expensive weapon weh them use in ah combat, so people don't forget, so people don't forgot, if you love you country you is a true patriot, but if you don't love it you is a foolish twat, you come from Jamaica, Grenada or monster-rock (Montserrat), you could be a Japanese, you could be a Jap, remember you culture you must not swap, if you do that you we get brainwash, some man wouldah do anything just fi drive a chariot. (Diamonds, 1985)

Trevor Natch suggested that although he was 'born in ah England under the Union Jack, from me's a bwoy me start to wear me thinking cap', he knew that this was his 'Mother Country', and that the very symbolism tied up with the flag excluded him because 'there ain't no black in the Union Jack, so all you niggers, fuck off back' as the old ditty goes. For many blacks throughout the Diaspora, like Trevor Natch, this chant acts as a reminder of how we are/were perceived in the white imagination, because there is clearly no black presence in the Union Jack. Exposure to this type of chant, and the lived experience of racial assault that Dego described above, made many of the immigrants from the colonies soon realise that in the eyes of their white 'brothers and sisters', they were nothing more than the bastard children of a scornful 'Mother'. For this reason the lyric Trevor Natch decided to 'write an arrange' describes a known blak reality based on knowledge that came from the community to which he belongs, means his lyrics constitute a truer reflection of a black youth's grass-roots perspective. However, I must make a confession, which will also act as an insight into why this perspective is relevant to my entire discussion, especially the notion of lyrics as sources of 'interior knowledge'.

I, along with many other performers, believed that Trevor Natch was born in Jamaica and had recently arrived on these shores, because the way he spoke, his cultural sensibilities and his mannerisms were more akin to a Yardy's than a 'typical' black youth born in Britain. When I expressed my surprise to Trevor Natch about his being 'born in ah England under the union Jack' (I never heard him speak 'Standard English' or cockney), he informed me that he went to live in Jamaica when he was young and spent most of his teenage years there. What I find of utmost significance is his revealing that it was his choice not to speak 'like ah white man', he saw himself as different from them, which for him was encapsulated in his stating that you must 'remember you culture you must not swap, if you do that then you get brainwash'. The suggestion being that for him as a blak youth his culture was Jamaican, in much the same way as a Japanese person born in England would still be regarded, rightly or wrongly, as a 'Jap'.

Cultural imperialism could be resisted by remembering your own 'culture', whilst being aware that there are many blacks who would sell you out for material gain, 'some man wouldah do anything just fi drive a chariot (car)'. That is why he argued that he always has to use his 'thinking cap' when dealing with white culture, because the best way to deal with the downpressor was to demonstrate, through your own usage of language, your blak awareness. It is this very point Asante was stressing when he suggested that the black intellectual must realise that, 'there can be no freedom until there is a freedom of the mind' (1995: 31), which according to Trevor Natch means resisting the 'brainwashing' tactics of your perceived cultural/racial enemy thereby using your 'thinking cap' to navigate your way through the social world.

Trevor Natch argues that by wearing your 'thinking cap' and challenging the assumptions that you believe do not reflect your reality; your perceptions of the world within, and through, language will change. The point is that the history of black cultural struggles for justice in the face of racial domination, demonstrates from the outset the necessity to reclaim the power to define your own 'reality' through a particular usage of language. The Deejay can, in this way, deal with a range of issues that span the breadth of everyday livity, because the language of conscious choice enables you to mould your critique and rhyme with reason, according to any given situation in a fashion that will be overstood by your peers.

Conclusion

Throughout this chapter I have presented an evaluation of the thought processes behind the messages, contained within Reggae-dancehalls, to highlight how certain black youth chose to intellectually challenge a dominant culture. I focused on the need for these youths to establish, often as the direct countering of a specific type of 'silence', their own 'voice' based upon 'what them see and know' as a more representative blak reality. This meant that I presented an argument as to why these accounts are regarded within the Reggae-dancehall as original/conscious/intelligent, in this my endeavour to substantiate how 'proper lyrics' are ultimately received as valid sources of knowledge. Consequently, the notion of what constitutes a 'proper lyric' is arguably a value judgement that is premised on a known aspect of the 'moral culture', that is an integral part of the Reggae-dancehall scene. The 'moral culture' of which I speak is premised on reasoning through various encounters with a dominant culture and then, in the form of the Deejay's account, voicing said reasonings as an alternative form of blak cultural politics. This is because by openly discussing the positive/negative aspects of these types of racialized encounter, in a language that you are seen to control, participants determine workable and practical solutions to what are indeed problems that affect the black community as a whole. For this reason to Deejay in this manner acknowledges the role the Divine plays as the provider of all things in the world as we know it, including the inspiration to chant down Babylon on the mic. A 'truths and rights'-driven factor that is a central feature of the 'moral culture' of the wider black community, therefore using the 'gift to uplift' is to carry out 'Jah works'.

The suggestion is that although the preferred language of expression was Patwa, the concerns it gave voice to were specifically dealing with the realities of urban life in Post War-Britain, especially when challenging our non-status as Britain's unwanted 'citizens'. Those who could not access the culture were in no position to accurately represent the mindset of black youth during this moment because the chosen language of expression, Patwa, was alien to them. Therefore its usage, according to many of these theorists, was symptomatic of a form of social self-exclusion that confirmed all of the negativity associated with the black youth presence. The fact that what was actually occurring in many cases countered their restricted theorisations, especially reasonings like 'head-decay-shun', did not figure in their reckoning. That is why Macka B's previous statement has such validity 'cau sometimes we gotta do what we gotta do no matter bout the consequences'; it exemplifies the counter-thought that consciously challenges certain racist preconceptions.

Thus the blak youth who were performing in the Reggae-dancehalls during this moment were far from uneducated and did in fact display levels of social/cultural and political awareness that are yet to be fully appreciated. Moreover, Deejays who use the culture in this fashion are regarded as 'original' because they naturally distance themselves from those who 'chat bollocks' or that 'Fantasy Island shit' which says nothing about the black British experience. This was the point Trevor Natch made when emphasising the difference between the Deejays who 'right an rahbit' and those who 'write an arrange', because making 'sounds' alone will not counter the racist, hegemonic force that seeks to destroy the Afrikan . For as will be evidenced in the final chapter, this notion of difference was to become even more significant as the originators of the 'critique from the street' began to be noticed in the wider public arena, which led to a series of conflicts with many who sought to control this 'hidden voice' that was, in essence, there to 'bun dem out'.

Chapter 7

'To who respect is due, respect it must goh through'!

Introduction

My thoughts on Outrage's involvement in banning Jamaican performers and interfering in the affairs of the black community? For me it's about controlling and censoring our most potent voice because generall4y where we air and discuss things is through music or performance, because everything else is white-dominated and white-controlled. (Henry, cited in Gabriel, 2005)

Old pirates yes they rob I, yes they thief a-way my lyrics, run gaan ah studio, an put them pon plastic (Asher Senator, Saxon 1983)

In this final chapter, I will focus on a shift in Deejay consciousness that led many to aspire to a level of professionalism, which was a consequence of the increasing visibility of a form that was now deemed by many in the music business to be commercially viable. Therefore the form, in some respects, became known beyond the boundaries of the Reggae-dancehall. Consequently the notion of Deejaying took on a new dimension when the performers recognised the potential to earn a living out of what was for many a natural mode of expression. Asher Senator uses the melody from Bob Marley's 'Redemption Songs' to cleverly deal with an aspect of piracy that had serious ramifications for the original Deejay. The main bone of contention was that those Deejays, who had access to recording studios/record companies, could pirate another Deejay's style, 'run gaan ah studio, put them pon plastic', and earn from the products of another's mind. Of even more importance many white people who owned record companies, saw the potential to exploit British Deejays, which meant they began to control

215

what was being said in the wider public arena. This also brought in the age of white control and censorship over an identifiably black cultural form, that has manifested in the racist tactics used by the white gay organisation 'Outrage', to ban many Jamaican Deejays from performing in contemporary British society.

I will therefore begin the discussion with a sample of the lyrics that described the shift in the Deejay's own awareness of how their role as 'entertainer' took on another dimension, as they became more professional. This meant that instead of just affiliating yourself with a Sound System (generally a local one), Deejays began to take seriously the level of professionalism that was now becoming part and parcel of this expressive culture that, unlike orthodox musicianship, has no recognised learning process. Therefore, it is how professionalism is viewed from within the culture that is of interest here due to the noticeable increase in the number of original lyrics one would hear that extolled the virtues of taking the business seriously. The idea of being more professional and serious about the business was taken to its extreme by Papa Levi in a lyric entitled 'Ram Jam Capitalism', which dealt with the theme of piracy from another perspective. Levi's account represents one of the most controversial tracks ever recorded by a British Deejay, questioning the rights and wrongs of white involvement in the culture. Questioning, was not just restricted to white involvement per se and often led to rivalry and open conflict between entertainers, producers, and radio disc jockeys, because, with the interest shown by British record labels, there was now more money to be made in the business. Many of the conscious Deejays expected payment for their 'works', whilst maintaining their blak orientation, which as will be shown in many cases led to a clash of social, cultural, political and racial values.

7.1   I'm not ah amateur, I man ah Pro

All professional musicians need money, and those who pay them have their own reasons for doing so. (Small, 1987:180)

Professional, I am professional, yeh, professional, I am professional, the hottest ting around since Echo General, so when me Deejay in the dance me want me collateral. (Welton Irie, Gemini Disco, 1981)

I used to stand up in front of Saxon as a youth and think them man deh can chat and one day I'm gonna chat like them and now it's how I earn my living. (C. J. Lewis, Personal Communication, 1998)

The above extracts speak to the reality of a shift in the self-perception of the Deejays that led to many of them assuming the mantle of professional entertainers. Again, as evidenced in Welton Irie's extract, it was the Jamaican Deejays who first articulated this shift. However, before I focus on how this shift was reflected in the lyricism of the British Deejays, I will provide some background information that will make the overall significance of this change in consciousness known. There was a realisation in the early 1980s that Deejays were now being separated from the Sound Systems to which they were affiliated and many were hired by promoters to feature in Deejay Jamborees. These Jamborees were massive events that featured various performers, sometimes from all over the country and often included Jamaican Deejays as recounted above in 5.4's **re-memories**. These events obviously appealed to a wider audience who could now partake in a novel Reggae-dancehall experience. A promoter could now hire the Saxon Deejays without having to pay for Saxon's Set, which meant that the Deejays were now regarded as entities in their own right. This occurrence caused all forms of contention as the Sound System owners often believed their names were being used in what they considered to be a very exploitative situation. However, this in itself was a reversal of the norm; it was usually the performers who openly expressed these grievances about non-payment to the various Sound System owners, their supposed 'employers'. It was widely recognised within the culture that many Sound System owners paid their Deejays little or nothing, often arguing that the money generated was spent on the upkeep of equipment, providing the 'Sound-van' and buying new tunes, dub plates etc. This type of scenario led to the Saxon Deejay Papa Levi going on 'strike' in 1983, during which time he performed on other Sets including Ghettotone, whilst refusing to chat Saxon, because:

It nuh easy fi write an time you lyrics, an then drop it in front ah 'crowd ah people', nuff bwoy try an fail which is why them haffi pay I an I fi perform cau each man fi get pay according to them works, literally. (Papa Levi, 1997)

217

Levi expresses the thought behind this change of emphasis in Reggae-dancehall Deejay culture; the Deejays realised that people were coming to the sessions to hear them chat 'proper lyrics' and not just to listen to the Set play music. Consequently many Deejays began to appreciate their own contribution to the Sound System performance as a totality and demanded that they be financially remunerated 'according to them works, literally'. Many of the British Deejays welcomed this change in emphasis as it meant that their status as originators, within the culture, was now being appreciated both outernationally and financially. This was because, as I mentioned above, many found themselves performing side by side in Deejay Jamborees with Jamaican Deejays, as was the case in my performing on Frontline with the Gemini Disco posse. However, as a Sound System co-owner/Deejay myself during this historical moment, I can fully appreciate both sides of the argument, for in this twilight world if a dance 'flopped' or the promoter 'head out' (made off with the cash), there would be no money to pay anyone. Moreover, due to the 'illegal' nature of the 'Blues-dance' business, these sessions could flop for various reasons: bad weather, police raids, 'fight bruk-out an mash it up', which often occurred. Such occurrences generally resulted in the promoter or Sound System owner ending up out of pocket because no cash would be generated to cover their initial expenditure. As a consequence many Sound System folk had occupations that were separate from the Reggae-dancehall scene and often funded their Sound Systems as a joint enterprise, hoping that one day the Sound would generate enough cash to 'run' itself. In fact as Dr Vibes stated:

> Once you decide seriously that you are going to set up a Sound, you have to know that it is not an overnight thing. Sometimes you don't make anything for a good while and it is during these times if you believe in what you want to achieve then you have to put you hand in you pocket. Most Soundman do something else otherwise you won't survive in the business. (Personal Communication, 2001)

Appreciating this very significant point about the nature of the culture makes it easier to comprehend why many Deejays performed out of an aesthetic appreciation of their own skills or natural ability, because Deejaying, much like Dr Vibes' perspective on Soundman, was generally separated from other types of financially rewarding 'work'.

More so when we consider that the Deejay performance was perceived to be a primarily 'oral/mental' activity as opposed to the 'physical' labour associated with stringing-up the Set. And as anyone who has experienced a dancehall event will testify, this type of 'physical' labour included heavy lifting and carrying out many an arduous task as part of the stringing-up process. A division of labour was often employed which logically viewed the maintenance and stringing-up of the Set as the priority in terms of payment, because it was based upon 'physical' and not 'mental' labour. Hence:

> The truly significant thing about the rise of the Deejay, though, is that it came from the people within their own arena in the most direct way possible. On the mic in the dance. The beauty of Deejaying has always been the lack of investment needed for talent to show up: even the smallest sound systems will attract their share of outgoing types who'll beg the operator to let them *hol' the mic, nuh,* and all that is needed is lyrics, an ability to ride a riddim, verbal dexterity and a quick mind. No cash up front for studio time or backing musicians...practically anybody could get up and have a go. (Bradley, 2001:504)

Bradley quite rightly states that to perform in this fashion is open to all who wish to 'have a go', although to suggest that all one requires to perform 'is lyrics, the ability to ride a riddim, verbal Deejaying dexterity and a quick mind', reflects the generally simplistic attitude towards the role of the Deejay. Perhaps this was true to an extent for many Deejays but, once the originators who wished to become professional entertainers recognised their own worth, they in the words of the Jamaican Deejay U Brown, 'can't tek the praise without raise' (1980). This track was featured on the B~SIDE of the late great Dennis Emmanuel Brown's popular tune 'Praise Without Raise'; what is really significant is that this tune along with Sugar Minnot's 'You give Me Penny For My Song' (1980) was requested by many Deejays who would then use the lyrics of these tracks to have a 'dig' at their 'employers' the Sound System owners. This was, as highlighted before, the rationale behind Levi's decision to go on 'strike', as the Deejay's role within the culture was somewhat undervalued because you failed to 'raise' any cash for your labour.

Once it was recognised that certain Deejays were in demand and required to perform at these Jamborees, those who realised how much effort they were putting into their performances quickly dispensed with the amateurish approach. This was a significant factor in the reasoning behind Benji's creation of the 'In Demand' lyric, featured in the previous chapter, as he believed that Big John and Percy failed to consider what it actually took to write, rehearse/memorise, and perform a lyric in the heat of the Reggae-dancehall. This is all the more perplexing when considering that most Sound System folk have regular meetings where new equipment is introduced and tested by the Operator, or new/special tunes are played and organised by the Selector; during which time the Deejays often grasp the opportunity to test out new styles/lyrics on the latest riddims. So one would naturally assume that, because other members of the Set would have this insight into this aspect of the Deejay process, a thorough appreciation of their 'works' would be forthcoming.

Equally, it cannot be overstated that the contribution and professionalism of the other members of the Set should also be valued and considered. For instance, the Selector would have to select prior to the event which records were appropriate for that specific occasion. For example, playing Specials/Dub plates all night long at a christening or birthday party would be seen as amateurish and would not go down well with the 'crowd ah people'. Similarly a Set would definitely 'get buried' if they played Commercial (recorded releases) in a Sound-clash because the audience expects to be entertained appropriately according to the type of occasion attended. I am suggesting that there are hidden (physical as well as mental) dimensions to all aspects of Sound System culture. Given that the focal point of this discussion is Deejaying, I argue that the actual 'product' of the Deejay's 'labour', the lyric, is often appreciated in the context of the live performance as a largely spontaneous 'oral/mental' exercise. This means that these observations are not generally based upon the 'insider knowledge' that appreciates the process of written creation and rehearsal that are crucial to the finished article and is why many commentators suggested that the culture is primarily spontaneous (head-top) and therefore non-scribal. For this reason I will in the next section present the Deejay's perspective on what it meant to perform, original lyrics, in front of 'crowdah people' during this moment.

7.2 It's ah job, Jahman it is ah job to entertain!

To who respect is due, respect it must goh through, me respect me mother me father me uncle me brother me sister too, me family always ah tell me seh Asher we proud ah you, them see me pon television an them say yes ah long time it due, me lyric pon sale in ah shop the demand ah the start of supn new, cau it is for sure 1984 me mek me record debut, them seh me professional now through certain tings me start fi do, first sign me name pon ah poster an me nuh like-it me wouldah screw, an wouldn't reach ah the dance unless in the end me feel too, but now somebody print me name me run find out is who, them don't want gimmie up-front fi the dance, good, all of them get sue, nuh fight nuh fuss nuh cuss no star don't even argue, cau to who respect is due, respect it must goh through. (Asher Senator, 1984)

The above extract demonstrates that there was a form of dialogue between the Deejays and those who required their services, which centred upon whether or not these interested parties realised that 'professional musicians need money'. To make the point clearer consider, for instance, when I previously suggested that Benji performed because, in his own words, he was a 'fanatic' and did it out of his love for the Deejay 'vibes'. The fact that he was a professional draughtsman lends credibility to this aesthetic argument because he had a viable source of income from his 'real 9 - 5 work' and thus his Deejaying was for non-financial reward. However, for Deejays like Tippa Irie this was not an option because for him Deejaying is his 'trade' and thus:

I caan Deejay fi free cau me family haffi live an me caan come from work an tell me family me work an nuh mek nuh money. Them wouldah check seh me mad cau I would be disrespecting myself. The only thing I know is how to entertain. Some man can do plastering or plumbing an them ting deh, but I have been chatting since I was a youth so this is my trade. Remember, how much times them print we up pon poster, people come, we chat, an don't mek nuh money. A long time me stop do them ting deh Lez, God know. (Personal Communication, 1999)

221

That is why Asher's suggestion that 'me lyric pon sale in ah shop, the demand ah the start of supn new', firmly places Tippa's observation in the context of this shift in self-perception, especially for those performers who did not have an alternative means of generating an income. Therefore, once this 'demand' for them to appear at various functions became economically viable, Deejays began a dialogue amongst themselves as to why their attitude must change from within and why they must become more professional. This change in emphasis led to a certain aspect of the culture becoming commercialised and therefore known within the mainstream public arena and:

> Radio DJs like Tony Williams, on the now defunct Radio London's *Rockers FM*, would constantly feature live DJing on his shows. This was to have a major influence on what we now readily recognise as freedom (pirate) radio stations, who adopted the sound system ethos to great effect. (Henry, 2002:287)

Ironically the increasing exposure of the British Deejays on 'Rockers FM' and Capital Radio's 'Roots Rockers' popularised the form in such a way that Sir Lloyd, a south London Sound System owner, whose Set carried this name as well, immortalised the British Deejay presence in a series of three live recordings (1983/4). This type of recording was already known in Britain because a Jamaican 'live' album entitled 'Lees Unlimited', featuring various Deejays was released in 1982, and a few more were to follow in its tracks by featuring the most popular Sets and performers. However, Sir Lloyd featured on his Set the cream of British talent in these Jamborees, which gave the performers a wider exposure than their Sound System cassettes could realistically achieve, in the alternative 'world music market'. This meant that the final product could be purchased from record shops and other outlets (many West Indian food shops, barber shops and hairdressing salons sell music) and played on the radio, which obviously increased the Deejay's profile in the wider public arena. Furthermore, these recordings actually allowed a comparison to be made, lyrically and style-wise, between the performers who were arguably the best exponents of their 'trade', because the albums featured various Deejays one after the other. It should come as no great surprise that certain renowned record producers/companies capitalised on this novel aspect of the culture as the 'demand' for British Deejay style spread from the live arena to the record shops, where studio recorded versions of popular lyrics became widely available. This subsequently challenged the predominance of the Jamaican Deejay style because more and more British black youths were chatting original lyrics in their own style. Consequently:

> By the 1980s, the British Deejays were achieving global recognition and sound systems like Saxon, Coxone, Frontline, Wasifa, Ghetto-tone, King Tubby's, Jamdown Rockers, Java High Power, Unity and a host of others became household names within the black community. (Henry, 2002:282)

As a 'household name' Asher Senator (1984) was now stating that, before he took the business seriously, he was content to 'screw' (become angry) when a promoter printed his name on a poster without his knowledge, only appearing at the event if he felt like it. As soon as he regarded himself as a 'professional', and knew that others associated with him echoed similar sentiments, 'them seh', he argued that if anyone 'print me name', without prior consent, 'me would run find out is who'. And if, 'them don't want gimmie up-front fi the dance, good, all of them get sue', which means that recourse to some type of legal settlement had now become an option for him in line with his professional approach to the business. Furthermore, he expected to be paid an 'up-front' (advance) for his services. Failure to do so would lead to the same sanction, because in his opinion you must 'respect' the performer in much the same way as you should highly respect your own family members. Asher's perspective reinforces the sentiments expressed by Tippa Irie who also expected the promoter to recognise his level of professionalism and act accordingly out of a mutual 'respect', 'nuh fight nuh fuss nuh cuss no star don't even argue, cau to who respect is due, respect it must goh through'. He therefore expected some type of reasonable solution, under the threat of suing the guilty promoter, whereas Trevor Natch's perspective, which we will now consider, was opposed to this form of resolution as he states:

> It's ah job, Jahman it is ah job to entertain, so when me hold the mic nuh bwoy cannot complain, cau several subjects my head contain, I don't plait-up my hair like Leroy from Fame, promoter check me, money him will gain, but if him don't pay, him wouldah get slain,

police man seh Trevor Natch you could-not be tame, cau me wife, me kid, me haffi maintain, me nuh fool like Michael Jackson breddah called Jermain, him manager rob him then run off to Spain, through that him shock himself with electric main, tree months later him consciously regain, but all him try him couldn't sex him galfriend the same, well that is that, and this is this, and so it shall remain, cau it's a job, Jah man it is ah job to entertain. (Trevor Natch, Diamonds 1985)

Trevor Natch clearly states in his account that he is a professional entertainer and therefore people, especially promoters, should realise, 'it is ah job, it is ah job to entertain'. This attitude clearly states his position as a professional who recognises his responsibility is to entertain the audience with 'proper lyrics' and he has readied himself to do so. Trevor Natch is arguing that from the moment he begins his performance he is professional enough, 'several subjects me head contain', to fulfil his obligation to both the 'crowd ah people' and the promoter, which is why 'nuh bwoy (the promoter) cannot complain'. Trevor Natch also informs the 'bwoy' in question that he should realise that he is not afraid to defend his position, physically, as he is not effeminate. This is the rationale behind his usage of 'I don't plait-up my hair like Leroy from Fame' who, like many other supposedly gay men, was only mentioned by performers as 'batty-men'; no threat to the Deejay's machismo. In Leroy's case this was based on aspersion, as far as I am aware, yet his name, like that of many 'gay-men' (most notably bwoy George), became a signifier for the archetype 'batty-man' within the culture.

It is therefore not unusual to hear performers diss one another by implying that 'them ah hug up one another like ah Rock Hudson, me prefer hold a daughter (a woman) an get person to person' (Supercat, Saxon 1985). Then as is still the case now, to be branded as a 'batty-man' is the ultimate mark of disrespect in Reggae-dancehall culture. We can pretend it isn't so to be 'politically correct' and cut/distort 'offensive' language until the proverbial 'cows come home', but that is a fact of life and livity in many black counter-cultures and you will not hear homosexuality promoted as a positive human experience within them. Furthermore, I resent people who do not appreciate this fundamental, assuming they have the power to control what can and cannot be said by Reggae-dancehall Deejays. These discussions need to be undertaken by us, those blacks/Afrikans who fully appreciate why certain things are said, which cannot be meaningfully discussed when separated from their historical context. Then, and only then, will we resolve the issues of homosexuality, misogyny and shadism that all too often feature in the lyricism of contemporary Deejays, to the overall detriment of the global black/Afrikan family.

However, in the context of this discussion, Trevor Natch makes it known that, unlike Asher, he is not interested in suing the guilty party as his logic dictates that, 'promoter check me, money him will gain, but if him don't pay, him wouldah get slain'. Knowing Trevor Natch personally as I did when he performed this lyric, he was, as they say in Jamaica, 'as serious as ah judge weh nah laugh'. By openly stating that 'police man seh Trevor Natch you could-not be tame'; he serves a further warning to the promoter that he was not unduly worried if they chose to involve the police, 'cau me wife, me kid, me haffi maintain', further emphasising Tippa's point that this was a 'trade', my skills for your money, and not a hobby. Hence Trevor Natch's sentiments reflect what was a growing concern about performers being swindled out of their royalties, which affected all of the Deejays who were now expressing an interest in signing contracts with record companies, managers/agents, or promoters. Those who had suffered these negative experiences made use of a form which allowed them to voice their opinions almost immediately within the Reggae-dancehall, thereby creating a dialogue about these most pressing concerns. Therefore tales of unscrupulous promoters, managers and record companies were rife within the culture and many Deejays were not afraid to voice their bad experiences during lyrical performances, because:

> When we tear down the lawn we always get nuff applause, so man ah rush me an Benji fi tun superstars, but before we sign contract we read every clause, cau them man know how to rob you without breaking any laws. (Lezlee Lyrix, Diamonds 1985)

I wrote these sentiments after a conversation I had with Benji in 1985, when the realisation hit us that the record label he was signed-up with, Fashion Records, paid their performers 8% royalties instead of the 'recognised' norm in the music business; which was the 10% that Greensleeves (who I was with at this time) paid their performers. Benji suggested that the reason why record company owners could 'try ah ting like that was cau them tek we fi fool', because, like many others, they often assumed that Deejays basically lacked intelligence/education and were therefore deemed to be ignorant on such matters. That is why I thought it was important to let potential signups be aware of these differences which, in the context of the more 'successful' performers, could amount to considerable sums of money. For this reason it was not unusual to hear (except in cases where the guilty party was a known 'bad man') the Deejays sounding out those who they believed had swindled/exploited them, which explains the reasoning behind Trevor Natch's (1985) usage of Jermain Jackson's well-publicised story.

Trevor Natch opined that this scenario would not have happened to him because 'me nuh fool' and would therefore not blindly trust anyone, especially a manager who Jamaicans often remind us can become a 'damager' and likewise a producer can become a 'reducer'. By stating that he would not consider suicide by electrocution, ('through that him shock himself with electric main'), Trevor Natch demonstrates that the reality of the music business is that all professional entertainers are susceptible to this type of unscrupulous act, irrespective of high-profile status, fame or fortune. Trevor Natch, then states that as a consequence of his unsuccessful suicide attempt, Jermain Jackson became the same type of guy as Leroy because, 'all him try him couldn't sex him galfriend the same'. Thus his manager not only robbed him financially but more significantly robbed him of his sexual prowess, which for Trevor Natch is the ultimate marker of manliness and therefore leads him to conclude: 'well that is that', meaning Jermain's reaction to being conned led to a form of self-harming that deprived him of his manhood; 'and this is this', Trevor Natch's reaction would lead to the promoter being harmed, 'and so it shall remain cau it's a job, Jah man it is ah job to entertain'.

7.3   'Hidden voices' in public spaces

As a result of the Deejay's public profile being increased, due to the interest shown in their potential by mainly white-owned record companies, a series of conflicts over commercialisation of the culture arose. These record companies viewed British Deejaying as an economically viable resource that was novel and therefore, in many ways, highly exploitable as long as the emphasis was placed on saleability and not conscious upliftment. For this reason many performers began to question who the 'hidden voice' was truly representing and, of equal importance, who stood to gain the most from its mainstream promotion and commercialisation. In many instances it was plainly obvious that the Deejays and the record companies, who were quick to sign them, were at polar extremes with regard to the role and ultimate purpose of this black cultural form. To embellish this point I will discuss extracts from Papa Levi's 'Ram-Jam Capitalism', one of the most controversial tracks ever recorded by a British Deejay, to explain the wider ramifications of the white appropriation of black cultural forms.

The 'Ram Jam' in the title of this track is a nickname given to the white Reggae disc jockey, David Rodigan, who at that time worked for London's 'Capital Radio' (he now works on Kiss FM, London). The notion of 'Ram Jam' comes from within Jamaican culture and literally means to 'jam-pack' a Reggae-dancehall session and is also where the notion of the shubeen—to shove in—comes from. The 'Ram Jam' was also a famous Rock Steady/Ska/Reggae venue in Brixton from mid-to-Late 1960s and the resident Sound System was Brixton's own 'Sir Coxone Outernational'. Levi suggests that after 'Ram Jam' Rodigan has rammed-up the session he then seeks to con the black performers out of the monies they have earned as professional entertainers, due to his power position within the culture. Rodigan's name is thus transformed by Papa Levi into the metaphoric, 'rob an gaan', which literally means he is accusing him of robbing black performers out of their session money/royalties and then making off with the cash. However what is even more significant is that by doing so Levi highlights the types of problems that occur once a counter-cultural form becomes regarded as an 'over the counter culture' (Cooper, 2000), where commercialisation undermines its potential as a blak radical voice. Hence according to Papa Levi:

Spoken intro: I dare any MC in this whole wide world to chat ah lyric, such as this.

Chorus: Ram Jam Capitalism, Papa Levi with chi Ram Jam capitalism, we cufn man, Ram Jam Capitalism, Papa Levi with chi Ram Jam Capitalism, well hear me man.

Deejaying: Certain Deejay love fi boost rob an gaan, I Papa Levi am not one, the little baldhead Caucasian who believe him ah don, practice everyday fi talk Jamaican, ah bade aafah artist an musician, seh in ah Jamaica an England, all the money weh him skank him buy house an land, ungle (only) conscious people understand, rob an gaan ah deal with exploitation, pon radio rob an gaan ah boost nuff man, ah talk bout them voice sound magnificent, but I bet you one hundred tousand grand, if rob an gaan hold one ah fi him session, no more dan, five hundred pound him wouldah put in ah them hand, an ram him pocket with all thirty grand, then that nuh.

Chorus: Ram Jam Capitalism, Papa Levi with chi Ram Jam capitalism, we cufn man, Ram Jam Capitalism, Papa Levi with chi Ram Jam Capitalism, well hear me man.

Deejaying: The bwoy ah put himself in ah the position, fi capitalise aafah the black nation, cau who support Reggae? Nuh we same one, it coming like we brainbox nah function, rob an gaan ah wuk him head pan man-an-man, pushing Dub Vendor music pon the radio station, any money that it earn, him hold ah portion, we nuh fi put we trust in ah that kindah man, cau fi money him ah rip off the musician, fi money wouldah condemn ah innocent man, fi money him wouldah sell-out ah whole nation, seh baldhead rob an gaan nuh have nuh good intention, but fi suck-out the corn (money) out ah we same one.

Chorus: Ram Jam Capitalism, Papa Levi with chi Ram Jam capitalism, we cufn man, Ram Jam Capitalism, Papa Levi with chi Ram Jam Capitalism, well hear me man.

Deejaying: Seh wah we need now is organisation, an conscious man like Louis Farrakan, fi tek control of the situation, an run-out the leeches like rob an gaan, an all ah the puppet pon string musician, who him give couple pound an tell them galang, an hope seh you come-een pon the next session, seh in the Academy downah Brixton, rob an gaan you need ah hair transplant, an mr rob an gaan you need ah hair transplant...(Papa Levi, 1986)

Levi begins his vitriolic assault on David Rodigan's credibility with an open challenge to every MC (Deejay) in the world as he dares one and all 'to chat ah lyric such as this' which sets the scene for what is to follow. Levi is arguing that too many black performers, managers and others involved in the business sit back and pay lip service to an industry, that allows white people to 'bade aafah artist an musician'. The notion of 'bade' being the literal 'bathing in money' by those whites who profit from a medium that uplifts the black sufferer, whilst chanting down our enemies. This, in and of itself, is in my opinion, being true to the ethos behind Reggae music's creation, which was to give the black sufferer a potent 'public voice'. Levi attacks those performers whom he believes give Rodigan too much respect, 'certain Deejays love to boost rob an gaan', to which he suggests 'I Papa Levi am not one'. Therefore, Levi's intention is clear in as much as he distances himself from those Deejays that he later describes as 'puppet pon string musicians'. Musicians who not only sell their services cheaply, but are also disrespected in the process by the 'leeches' like 'rob an gaan' who 'give them couple pound an tell them galang'. A not too difficult task according to Levi as the exploiter/capitalist, in this instance, is a 'little baldhead Caucasian who believe him ah don, practice everyday fi talk Jamaican'. The inference being that he can control these performers by speaking to them in Patwa, because he is conversant, through daily 'practice', with Jamaican language and—as he is married to a Jamaican woman and frequents the Island on music business—with Jamaican cultural sensibilities as well.

'Rob an gaan' also wishes to establish himself in Jamaica because 'the money weh him skank him buy house an land', which is how property ownership is described in the Jamaican context and not normally used to describe purchasing a property in Britain. Therefore, 'rob an gaan' is no different from those whites who historically exploited the chattel slaves and ended up with the prime land on the island of Jamaica and equally determine the 'structural placement' of those they control racially, politically, culturally and economically.

Levi then shifts his focus to another aspect of 'rob an gaan's' overall method to deceive the black community when he argues 'ungle conscious people understand', that is those who are aware of the history behind the ploy 'rob an gaan' uses to ensure that his capitalistic enterprise is maintained. This, Levi suggests, is the manner in which he uses his power position, as a radio personality, to 'boost' certain 'puppet pon string' Deejays that Levi believes are untalented, weak willed, and therefore easily controlled. The accusation of Radio DJ favouritism are commonplace in the music industry, yet Levi's point seems to transcend banal accusations, as the suggestion is that it is the integrity of the Deejays that is in question due to the black consciousness they fail to represent. Levi points out the obvious disparity in supposed earnings, 'no more dan five hundred pound him wouldah put in ah them hand, an ram him pocket with all thirty grand'. Levi's skill as a master crafter of words captures the exploitative nature of this lopsided exchange, as it is not too difficult to imagine 'rob an gaan' visibly 'putting' the money in the Deejay's 'hand', whilst 'ramming' his own pockets with his portion of the monies accrued from the 'Ram Jam' session.

Levi further suggests that black people are in this instance responsible for perpetuating their own exploitation because although 'the bwoy ah put himself in ah the position, to capitalise aafah the black nation', it is our fault for not thinking more carefully about what is really occurring. Why? Obviously because, 'who support Reggae? Nuh we same one, it coming like we brainbox nah function'. The inference being that we cannot see that the relationship is wholly exploitative and for this reason it is easy for 'rob an gaan to wuk him head pon (outthink) man an man' and constantly deceive the black community. Furthermore, the manner in which this deception is maintained is based on the idea that 'rob an gaan' has a vested interest in a white-owned record company, 'Dub Vendor', which is also the home of 'Fashion Records'. I must state at this point that Rodigan has always denied this allegation and has always assured me that it is totally untrue, as he has no vested interest in any record company whatsoever. However, Levi's point about the disproportionate amount of airplay accorded to Dub Vendor music on Rodigan's radio show was well known within the culture and many resented Rodigan's alleged partiality. In fact there was an occasion when Rodigan informed his listeners, in an emotive outburst on one of his shows, that certain producers were threatening him with violence if he did not play their tunes on his program. One such producer who openly admitted to 'roughing up the bwoy' was 'The Mad Dread', who argued:

> I draped him—Rodigan—up and threatened him because he was only playing certain an certain man's tunes an I told him to stop fuck himself cau ah nuh only white-man fi eat ah food out ah this ting yah. (Personal Communication, 1996)

It must also be noted that 'The Mad Dread' informed me that he thought Levi's tune Ram Jam Capitalism was misguided, because at the end of the day we rely on disc jockeys like Rodigan to 'promote our tunes'. However, he went on to suggest:

> That doesn't mean the bwoy (Rodigan) can tek the piss out ah we, cau Tony Williams (Rodigans main rival during this moment) wouldah play ah tune an tell you seh him nuh like it but is the listeners who must decide fi demself if them want hear the tune pon the radio.

It is noticeable that 'The Mad Dread' is not overly concerned with whether or not 'rob an gaan' has a vested interest in 'Dub Vendor'. He was only concerned with the fact that his tunes were not receiving, in his opinion, the levels of airplay accorded to Fashion Records. That is why he cites Tony Williams as an example of how the business could be impartial because Williams would inform the listeners that he often played records that he may not like, but has an obligation to let the people hear them anyway. Whereas, in the case of 'rob an gaan', the argument is that his alleged discreet relationship with Dub Vendor meant that by playing their/his tunes 'any money that it earn, him hold ah portion', therefore 'we nuh fi put we trust in ah that kindah man'. Levi argues that it is no problem for him to take Reggae music and use it to 'sell-out ah whole nation', because 'baldhead rob an gaan nuh have nuh good intention, but fi suck-out the corn out ah we same one'; which means that Reggae-dancehall music's potential to strengthen the economic position of the black community is muted by his lack of 'good intention'. Therefore the perceived lack of 'good intention' toward the black community by white people in the business was a consequence of their failure, in many cases, to appreciate the profundity of the 'hidden voice' that dominated the Reggae-dancehalls with its blak radicalism. Hence:

> To the outside world, including an enormous proportion of Reggae's recent converts, toasting was never a valid art form in itself; it was either a pointless, almost parasitical abomination or consigned to the drawer marked 'novelty'. This latter aspect wasn't helped much by a clutch of opportunistic Deejays who believed the best way forward

was through gimmickry - step forward, Smiley Culture and a host of others who know who they are, which in itself must be penance enough. (Bradley, 2001:504)

Bradley's comments capture the differences in the manner in which the worth of the form was perceived from 'within' the culture by the performers and those who inhabit the 'outside world', the record company owners. Although it must be noted that these types of 'gimmickry' were not created solely for the purpose of selling records to a wider market; in fact, Smiley Culture's 'Police Officer' and 'The Cockney Translation' and other popular Deejay tunes that featured on the national charts were already known within Reggae-dancehalls. Moreover, the style in which the lyrics were delivered, in Smiley's case on Saxon's Set, was not dissimilar from the studio version that featured in the record stores, so what is at stake is more complex than Bradley's notion of 'gimmickry'. I demonstrated at various points above that original Deejays will chat 'all kindah style', which is 'more like when you ah reason an mek two joke'; this means that the 'hidden voice' expresses all aspects of an urban black experience. Therefore the reality was that the potential for the 'hidden voice' to uplift, as an Africentric tool for liberation, was subsumed under the weight of white expectation, which obviously meant that 'gimmickry' became the register by which the form was judged and accepted within the wider public arena.

Whether this expectation was real or imagined is of no consequence, the fact is that this was the argument used by Levi and many others to state what was happening to our 'voice' once it became known in the 'white world'. This is because we recognised that we were professional entertainers, in much the same way as the record company owners had their professional approach to the music business in general. However, what needs to be acknowledged is that 'conscious Deejays' viewed their professionalism in concordance with an Africentric standpoint, so there were in essence two different notions of the professional economics of representation: one which spoke to the expectance of the white world, which viewed the form as a means of generating a profit from a novelty; the other was how we regarded the form as our most potent voice in the alternative public arena out of which we could also earn a living. According to Sister Audrey (1999):

They've got all these Deejays in the pop charts singing rubbish! What about the singers who sing about the things that affected the people that came from the Caribbean in the 1950s and are still affecting people now? Do you hear them on popular radio stations? This is an example of how things get lost, things that are really important to the generations of blacks born in Britain. (Personal Communication, 1999)

Considering the seriousness of Sister Audrey's comments it is not that surprising that the Deejays who are not content to enter the 'pop charts singing rubbish' would, as in Levi's case, offer a proviso for the 'conscious' people who wish to combat this white, record industry, menace. Levi introduces the type of player who can provide the guidance we require to 'run out the leaches like rob an gaan', in this instance it is Minister Louis Farrakhan, the Leader of the Nation Of Islam. The fact that Levi, a Rastafari, cites Farrakhan is significant as there was, during the mid 1980s, a rekindling of black interest in the alternative politics of the 'Nation Of Islam', who preached among other things the need for black people to be more professional in our dealings with white society. That is why Levi demonstrates that he is Rastafari in a more profound sense than merely his choosing of the Twelve Tribe name, Levi, and as such is not afraid to state this actuality in his challenging of white domination through exploitation/commercialisation. For by this time many of the advocates of Rastafari, especially those affiliated to 'The Twelve Tribes of Israel', were openly welcoming white people into their organisations: I know this for a fact as I attended Twelve Tribes' meetings and dances during that time. The pro-black stance that sought to perpetuate upliftment as something more than a rhetorical device was lacking and many black youths, like Levi, were seeking an alternative blak cultural politics that was aligned to Garvey's 'Africa for the Africans' and 'Race First'. Consequently many began to embrace figures like Malcolm X, Claudia Jones, Walter Rodney, Angela Davis, Kwame Ture and Elijah Muhammad, as these were the teachings they were receiving from the 'followers of Farrakhan', many of whom were their bredrin or sistrin. In fact a Rastafari sistrin, Christine Asher, who was affiliated to 'Twelve Tribes' until the mid-1980s, argued:

233

You caan blame the youth them fi looking fah supn better cau when them go-ah Twelve Tribes meetings or dances them seem to be more interested in colours (they have regular dances where the wearing of a particular colour is encouraged) than why we ah suffer through we colour. You hear the Deejay them ah taak one bag ah culture then look in ah the crowd an you we see supn different. Ah bear mix-up mix-up did ah gwaan, an still ah gwaan to this day, cau them mek Rastafari into a commercial joke ting. Wah you wouldah see pon the TV, an them stupidness deh like 'funky dread' is not Rasta dem is rastitute and renta-dread. (Personal Communication, 2001)

It is the notion of commercialisation that is most significant in Christine Asher's account, for it allows us to see why it was necessary for many British born blacks to re-think their affiliations to 'black' organisations like 'Twelve Tribes' and subsequently posit the more Africentric notion of 'blak' as suggested above. That is why for her 'Twelve Tribes' gatherings became more of a 'commercial joke ting' where people were more focussed on the colour of your outfit than the colour of your consciousness. Christine Asher saw these particular gatherings as oppressive due to the shift in emphasis with regard to what black people are struggling against as the most visible recipients of racist exclusionary practices. That which, she argues, cannot be negated by adorning ourselves (and others) in pretty colours and then dancing the night away like 'rastitutes'or 'renta dreads' - dreadlocks who prostitute themselves to benefit white people. As the Reggae-dancehall was a site for blak upliftment by virtue of the potency of the roots singers and conscious Deejay's portrayal of social realism that spoke to the reality of being black in racist Britain. This means that once the culture is appropriated in this negative fashion, its role and purpose becomes confused, as it no longer serves the cause of blak upliftment and social advancement. Therefore the idea of not wishing to partake in these meaningless events was the rationale behind her usage of the term 'mix-up', because as Sister Audrey suggested this too is an 'example of how things that are really important to us get lost'. In this context the 'mix-up' is the usage of a cloak, your adornment in 'colours', to mask the differences between you and those whites that are welcomed with open arms by an organisation that was birthed from the Afrikan struggle for liberation from the tyranny of white downpression. Therefore, it is not possible for Christine Asher to ignore the fact that

Reggae music constantly reminds us 'why we ah suffer through we colour' because, as she suggests, the music has a libratory potential that should not be compromised or turned 'into a commercial joke ting'. Hence 'you hear the Deejay them a talk one bag ah culture then look in ah the crowd you we see supn different', which is why a conscious person seeks 'supn better' because 'we're not preaching to go out and kill anybody, we're just preaching about the injustices and trying to right certain wrongs that were done to Afrikans by racist Europeans' (Macka B, 1999).

The 'supn better' Christine Asher spoke of which could be used to 'right certain wrongs', was for black youths, like Papa Levi, found in the words of a 'conscious man like Louis Farrakhan', whose example we needed to follow in our endeavours to organise and then be in a position of strength to 'run-out the leeches like rob an gaan, an all ah the puppet pon string musician'. For it was in many ways the inspiration these black youths received from the alternative politics of organisations like the Nation of Islam, and conscious Rastafari who preached self-empowerment as Garveyite philosophy, that led to a reformulation of what it meant to be black in Britain. That is why Levi's mentioning of Louis Farrakhan is not surprising in the context of a fearless blakman, in this instance Levi himself, advocating the overthrow of white oppression/exploitation. Furthermore, by doing so he offered a solution to those who, like himself, were fed up of being exploited by our most recognisable historical enemy, the white capitalist. However, with all this said, it must be noted that Levi had another, and by far more personal, motive for this assault on Rodigan's credibility, which was evidenced in the final verse of the extract. This is where he informs the listener of an incident that took place at a 'rob an gaan' session, in which he was one of the main attractions during a 'Capital Radio Live to London' event in 1984. It shows how becoming a 'professional' entertainer, and thereby gaining wider exposure within the mainstream public arena, had its own set of problems that stemmed from a confusion of perspectives when a counter-culture's potency is confronted with commercialisation.

In Levi's take on this particular occurrence is surprising, bearing in mind the totality of his condemnation of 'rob an gaan' and his so-called minions of 'puppet pon string musicians', to which he himself had suggested most forcefully 'I Papa Levi am not one'. The definitive 'not one' as a signifier of his disapproval at any-'one' who would 'boost', support/feed this enemy presence by appearing at any of his exploitative shows. To do so would be to not only 'ram' his pockets with our cash, but also to tarnish your own reputation as a 'conscious Deejay'. However, the reality is that Levi did appear on this particular show at the Brixton Academy as a headline artiste and had featured several times on Rodigan's Capital Radio show, 'Roots Rockers', where he and many other Saxon Deejays performed live on the air in the studio. It was in this context that he appeared as one of the acts on Rodigan's 'Live to London' show on a Saturday evening and what transpired during this particular moment is an exemplar of what happens when the 'hidden voice' is exposed in the wider public arena.

The lyric that Levi performed in the Brixton Academy in October 1984, which so panicked Rodigan, was a version of one of Reggae music's all time favourite dancehall tunes entitled 'Bobby Babylon'. The original version was recorded for Coxsone Dodd's Studio One Label, during the 1970s, by Freddie McGregor and was an account of the ill treatment Rastafari receive at the hands of Jamaican downpressors. Levi retained the original melody and changed up the words; although this is a regular occurrence in Reggae-dancehall culture, Levi's lyric was exceptionally cutting as it berated the then Prime Minister, Margaret Thatcher. Thus, as soon as Rodigan realised what Levi was actually saying he cut the music and attempted to usher Levi off stage as McGregor's immensely popular chorus line of:

> Bobby Bobby Babylon you run come, Bobby Babylon, don't touch the Nyahman. – **Became** - Maggie baggie (her knickers) smell strong like ah rotten yam, Maggie baggie smell just like ah onion...

Rodigan eventually persuaded Levi to leave the stage but by then the damage had been done, he had buried the Prime Minister 'Live to London' and it was rumoured that Rodigan almost lost his job over the incident. For Levi it spelt the end of his affiliation with Island Records who arguably 'shelved' him until his contract expired and then dropped him from their label altogether. Whilst reasoning with me about this incident Rodigan suggested that:

> Levi should have known that he couldn't chat a lyric like that on the air because some of what he said was highly offensive, like her

husband (Dennis Thatcher) having shit on his fingers from touching her baggie. I myself was surprised and disappointed with him as I wanted him to perform with me at other shows and not just in England, because he was one of the best Deejays. But after that I couldn't take that kind of chance and I know that he blames me for what happened to his career after that show at the Academy. (Personal Communication, 2001)

I agree with Rodigan's suggestion that Levi should have known that to attack the Prime Minister was foolhardy in this instance, as it was not within the confines of the culturally fortified Reggae-dancehall, and can appreciate why he expresses his 'disappointment' at Levi's lack of sound judgement/professionalism. The most important factor is that Levi failed to appreciate that this aspect of the Deejay 'voice', where you can bury an adversary, any adversary without mercy, was 'hidden' from the wider white public and more importantly the downpressor's gaze. That is because Deejays were expected to rely on 'safe' gimmicky type tunes like the aforementioned 'Police Officer', 'Cockney Translation', or 'Hello Darling' when they were performing in 'public'. For a 'black youth' to bury 'maggie' in this very public fashion was totally unacceptable, and yet within the safe haven of the Reggae-dancehall the 'maggie baggie' lyric was one of Levi's most popular. This means that there was indeed a conflict of interests between what Deejays could say in the 'public' and 'alternative public' arenas. Moreover, it was this type of conflict that ended my affiliation with 'Greensleeves UK Bubblers Label' in 1985, as I refused to be dictated to by the white owner/producer who wanted me to chat 'slackness' and the 'Fast Style':

> I went to Greensleeves and Chris Cracknel who was the manager said to me you have to do this, and you have to do that, I said I don't have to do none of that. Why do I have to do that? I'm not beholden to you for anything so you can get fucked, you know, I'm quite happy to be a plumber. (Henry, 2003:449)

The point I am making is that I know that if it was not for the power of the word I received from pro-black, Africentric, counter-cultures like Reggae music and Rastafari, I probably would be walking around as another victim of the white man's 'brainwash education'. Living in Babylon is dread and uncompromising and, as such, that is what we have to be, as Afrikans, if we are to retain our sanity in an insane society. That is why I will not have anyone who is not of me, and of my social, racial and cultural experiences tell me what is to be me and, by definition, tell me what is best for me. I would rather remain a 'plumber' to feed and maintain my family and keep sane, than become a traitor who is nothing more than a living coconut. That applies twofold, given that I now have Dr. before my name and know how titles can 'tun nuff ah we fool against ourselves' and create even more compromised Afrikans. Moreover, many other uncompromising Deejays have spoken of similar experiences where their perspective on the role and purpose of the culture is at odds with their would be employers. The seriousness of this stance was evidenced in Benji's 'In Demand' lyric where he clearly stated 'me nuh chat no fantasy and no soft porn, cau if me chat slack I seh me might get scorn'. The supreme irony here is that by maintaining this 'conscious' stance, the Deejays who viewed this as necessary to their 'professional' outlook were 'scorned' by certain blacks in the business and white-owned record companies. For instance, after Benji recorded his first track for Fashion Records, 'The Fare Dodger' (1985), which was a gimmicky tune he regularly performed on Diamonds Set, he noticed that:

> They (Fashion) were not really interested in anything that was more educational and profound, cos lyrics like these are licking out against the system. (Personal Communication, 1999)

Benji sums up perfectly what the Deejays faced when they wished to remain true to the ethos of the culture and gives yet another example of the continued exploitation of black cultural expression by those, blacks and whites, who shy away from its revolutionary potential to liberate the Afrikan mind. Hence I informed Benji that one of the best lyrics I heard was his 'Shame and Scandal' lyric, which would not appeal to record companies like Fashion because of its intelligent social realism. In the lyric he detailed the confessions of the British royal family and stated:

> **Chorus:** Ah shame an scandal in the royal family, say what ah shame an scandal in ah the royal family.

Deejaying:...Nuff German blood in ah the English Monarchy, the ting that mek them royal is them bag ah money, so nuh badder you goh marvel at the tings that you see, like Princess Diana on ah spending spree, one hundred thousand pounds on dress an mini, while two thirds of the world them ah dead fi hungry...You still not convince an you think it's ah joke, the queen have ah sister an she can't stop smoke, everyday she have ah cigarette hitch in her mouth, we should ah grateful that she don't snort coke, cau that would cost the government nuff pound note, we cold in ah England in the sun she ah soak, on ah Caribbean Island with ah nice young bloke...It's not no surprise to me them have ah Nazi relation, cau every Christmas the queen of England come pon television, she love talk from her palace the place buckinham, how black an white people bowyah should live as one, but me know prince charles couldn't marry no black woman, even though him love the Three Degrees an nuff black band, him even try fi body-pop like ah Blackman, but behind closed doors it's a different situation as England is very friendly with the South African, them know nuff ah the youth them ah die but the government don't care ah damn, as long as them dig fi gold an nuff diamond, me have couple gold ring but me nah goh wear nuh Krugerand, cau we all ah die an ah starve cau fi we land them get from. (Diamonds, 1985)

It is obvious that the links Benji makes between the royal family, their colonial/imperial history and their role in the continued exploitation of the Afrikan, as well as the British tax-payers who fund their lavish life-style are too hardcore and raw. For to state so plainly that 'the ting that mek them royal is them bag ah money'...'while two thirds of the world them ah dead fi hungry', demonstrates why they are in such a powerful position, and that is why you shouldn't 'marvel at the tings that you see'. In essence he encourages us to see them as the exploiters that they are, for this is the reality of their continued existence. Other performers were faced with the same problems when licking out against racism because chatting lyrics that promoted blak upliftment were not always welcomed:

I recorded three singles for Fashion in 1984 and things seemed to be going okay until I approached them with a lyric entitled 'Apartheid Must Be Destroyed'. It seemed that my stance was too strong for them as I was told by John and Chris that it was too controversial and anyway they believed that Mandela would be freed next year,

1985. That's when I decided to leave and recorded for Prof. (Mad Professor's Ariwa Sounds Label) cau them man deh know what the struggle is about. (Makca B, Personal Communication, 1999)

Macka B argues that once he expressed a wish to deal with the global aspect of Afrikan downpression, by suggesting that 'Apartheid Must Be Destroyed', Fashion's owners seemingly had no desire to associate their label with this type black consciousness. Thus, although many Reggae-dancehall Deejays were 'rushed' to become 'superstars', it was often only in the event of them voicing that 'coon-like' stuff that is the staple of the mainstream pop market. This said, it must be noted that Fashion/Dub Vendor continue to promote and release British Deejay tunes, whereas Greensleeves have seemingly distanced themselves from the genre since the 1980s, because:

Once the DJs had outlived their commercial usefulness they were subsequently discarded by the predominantly white-owned record companies, who did not generally recognise this type of expression from a black perspective. (Henry, 2002:282)

Thoughts of promoting blakness as a means of upliftment and transcendence were not expected in the commercialised spaces that are sustained by a diet of harmless 'gimmickry'. The suggestion is that conscious blacks/Afrikans cannot allow anyone to encourage them to forget, that which only their counter-cultures ensure that they remember in the first place. To do so merely perpetuates our condition as those who do not control their own destiny, always allowing others to interfere with our capacity to think ourselves into being, as valid members of the human family, along the principles of Africentric thought and action.

Conclusion

It is critical for us to appreciate how this shift in the Deejay's perspective on the role and purpose of the culture, with regard to financial remuneration, led to another set of concerns about who or what the culture represented. When the British Deejays became known as entities in their own right, in many ways the umbilical link was severed between them and the Sound Systems with which they were often synonymous. This meant that they became free agents, and in a practical sense, free to pursue the financial rewards that were being dangled in front of them by these largely white-owned record companies. However, the case of 'rob an gaan' makes known what is truly at stake when Deejays, like Papa Levi, believed they have the freedom to express that which was in essence most representative of the 'hidden voice' in the wider public arena. This scenario perfectly captures why this dimension of the 'voice' has to remain 'hidden', its role and purpose is to disrupt the sensibilities of the dominant white culture in those 'fortified' spaces where Deejays have a platform to freely articulate their concerns without compromise.

Appreciating the profundity of this argument leads to a greater consideration of the Deejay's contribution to black British discourse on racist exclusionary practices, because this aspect of the culture is the outernational 'voice' that speaks for the Afrikan downpressed. It is the conscious Deejay's duty to maintain a tradition of defiance otherwise, as Sister Audrey suggested above, 'they are not reminding people of the Afrikan struggle'. This means that there will always be a level of confusion regarding exactly whom the Reggae-dancehall Deejays are representing, a consequence of the manner in which Reggae music is generally perceived in the 'public arena'; a panacea for all the world's oppressed peoples. More importantly, what then happens is that any 'voice' that runs counter to this perspective, which denies the specificity of the relationship that black people have with a 'white world' as outlined above, is often treated with disdain. The very same point I made in the opening chapter, when redefining what it meant to be blak in a racist society, where any attempt to give 'voice' to the 'voiceless' is perceived as a threat to racial harmony. That is why to sum up my overall argument I wish to close with the sentiments of Desi B who states:

> Lez, when have white people listened to what we have to say unless they can make something out of it? It surprises me when white people think they can tell us who the music is for or what we should value. When I used to chat I knew who I was chatting for and because I had my profession (Desi B is an accountant) they couldn't tell me what I could and couldn't say. (Personal Communication, 1997)

Forward again!

> Academic texts are surely by definition principally about representative accuracy, politics is about symbolic identification, aesthetics is about symbolic attraction. These realms are not identical; the languages at work invoke different grammars of understanding, different chains of signification. (Keith, 1992:559)

It is imperative for contemporary scholarship to recognise the potency of the types of resistant forms that furnish the downpressed with coping and transcendental modes of thought and conduct, that are concealed within what appear to be sub-cultural forms. That is why I have argued throughout this book that there are 'hidden' dimensions to the interpretation of counter-cultural forms which, when unveiled, enable the culture to be 'known/overstood/read/interpreted/rendered' in a more interesting and significant way. Therefore by furnishing the downpressed with a platform to speak to their condition, the manner in which the telling of history, the conceptualisation of cultural politics and the frameworks for understanding difference can be re-thought. By doing so, the differences between the 'public' and 'alternative public' arenas can be interrogated in a space where the subjectivity and 'voice' of those who encounter racism can come to the fore in discussions around identity and belonging. The point is that the Afrikan downpressed are not content to 'resist' through mere symbolic codes or 'ritualised' forms of behaviour that do not dramatically alter our condition in the here and now, because transcendence is the key to our continued survival in Babylon shitstem. Therefore it is crucial that those with 'insider' knowledges, who have the methodology to make these cultural forms known in a more representative light, use the space to present these alternative ways of seeing the world, with a more 'representative accuracy'. For this reason I opened this discussion with an evaluation of much that had been written about the 'black youth' presence in Britain during the 'crisis' periods of the 1970s and 1980s, especially with regard to their outward displays of 'deviant' types of behaviour. Moreover, I stated there was an 'adaptive response' to racist exclusionary practices that led to a certain section of the black British community, reconfiguring what it meant to be alienated in the land of their birth, culminating in the usage of a 'self-generated concept' like blak as the reaffirmation of an Afrikan identity that is seldom acknowledged.

It was therefore not enough for these black youth to physically populate the British Isles as the silent unwanted other, which for many is what their parental generation were seemingly contented to do. These young men and women (black youth), who knew no other place as home, made a 'conscious' decision to 'populate' the words of the dominant culture, thus 'appropriating' them and making them their 'own'. This means that we draw on a culture that inform us of our 'similar style of life' by virtue of our global condition as the historical objects of white supremacist thought and action. Objects do not have the power of self-commentary as they are invariably commented upon, and those who are in a position to comment upon the object do so through the definitive power of description by inscription. Therefore as the nature of the object is defined, the objectified nature becomes synonymous with the inscribed/written 'reality', which is the consequence of the 'author' as the producer of a 'text' that does not necessarily represent the lives of 'real people'. Hence the description becomes synonymous with the traits that the object is supposed to possess (in much social theory), even in cases where the 'reality' is quite different, as we saw in the depictions of 'black youth' posited in the sociology of race in the A~SIDE. In fact the object often ceases to be perceived as such when it is 'discovered' that it possesses its own 'voice', which does not mean that it did not possess one. It could actually mean that it did always have one but, due to its alternative claims and location, the 'voice' remained 'hidden'. In other words although there is a relationship with the wider community, the partakers in the culture determine the parameters for discursive debate which is the subject of ongoing reasoning. Thus there is a notion that, within these sites of resistance and transcendence, that which is being discussed is governed by an aesthetic 'cultural code' based on blak sensibilities that is used to reject white standards of normality and belonging.

A fundamental reason for this occurrence is the fact that many of the strategies employed by black people to cope with racism and other forms of exclusion, based upon resistance and transcendence, are ongoing and less than spectacular. For example, that my wife hardly speaks Standard English at home, she argues, is 'logical because a natural part of me retaining my Jamaican identity is to chat Patwa'. Furthermore, upon arrival in Britain as a child, she soon realised 'to chat Patwa' was expected within her family home, irrespective of how 'well' they spoke when 'out ah road' (in public). This is also the main reason why I too 'chat Patwa' because in my family those of us who were born in Britain were immersed in, and influenced by, the Jamaican cultural sensibilities of our parents and elder siblings. Thus we were acculturated and socialised by Jamaicans living in London and were expected to partake in the 'verbal exchanges' that were regarded as crucial to fostering an alternative worldview.

The need for the retention of Jamaican/Caribbean language/culture is evidenced in the actual deed, the speaking of Patwa in the private space that is the home environment, which is then transposed into the Reggae-dancehall arena. This, more than any other aspect of our acculturation, explains why it was 'natural' for many black youth in Britain to express themselves in this language as the private space was extended into the alternative public arena. Moreover, the cultural template was already there for us to do so, as provided by the Jamaican Deejays featured on the Yard-tapes that were critical to our development as performers and social commentators. Therefore, our 'cultural identities', a mixture of British, Caribbean and Afrikan influences, did in many ways allow us to identify with the position of the Jamaican sufferer through our exposure to Reggae music and Rastafari teachings about the white man's system of head-decay-shun. This freed us from the constraints of Standard English, as it was 'natural' for us to communicate in Patwa when amongst like-minded black people (Deejaying live) or on occasions when the intention was to ensure that white people were excluded from our reasonings.

The most significant point here is that notions of 'code switching', as gimmicky 'London Jamaican', fail to do justice to the instrumental nature of that which enabled black youth, whose mouthpiece was often the Deejay, to counter the hegemonic force of the English language. A factor which makes known that there is still much confusion as to the outernational nature, role and purpose, of black music/culture in general, and Reggae-dancehall music/culture in particular, as viable sources of knowledge. Hence the exclusionary nature of white racism, and its myriad manifestations, means the conscious Deejays recognise that we inhabit different social worlds from many of our critics, based on quite often diametrically opposed realities. Reggae-dancehall music's blak message is not fully appreciated beyond its own frames of reference and therefore becomes 'unacceptable' to many who would seek to capitalise on its commercial potential, yet are unfamiliar with the history of where and why this cultural form arose. In fact, this exemplifies what is at stake when the 'hidden voice' is made known to many who believe that they understand 'black music', and were clearly unaware that Reggae-dancehall music contained this 'hidden' dimension that ensured that the conscious Deejay could never 'bow to the marketing strategies of the international recording industry' (Cooper 2000).

I demonstrated how a wider exposure to this 'hidden voice', within the mainstream public arena, had dire consequences for those performers who aspired to be professional entertainers, whilst never fully appreciating that the gimmickry that was expected within these spaces did little to promote blak liberation and upliftment and led to various types of conflict. This was because there is a way of viewing the black subject from 'within', which is grounded in an experiential 'reality' that is generally unknown to many who, as Christine Asher suggested above, are not interested in 'why we ah suffer through we colour'. This was one of the substantive contributions I forwarded in the A~SIDE, when I suggested that the ethnographer should recognise the validity of systems of inherited beliefs that are validated within the 'moral culture'. Not only with regard to the 'moral culture' that is under scrutiny, but also from the ethnographer's own epistemological standpoint as the recipient of knowledges that posit white superiority through everyday language and discourse in this Eurocentric 'moral culture'. Hence:

> Me born ah England, me know me blak me nar seh me British, cau to some of de politician blak man don't exist, me nuh care bout de liberal, tory or socialist, cau long time now blakman we ah fight prejudice, through some live good in them neighbourhood them lack awareness. (Papa Benji, 1984)

WHAT THE DEEJAY SAID

Evidenced in Benji's lyric is that ambivalence the "thoughtist" experiences when just because you 'live good' in your 'neighbourhood' you should not 'lack awareness' of who you are, where you are, and more importantly why historically you are here, in Babylon, in the first place. The Deejay's task is to demonstrate, through the associative power of their particular take on the English language, how they counter the white supremacist thinking that shackles the Afrikan mind by using language as an idiom for the transmission of an alternative blak aesthetic. Consequently operating out of this aesthetic I have extensively argued that those who overstand the linguistic form have access to the spaces and the messages contained therein, because the message is generally a song of themselves. Thus within these spaces the Deejays conveyed to the crowd ah people the specificity of a racialized experience on their own terms in a language they regarded as their own. I am arguing that identification as an autonomous self (as either Deejay or audience member) and your predicament in the personalised narrative (the lyric) is what makes this form so relevant to an endeavour that seeks to use biographical detail to posit a more inclusive and positive black historical presence in British society.

Future Prospects

I have focused on giving voice to the voiceless in this work as a means of contributing to the current debates on overstanding the history of black communities in Britain, by signifying the relevance of an outernational consciousness in the nature of interconnections across the Afrikan Diaspora. This means that Afrikan centred subjectivities cannot be overlooked in these debates, as it is they that often give rise to the 'self-generated concepts' that allow the downpressed to remove themselves from their peripheral placement in Europe's New World. I am speaking of a practical way for those who recognise themselves as blak to think themselves into being in a fashion that is not dependent on outward displays of 'Africanisms', which often do little to improve our overall condition as the recipients of white racism. That is why my usage of the concept blak in this study acts as disruptive sign that offers an alternative reading of history that places the Afrikan in time, as a sentient being, and across time as an autonomous historical being, whose modes of resistance and transcendence resonate and manifest in

246

the present as Reggae-dancehall music/culture. Therefore, I am offering a way for future studies of countercultural forms to use ethnographic renderings of biographical accounts to tell the story of 'real people', by focusing the analysis on the cultural artefacts the downpressed produce to pass on their personal narratives through the generations. That is why the metaphor of the 45 single is central to this discussion as it posits a practical way for us to view how all who are affected by racist exclusionary practices, irrespective of generational or gendered differences, constantly rework historical narratives in the present. By this I mean that the riddim track on which the Deejay performs is often the cultural product of another era, for instance a classic Studio One tune like Armageddon Rock that was created in the early 1970s, is still used in its original form to express contemporary concerns.

This speaks to the manner in which the cultural templates are used in a way that cannot be regarded as 'sub' anything, for it is an essential aspect of the culture that allows us to speak across and through various generations. I suggested above Sounds travel on tapes in alternative public arenas as Sets play the music that contain the Deejay's narratives, which link the disparate elements of our history, thus making it outernational and, therefore, whole. This means that we need to see these patterns of behaviour as the types of conscious thought and action that produce meaning by being constantly reflective, whilst at the same time future oriented, in a way that brings its alternative claims to the foreground. That is why future studies of these types of culture should perhaps consider self-overstanding to overstand self. Such a stance would ensure that these types of critical engagement with the 'white world' are recognised as the conscious reflections on the cultural struggles of the downpressed, who seek to negotiate a sane path through a hostile racist environment. This is borne from the recognition that you cannot escape the tendrils of a global system such as white racism/supremacy, which was designed by a global minority—the European—to control the actions of the global majority—the non-European—irrespective of where we happen to dwell on this planet. This means that, simply put, running away from reality is counterproductive and the only way for real and meaningful change to occur is for our stories, warts and all, to be told and listened to in the wider public arena. This I believe was/is the role and purpose of the conscious Deejays who sought/seek to challenge the status quo by giving voice to the voiceless in a manner that refuses to be compromised. For as Chinua Achebe suggests 'if we do not tell our own stories as Afrikan people, we will disappear' (1998), so perhaps it is time to take note of 'what the Deejay said' because:

Deejaying: Them ah seh me too blak ah weh them ah talk bout, through me know myself them want fi fill me with doubt, the blackman's burden was ah gag pon me mouth, knowledge take it off now ah time fi lick out, lickout gainst a system that seh white is right, from you pro black them want give you ah fight, them seh them don't want listen to Lezlee, them wouldah much prefer listen to presley, who pirate the rock n roll, thief weh the blues, then said ah nigger's only fit to shine his shoes

Chorus: It's time to make a change, black people gotta get get up, it's time to make a change, black people gotta step up, it's time to make a change you really gotta overstand you gotta educate yourself as an Afrikan. It's time to make a change, black people need to wake, it's time to make a change, black people need a shake up, it's time to make a change you really gotta free yuh mind and then we step step step up in ah life. (Lezlee Lyrix, 1997)

Hotep!!

Appendix: Glossary of terms

Aanyah	Here
Anyweh	Anywhere
Babylon / Beast	Police/enemies
Breddah	Brother
Bredrin	Brother(s)
Bruk	Break or broken
Buck-down	Sound clash
Bun	Burn
Chuck-it	Cause trouble
Cokey	Caucasian
Cuss	Curse
Combi	Combination - duet
Daughtah	Black Woman
Diss	This or to disrespect
Downpress	Pressed down by system
Dropped	Chatted/performed
Dub plates/Specials	Exclusive metallic discs
Dutty	Dirty
Extra	Showing off
Fi	To/For
Friars	Foolish person
Fronters	National Front/racists
Gaff	Place of residence
Galang	Go/Go Away
Gwaan	Go On
Haffi	Have to
Heartical	Sincere/true
Hitch-it/Pull-up	Restart the record
Innah	inside
Itrol	Control
Iyah	Rastaman
Juggled	Play records or chat lyrics
Kick-up	Crowd respond favourably
Leggo	Let go
Livity	Rastafari concept of all aspects of human existence

Nagah	Negro/nigger
Natch	Top notch
Oppah	Operator
Overstand/Over	Fully comprehend
Pickney	Child
Pirate	Deejay who steals another's ideas/lyrics/style
Prento	Apprentice
Rail-up	Crowd respond favourably or take offence
Riddims	Rhythm tracks
Shitstem	Corrupt System
Skank	A con trick or a dance also known as Ital Steppin
Siddong	Sit-down
Sistrin	Sister(s)
Soh/Suh	So
Supn	Something
Till	Tell
Trace	Insult - generally without currsing
Unnuh	All of you
Vank	Vanquish
Yah	Here
Yard	Jamaica
Wackad	Wicked
Wah/Weh	What

References

Bibliography

Allen, Sheila. (1982) "Confusing Categories and Neglecting Contradictions" Cashmore, Ernest. and Troyna, Barry. (eds) Black Youth In Crisis, London: George Allen & Unwin Publishers.

Alleyne, Mervyn. (1988) Roots of Jamaican Culture, London: Pluto Press.

Amos, Vincent. Gilroy, Paul. and Lawrence, Erol. (1981) *White Sociology: Black Struggle*, (unpublished paper).

Anderson, Claud. (1997) *Dirty Little Secrets About Black History, It's Heroes, And other Troublemakers*, USA: PowerNomics Corporation of America.

Asante, Molefi (1995) *Afrocentricity*, Trenton, NJ: Africa World press.

Back, Les. (1988) "Coughing Up Fire: Sound systems in south-east London", *New Formations 5*, (summer) 141-52.

—(1996) *New Ethnicities and Urban Culture*, London: UCL.

Back, Les. & Solomos, John. (2001), (eds) *Theories Of Race And Racism: A Reader*, London: Routledge.

Baker, Houston. (1987) *Modernism and the Harlem renaissance*, USA: University of Chicago Press.

Bakhtin, Mikhail. (1981) *The Dialogic Imagination* (ed) Holquist, Michael. (trans) Emerson, Caryl. & Holquist, Michael., Austin, USA: University of Texas Press.

Besson, Jean. & Momsen, Janet. (eds) (1987) *Land and Development in The Caribbean*, London: Macmillan Press.

Barrett, Leonard. (1971) *The Sun and the Drum: African Roots Jamaican Folk Traditions,* Jamaica: Sangster.

—(1988) *The Rastafarians*, Boston, USA: Beacon press.

Berger, Maurice. (2000) *White Lies: Race and the Myths of Whiteness*, USA: Farrar Strauss Giraux.

Besson, Jean. (1993) "Reputation and Respectability Reconsidered" in *Women and Change in the Caribbean: A Pan Caribbean Perspective*, Momsen, J. (ed) London: James Curry.

Bhabha, Homi. (1993) "Remembering Fanon: Self, Psyche and the Colonial Condition" in Williams, P. and Chrisman, L. (eds) *Colonial Discourse And post-Colonial Theory: A Reader*, England: Prentice Hall.

Black, Marlon. (2001) *The Daily Gleaner*

Bolinger, Dwight. (1980) *Language the Loaded Weapon: the use and abuse of language today,* London: Longman.

Boulaye, Patti. (1998) article in *The Mirror,* 12/11/98, London.

Bourdieu, Pierre. (1989) *Distinction: A Social Critique of the Judgement of Tatse,* translated by Richard Nice, London: Routledge.

Bourne, Jenny. (1980) "Cheerleaders and Ombudsmen": the Sociology of Race Relations in Britain", *Race and Class,* Vol. 21 No.4 Spring: pp. 331-352.

Bradley, Lloyd. (2001) *Bass Culture: When Reggae Was King,* London: Penguin Books.

Brake, Mike. (1980), *The Sociology of Youth Culture and Youth Subcultures,* London: Routledge & Kegan Paul.

Brathwaite, Edward. (1984) *History Of The Voice, the development of nation language in anglophone Caribbean poetry,* London: New Beacon Books.

Bulham, Hussein, Abdilahi. (1985) *Frantz Fanon and the Psychology of Oppression,* New York: Plenum Press.

Bygott, David. (1992) *Black and British,* Oxford: Oxford University Press.

Campbell, Horace. (1985) *Rasta and Resistance: From Marcus Garvey to Walter Rodney,* London: Hansib Publishing Ltd.

Carby, Hazel. (1999) *Cultures in Babylon: Black Britain and African America,* London: Verso.

Carmichael, Stokely. and Hamilton, Charles. (1967) *Black Power: The Politics of Liberation in America,* Great Britain: Pelican Books.

Cashmore, Ernest. (1979) *Rastaman: The Rastafarian Movement In England,* London: Unwin Paperbacks.

Cashmore, Ernest. and Troyna, Barry. (eds) (1982) *Black Youth In Crisis,* London: George Allen & Unwin Publishers.

Cashmore, Ellis. (1997) *The Black Culture Industry,* London: Routledge.

Centre For Contemporary Cultural Studies (1982) *The Empire Strikes Back,* London: Routledge.

Chambers, Ian. (1986) *Popular Culture: The Metropolitan Experience,* London: Methuen & Co. Ltd.

Clarke, Sebastian. (1980) *Jah Music: The Evolution of the Popular Jamaican Song,* London: Heinemann Educational Books Ltd.

Clifford, James. (1986) "Partial Truths" (in) Clifford, J. & Marcus, George (eds) *Writing Culture: The Poetics and Politics of Ethnography*, London: University of California Press, Ltd.

Coard, Bernard. (1991) *How The West Indian Child is made Educationally Sub-Normal In The British School System*, London: Karia Press.

Cohen, Anthony. (1994) *Ethnicity, identity and music: the musical construction of place*, Stokes, M. (ed), UK: Berg.

Cooper, Carolyn. (1993) *Noises in the Blood: Orality, Gender and the 'Vulgar' Body of Jamaican Popular Culture*, London and Basingstoke: Macmillan Education Ltd.

—(2000) "Rhythms of Resistance: Jamaican Dancehall Culture and the Politics of Survival" (Paper received via email, May 2000).

—(2004) *Sound Clash: Jamaican Dancehall Culture At Large*, New York: Palgrave Macmillan.

Davis, George. (1989) *I Got the word in me and I can sing it, you know:A study of the performed African American Sermon*, Philadelphia: University of Pennsylvania Press.

De Beauvoir, Simone. (1972) *The Second Sex,* Trans (ed) by Parshley, H.M. London: Cape.

Dent, Gina. (ed) (1992) *Black Popular Culture: A Project by Michelle Wallace*, Seattle: Bay Press.

Desai, Phil. (1999) *Spaces of Identity, Cultures of Conflict: The development of new Asian masculinities*, PhD thesis, Goldsmiths College, University of London.

Du Bois, William. (1990) *The Souls of black Folk*, New York: Vintage Books.

Edgar, David. cited in Gilroy, Paul. (1982) "Steppin out of Babylon", *The Empire Strikes Back*, London: Routledge.

Ekwe Ewke, Herbert. (1994) *African Peoples Review*, Vol III, No.2, pp16, July-September, Reading, England: The International Institute For Black Research.

Fanon, Franz. (1986) *Black Skin, White Masks*, London: Pluto Press Ltd.

Finkenstaedt, Rose. (1994) *Face To Face blacks in a America: white perceptions and black realities*, USA: Morrow.

Fisher, G. and Joshua, Harris. (1982), "Social Policy and Black Youth", in Cashmore, Ernest. and Troyna, Barry. (eds) *Black Youth In Crisis*, London: George Allen & Unwin Publishers.

Foehr, Stephen. (2000) Jamaican Warriors: Reggae, Roots & Culture, London: Sanctuary Publiching Limited.

Foster, Chuck. (1999) *Roots Rock Reggae: An Oral History of Reggae Music from Ska to Dancehall*, New York City: Billboard Books.

Frith, Simon. (1996) *Performing Rites: On the Value of Popular Music*, Oxford: Oxford University Press.

—(1983) *Sound Effects: Youth, Leisure and the Politics of Rock 'n' Roll*, London: Constable.

Frith, Simon. and Goodwin, Andrew. (1990) *On Record: Rock, pop and the Written Word*, London: Routledge.

Fryer, Peter. (1984) *Staying Power: The History of Black People in Britain*, London: Pluto.

Gandy, Oscar, H. (1998) *Communication and Race: A structural perspective*, London: Arnold.

Garrison, Leonard. (1979) *Black Youth, Rastafarianism and the Identity Crisis in Britain*, London: Afro-Caribbean Education Resource Project.

Garvey, Amy. Jaques. (1986) *The Philosophy And Opinions Of Marcus Garvey*, USA: The Majority Press.

Gates, Henry Louis. (1988) *The Signifying Monkey: The theory of Afro-American Literary Criticism*, Oxford: Oxford University Press.

Gilroy, Paul. (1982) "Steppin out of Babylon" in CCCS, *The Empire Strikes Back*, London: Routledge.

—(1987) *There Ain't no Black in the Union Jack: The Cultural Politics of Race and Nation*, London: Hutchinson Education.

—(1991) "Sounds Authentic: Black Music, Ethnicity and the Challenge of the Changing Same" in *Black Music Research Journal*, Vol 11, No2, Fall.

—(1993a) *The Black Atlantic: Modernity and Double Consciousness*, London: Verso.

—(1993b) *Small Acts: Thoughts On The Politics Of Black Cultures*, London: Serpents Tail.

—(1994) "After the love has gone": bio-politics and ethno-poetics in the black public sphere. *Public Culture*, Vol.7, 49-76

Gordon, Avery. (1998), *Ghostly Matters: Haunting and the Sociological Imagination*, Minneapolis: University of Minnesota Press.

Griffin, John. (1984), *Black Like Me*, London: Granada Books.

Gutzmore, Cecil. (1993) "Carnival, the State and the Black Masses in the United Kingdom" (in) James, Winston. & Harris, Clive. (eds) *Inside Babylon: The Caribbean Diaspora In Britain*, London: Verso.

Hall, Stuart. Critcher, Charles. Jefferson, Tony. and Roberts, Brian. (1978), Policing the Crisis: Mugging, the State and Law and Order, London: Hutchinson.
Hall, Stuart. (1993) "New Ethnicities" in Morley, David. and Kuan-Hsing, Chen. Stuart Hall (eds) Critical Dialogues in Cultural Studies, New York: Routledge.
Hampton, Henry. Fayer, Steve. Flyn, Sarah. (1990) Voices of Freedom: an oral history of the Civil Rights Movements from the 1950s through the 1980s, New York: Bantam.
Heaney, Seamus (2003) - http://news.bbc.co.uk/1/hi/entertainment/music/3033614.stm-
Hebdige, Dick. (1977) "Reggae, Rastas and Rudies" in Curran, J. Gurevitch, Michael. and Woollacott, Janet. (eds) Mass Communication and Society, London: Edward Arnold (publishers) Ltd.
—(1979) Subculture: The Meaning of Style, London: Methuen.
—(1987) Cut 'N' Mix: Culture, Identity and Caribbean Music, London: Routledge.
Henry, William. (2002) "Lovers Rock" (in) Donnell, A. (ed) Companion to Contemporary Black British Culture, London: Routledge.
Henry, William. (2002) "Sound system DJs" (in) Donnell, A. (ed), Companion to Contemporary Black British Culture, London: Routledge.
Henry, William. (2003) "Chatting For Change" (in) Back, L. & Bull, M. (eds) The Auditory Culture Reader, Oxford: Berg.
Henry, William. (2005) "Projecting the 'Natural'; language and citizenship in outernational culture", Besson, Jean. & Fog Olwig, Karen. (eds) Caribbean Narratives Of Belonging: Fields Of Relations, Sites Of Identity, Macmillan Education: Oxford.
Herskovits, M.J. (1990) The Myth of the Negro Past, Boston: Beacon Press.
Hewitt, Roger. (1986) White talk, black talk: inter-racial friendship and communication amongst adolescents, London: Cambridge University Press.
Hutchinson, Earl (1997) The Assassinatioon Of The Black Male Image, Touchstone: New York.
Jah Bones. (1986) "Reggae Deejaying and Jamaican Afro-Lingua" (in) Sutcliffe, David. and Wong, Ansell. (eds) The Language of the Black Experience, Oxford: Basil Blackwell Ltd.
James, Winston. "Migration, Racism and Identity Formation: The Caribbean Experience in Britain", (in) James, Winston. & Harris, Clive.

(eds) (1993) *Inside Babylon: The Caribbean Diaspora In Britain,* London: Verso.

Jefferson, T and Clarke, J. (1973) "Down These Mean Streets...The Meaning of Mugging" (cited in) Jones, Simon. (1986) *White Youth And Popular Jamaican Culture,* PhD thesis for Centre

Jones, Leroi. (1995) *Blues People,* Edinburgh: Payback Press.

Jones, Simon. (1986) *White Youth And Popular Jamaican Culture,* PhD thesis for Centre for Community and Urban Studies, Faculty of Arts, University of Birmingham.

—(1988) *Black youth, white culture: the Reggae tradition from JA to UK,* London: Macmillan.

—(1993), "From Punishment to Discipline? Racism, Racialization and the Policing of Social Control" (in) Cross, Malcolm. and Keith, Michael. (eds) *Racism, the City and the State,* London: Routledge.

Keith, Michael. and Rogers, Alisdair. (eds) (1991) *Hollow Promises: Rhetoric and Reality in the Inner City,* London: Mansell.

Keith, Michael. (1992) "Angry Writing: (re)presenting the unethical world of the ethnographer" (in) *Society and Space,* Vol. 10, pp 551-568.

Kelly, Robin. (1999) (in) Neal, Mark (1999) *What The Music Said: Black Popular Music and Black Public Culture,* London: Routledge.

Lamb, Donna. (2004) "Post-Traumatic Slave Syndrome" http://www.globalblacknews.com/ lamb71.html.

Lawrence, Erol. (1982) "In the abundance of water the fool is thirsty: sociology and black pathology" (in) CCCS, *The Empire Strikes Back,* London: Routledge.

Lazarre, Jane. (1997) *Beyond the Whiteness of Whiteness: Memoir of a White Mother of Black Sons,* Durham and London: Duke University Press.

Lea, John. and Young, Jack. (1984) *What is to be done about law and order?,* Harmondsworth: Penguin.

Leary, Joy DeGruy, *Post Traumatic Slave Syndrome: America's Legacy of Enduring Injury and Healing*

Levine, Lawrence. (1977) *Black Culture And Black Consciousness: Afro-American Folk Thought From Slavery to Freedom,* Oxford: Oxford University Press.

Little, Daniel. (1991) *Varieties of Social Explanation: An introduction to the Philosophy of Social Science,* Oxford: Westview Press, Inc.

Liverpool, Hollis. (2001) *Rituals Of Power And Rebellion: The Carnival tradition In Trinidad & Tobago 1763-1962*, Chicago: Research Associates School Times Publication.

Longhurst, Brian. (1995) *Popular Music and Society*, Cambridge, UK: Polity Press.

Martin, Tony. (1986) *Race First: The Ideological and Organizational Struggles of Marcus Garvey and the Universal Negro Improvement Association*, USA: The Majority Press.

Maultsby, Portia. (1991) "Africanisms in African-American Music", (in) Holloway, Joseph. (ed), *Africanisms in American Culture*, Bloomington, IN: Indiana University Press.

Melville, Casper. (1997) *New Formz and Metal headz: Jungle, black music and breakbeat culture*, (unpublished) MA Thesis, Goldsmiths College, University of London.

Masouri, John. (1998) article in *Echoes*, London.

Mercer, Kobena. (1990) *Powellism: race, politics and discourse*, PhD thesis, University of London.

—(1994) *Welcome To The Jungle: New positions in Black cultural Studies*, New York & London: Routledge.

Mintz. Sidney. (1989) *Caribbean Transformations*, New York: Columbia University Press.

Morrison, Toni. (1987) *Beloved*, New York: Knopf.

Mühleisen, Susanne. (2002) "black British Englishes" (in) Donnell, Alison. (ed) *Companion to Contemporary Black British Culture*, London: Routledge.

Mullane, Deirdre. (1993) *Crossing The Danger Water: Three Hundred Years of African American Writing*, New York: Doubleday.

Nettleford, Rex. (1999) "Discourse on Rastafarian Reality" (in) Murrell, Nathaniel. Spencer, William. and McFarlane, Adrian. (eds) *Chanting Down Babylon The Rastafari Reader*, Kingston, Jamaica: Ian Randle Publishers.

Newland, Courttia. (2000), 'Introduction', (in) Newland, Courttia. and Sesay, Kadija. *IC3: the Penguin Book Of New Black Writing in Britain*, London: Hamish Hamilton.

Nketia, Kwabena. (1974) *The Music of Africa*, New York: W.W. Norton.

Okokon, Susan. (1998) *Black Londoners 1880-1990*, Gloucestershire: Sutton Publishing Ltd.

Oliver. Paul. (ed) (1990) *Black Music in Britain: Essays on the Afro-Asian Contribution to Popular Music,* Milton Keynes: Open University Press.

Ong, Walter. (1991) *Orality and Literacy: The Technologizing of the Word,* London: Routledge.

Oxford Concise Dictionary, (1998) Oxford: Oxford University Press.

Prah, Kwesi. Kwaa. (1992) *Capitein: A Critical Study Of An 18th Century African,* Trenton, NJ: Africa World Press.

Prescod, Colin. (1979) "Back thought", *New Society,* 48, no. 865 (3 May), 280-81.

Pryce, Ken. (1979) *Endless Pressure: A Study of West Indian Lifestyles in Bristol,* Harmondsworth: Penguin.

Pryce, Ken. (1986) *Endless Pressure: A Study of West Indian Lifestyles in Bristol,* (2nd ed), Bristol: Bristol Classical Press.

Reynolds, Simon. (1990) *Blissed Out,* London: Serpents Tail.

Rex, John. and Tomlinson, Sally. (1979) *Colonial Immigrants in a British City: A Class Analysis,* London: Routledge.

Rigby, Peter. (1996) *African Images: Racism And the end Of Anthropology,* Oxford: Berg.

Roosevelt, Thomas Jr. (1996) *Defining Diversity,* USA: Amacom.

Said, Edward. (1978) *Orientalism,* London: Penguin.

Said, Edward. (1993) *Culture and Imperialism,* London: Chatto & Windus.

Saunders, Charles. (1998) "Assessing Race Relations Research" (in) Ladner, Joyce. (ed) *The Death Of White Sociology,* Baltimore: Black Classic Press.

Scafe, Susan. (1989) *Teaching Black Literature,* London: Virago Press Ltd.

Sebba, Mark. (1993) *London Jamaican: Language Systems In Interaction,* London: Longman.

Small, Christopher. (1994) *Music of the Common Tongue,* London: Calder.

Solomos, John. (1988) *Black Youth, Racism and the State: the Politics of Ideology and Policy,* Cambridge: Cambridge: University Press.

Solomos, John. and Back, Les. (1996) *Racism and Society,* Basingstoke: Macmillan.

Spencer, Jon. Michael. (1995) *The Rhythms of Black Folk: Race, Religion and Pan-Africanism,* Trenton, NJ: Africa World Press, Inc.

Stolzoff, Norman. (2000) *Wake The Town & Tell The People: Dancehall Culture in Jamaica,* Durham and London: Duke University Press.

Tagg, Philip. (1982) "Analysing Popular Music: Theory, Method, and Practice" in *Popular Music*, Vol. 2.

Tagg, Philip. (1989), "Open letter: Black music, Afro-American Music and European Music" in Popular Music, Vol.8, No.10.

Thompson, Becky. "Afterword" (in) Ladner, Joyce. (ed) *The Death Of White Sociology*, Baltomore: Black Classic Press.

Tilley, Christopher. (1990) *Reading Material Culture: Structuralism, Hermeneutics and Post-Structuralism*, Oxford: Basil Blackwell.

Toop, David. (1985) *The Rap Attack*, London: Pluto Press.

—(1991*), Rap Attack 2*, London: Serpents Tail.

Troyna, Barry. (1977) "The Reggae War", (in) *New Society*, March 10th.

—(1978) *The significance of Reggae music in the lives of black adolescent boys living in Britain: An exploratory study*, MPhil Dissertation, University of Leicester.

—(1979) "Differential Commitment to Ethnic Identity by Black Youths in Britain", (in) *New Community*, vol.17, no.3, pp. 403-414.

Ture, Kwame. and Hamilton, Charles (1992) *Black power: The Politics of Liberation in America*, USA: Vintage Books.

Ugwu, Catherine. (1995) (ed) *Let's Get It On: The Politics of Black Performance*, Seattle: Baypress.

Walters, Basil. 'My lyrics must suit my children', article in *The Sunday Observer*, Kingston, Jamaica.

Websters Encyclopaedic Dictionary, (1997) Massachusetts: Merriam Webster.

Weinreich, Peter. (1979) "Identity diffusion in immigrant and English adolescents", in *Race, Education and Identity*, Verma Gajendra. and Bagley, Christopher. (eds) London: Macmillan.

Willis, Paul. (1977) *Learning to Labour*, London: Saxon House.

Wong, Ansel. (1986) (in) Sutcliffe, David. and Wong, Ansel. *The Language of the Black Experience*, Oxford: Basil Blackwell Ltd.

Wood, Andy. (2002), "Reggae" (in) Donnell, Alison. (ed) *Companion to Contemporary Black British Culture*, London: Routledge.

Woolgar, Steve. (1990), (in) Lynch, Michael & Woolgar, Steve. (eds) *Representation in Scientific Practice*, Cambridge, Mass: MIT Press.

Personal Communications
Asher Senator & Papa Benji, (1999) recorded reasoning session, London, England.

Caesar, (1997) field notes from reasoning session, London, England.

Champion, (2001) field notes from reasoning session, London, England.

Chubby, (2005) field notes from reasoning session, Birmingham, England.

Christine Asher, (2001) field notes from reasoning session, London, England.

Cocksman, (1998) field notes from reasoning session, London, England.

C. J. Lewis, (1998) field notes from reasoning session, London, England.

Derek, (1999) recorded reasoning session, London, England.

Desi B, (2001) field notes from reasoning session, London, England.

Dr Vibes / Rankin, (2001) recorded reasoning session, London, England.

The Mad Dread, (1996) field notes from reasoning session, London, England.

Dirty Desi, (2001) field notes from reasoning session, London, England.

Hayes, Lawrence. (1996) recorded reasoning session, London, England.

Lewis, Rupert. (2001) recorded reasoning session, Kingston, Jamaica.

Macka B. (1999) 18th November 1999, recorded reasoning session, London, England

Macka B. (2001) field notes from reasoning session, London, England

McGrath, Ronnie. (2002) field notes from reasoning session, London, England.

Mikey Reds, (1998) recorded reasoning session, London, England.

Nehusi, Kimani. (2000) field notes from reasoning session, London, England.

Papa Benji, (2000) recorded reasoning session, Portland, Jamaica.

Reds, (1999) field notes from recorded reasoning session, London, England.

Rodigan, David. (2001) field notes from reasoning session, London, England.

Rubin Ranks, (1997) field notes from reasoning session, Kingston, Jamaica.

Sister Audrey, (1999) recorded reasoning session, London, England.

Tippa Irie, (1998) field notes from reasoning session, London, England.

Yard/Session-tapes

Capleton, 'Black Star Sound System', (1999) Kingston, Jamaica.
Lezlee Lyrix 'Capital Rap Show', interview with Tim Westwood, (1989)
Capital Radio 95.8 FM, London, England.
Charlie Chaplin & Papa San, (1983) 'Creation Sound System', Kingston,
Jamaica.
Cinderella, Lezlee Lyrix, Papa Benji & Trevor Natch, (1985) 'Diamonds
The Girls Best Friend Sound System', London, England.

Gemini Disco Sound System (1981)
Burru Banton
Johnny Ringo
Welton Irie

Ghettotone Sound System (1983)
Asher Senator
Champion
Daddy Dego
Dirty Desi
Lezlee Lyrix
Nico D
Papa Levi
Reds
Smiley Culture

Jack Ruby Hi Fi Sound System (1980)
Nicodemus

Jah Love Sound System (1980)
Brigadier Jerry
King Yellowman
Lord Sassa Frass

Jamdown Rockers Sound System (1983)
Champion

Killamanjaro Sound System (1984)
Puddy Roots

Ray Symbolic Sound System (1980) <u>Saturday Night Jamdown Style</u>, (Live LP)
Ranking Joe

Saxon Sound System (1983)
Asher Senator

Saxon Sound System (1987)
Daddy colonel
Papa Levi
Super cat
Tippa Irie

Sir Lloyd Sound System (1983), "Live LP", recorded at Dick Shepherd School, Brixton: Raiders Records.
Lana Gee
Lezlee Lyrix

Stereophonic Sound System (1980)
General Echo/Rankin Slackness
Donovan

Recorded Releases
Achebe, Chinua. (1998) 'Chinua Achebe' (Documentary) Channel 4.
Asher Senator (1984) "To Who Respect Is Due" (Disco 45) Fashion Records, London.
Brown, Barry. (1983) "Thank You Mama" (Dub Plate Special).
Brown, Dennis. Emanuel. & Brown, Hugh. (1981) "Praise Without Raise" (Disco 45), Yvonne Special, Kingston Jamaica.
Brown, Hugh (1980) "Praise Without Raise", Cash an Carry Records, Kingston, Jamaica.
Crucial Robbie, (1985), "Proud to be Black" (white label pre-release).
Daddy Colonel (1998) "Fraid of the Bible" (Disco 45) MCS Records, London.
Jolly Brothers, (1978) "Conscious Man", White Label.
Leroy Smart, (1979) "Be Conscious", Ghettotone Sound System Session-tape, (1982).

Lezlee Lyrix, (1984) "Blind Date/Put Back You Truncheon", (Disco 45) Greensleeves UK Bubblers, London.
- (1996) "Afrikan Body, white man mind", (recording), MCS Records, London.
- (1998) " Time To Make A Change" (Disco 45) MCS Records, London.
Macka B, (1987) "We've Had Enough", We've Had Enough, (Album) Ariwa Records, London.
- (1988), "Proud to be Black", Looks Are Deceiving (Album) Ariwa Sounds, London.
- (1990), "Get Conscious", Natural Suntan (Album) Ariwa Sounds, London.
- (2000) "African Slavery", Global Messenger (Album) Ariwa Sounds, London.
Manzie, (1979) (Sleeve-note) General Echo, Rocking and Swing, (Album) Rock-it Records, Kingston, Jamaica.
Muhammad, Khalid. (1997) Afrikan Hellocaust (Video Lecture) Tree Of Knowledge, Manchester.
Papa Levi, (1984) "Riot Innah Birmingham" (featured on Tony William's 'Rockers FM' cassette recording).
- (1986), "Ram jam Capitalism" (45 Single) Treco Records, London.
- (1994), "Nuff Black", Back to Basics (Album) Ariwa Records, London.
Shabazz, Menelik. (2005) Burning an Illusion, DVD Release, United Kingdom : BFI
Sugar Minott. (1981) "Penny for My Song" (Disco 45) Black Roots label, Kingston, Jamaica.
Van Sertima, Ivan. (1986) "Blacks in Science Ancient and Modern" (Video Lecture) London.
Wheeler, Caron. & Macintosh, Carl. (1991) UK BLAK, EMI Records, London.
Williams, Willie. (1976) "Armagideon Rock" (45 Single), Studio One, Kingston, Jamaica.

Index

V

Van Sertima, Ivan, 37

W

W.E.B Du Bois, 7
Welton Irie, 160, 193, 195, 216, 217
Welton Youth, 166
West End, 5, 161
West Indian cricketers, 39
West Indies, 63, 65, 68, 70, 79
Wheeler, Caron, 26, 27, 45

Williams, Tony, 171, 222, 231
Wilson, Amos, 41

Y

Yard/Session-tapes, 14, 80, 101, 103, 109, 113, 166
Yard-tape, 9, 10, 11, 84, 101, 102, 105, 106, 107, 109, 110, 111, 112, 150, 153, 156, 158, 160, 162, 166, 168, 185, 192, 195, 197, 244
Yellowman, 106, 107, 108, 109, 153, 156, 162